AF334882

WORD AND WORK
IN THE POETRY
OF JUAN RAMON JIMENEZ

MERVYN COKE-ENGUIDANOS

WORD AND WORK IN THE POETRY OF JUAN RAMON JIMENEZ

TAMESIS BOOKS LIMITED
LONDON

Colección Támesis
SERIE A - MONOGRAFIAS, LXXXVIII

ISBN 0 7293 0139 7

Depósito legal: M. 34708-1982

Printed in Spain by Talleres Gráficos de Selecciones Gráficas
Carretera de Irún, km. 11,500 - Madrid-34

for
TAMESIS BOOKS LIMITED
LONDON

To Miguel

CONTENTS

I am indebted to Girton College of the University of Cambridge, England, for its scholarly and financial support for the publication of this book.

PREFACE

Between the year 1935 which saw the publication of E. Nedderman's *Die symbolistischen Stilelemente im Werke von Juan Ramón Jiménez* and the year 1977 when R. A. Cardwell brought out his *Juan R. Jiménez, The Modernist Apprenticeship 1895-1900,* a considerable number of major books of critical scholarship on the work of Juan Ramón Jiménez have appeared, as well as many essays, articles and monographs. However, none of these has studied in a detailed and systematic way the relation between the poetic conception of Word and Work and both his literary and his creative writing.

The terms «Palabra» and «Obra» were constantly reiterated by Juan Ramón, both in conversation and in his writings, prose and verse alike. It seemed to me that insufficient serious attention had been given by critics so far to the significance of the usage of these capitalized words. It may be that the terms have been overlooked or ignored largely on the basis of the assumption that they comprised just one more of the many obsessive eccentricities of a poet already famed for his personal and literary peculiarities. But it is my belief that Juan Ramón has not been credited with the consideration he properly intended with regard to his special conception of «Palabra» and «Obra»: that « ¡Palabra justa y viva, / que la vida interior brota! »; and that «Obra» which induced such lines as « ¡Qué puro el fuego cuando se ejercita / — ¡corazón, hierro, Obra! ».

With regard to bibliographical data, my chief sources have been the excellent revised edition of G. Palau de Nemes's *Vida y obra de Juan Ramón Jiménez* (Madrid, 1974); D. F. Fogelquist's *Juan Ramón Jiménez* (Boston, 1975); F. Garfias's *Juan Ramón Jiménez* (Madrid, 1958); A. Campoamor González's *Vida y poesía de Juan Ramón Jiménez* (Madrid, 1976); and R. Gullón's *Estudios sobre Juan Ramón Jiménez* (Buenos Aires, 1960), together with the supplementary biography contained in his *El último Juan Ramón Jiménez* (Madrid, 1968).

The study of Juan Ramón's relationships with his various contemporaries is a field in which much work has been carried out. His relationship with Rubén Darío, for instance, has been the subject of studies by such scholars as J. M. Aguirre, J. L. Cano, G. Díaz-Plaja and D. F. Fogelquist, whilst M. Fernández Almagro has written on Juan Ramón with respect to his situation with other contemporary Andalusian poets. My own examination of Juan Ramón's aesthetic concepts, however, necessitated a survey of the poet's European context also. Comparisons with Mallarmé, Yeats and Eliot for example indicate the value placed upon the poetic Word by European contemporaries.

Much has been written on Juan Ramón in the context of «modernismo», notably by R. A. Cardwell and by R. Gullón, whose compilation of the notes taken from the poet's own lectures under the heading *El modernismo, notas a un curso (1953)* (México, 1962) has proved an invaluable fund of information. G. Díaz-Plaja, E. Díez-Canedo and G. Figueira are amongst those who afford a general review of the poetry of Juan Ramón; but for a knowledge of close textual analysis to date, I have turned to critics such as Carlo Bo, L. R. Cole, B. Gicovate, R. Gullón, E. Nedderman, M. P. Predmore, A. Sánchez-Barbudo and H. T. Young. My own study diverges from these in its discussions of the theory of Juan Ramón's concept of the Word; its origins both lay and religious; the poet's rejection of the scepticism manifested by contemporary philosophers and phenomenologists with regard to the power of the Word; and the gradual advance toward his paradoxical goal of Silence as the transcendence of language. The Work—the product of the Word—is shown as both vital organism and vessel of Salvation. The intimate relationship between the poet and his Work, and their mutual growth, raises discussion on the problem of orthodox chronology and the «tiempo verdadero» of the inner life. The tenuously referential «matter» of the Work is defended on the poet's own grounds—namely, that the Word is an aesthetic, not an ethical preoccupation. The study concludes with a consideration of the prose poem «Espacio», essential reading for which was M. T. Font's *Espacio: autobiografía lírica de Juan Ramón Jiménez* (Madrid, 1972). My own approach differs in that it attempts to show «Espacio» as the microcosm of the total Work and as a major breakthrough in the use of the Word. The new poetic diction is seen as the literary equivalent of contemporary scientific and psychological advances. Whilst taking careful stock of the existing body of critical opinion therefore, my arguments here are in the main my own rather than the extension of an already expressed line of thought. The exception to this is my discussion of the effect produced upon Juan Ramón's aesthetics by his transatlantic voyages. In this, the important works of A. Sánchez-Barbudo and R. Gullón respectively have provided the basis of my own findings in relation to the concept of the «Obra», although at times the accord was independently reached. Finally, in those cases where I have found it necessary to call on personal testimony to some statement made by Juan Ramón or to some event in his life, I have had recourse mainly to J. Guerrero Ruiz's *Juan Ramón de viva voz* (Madrid, 1961) and to R. Gullón's *Conversaciones con Juan Ramón Jiménez* (Madrid, 1958), from both of which sources I have quoted freely.

My references to the poetry of Juan Ramón are taken from *Primeros libros de poesía* (Madrid, 1973); *Libros de poesía* (Madrid, 1972); and the *Tercera antolojía poética* (Madrid, 1970). These sources are quoted throughout with the abbreviated forms of *PLP, LP* and *TAP* respectively. For the sake of brevity, and also in accordance with the poet's own custom, I have referred to Juan Ramón Jiménez with the initials JRJ both in the text and in those titles of books and critical works in which his name appears. In the title, as in the text, of this book I have chosen to use the English translation of «Palabra» (Word) and «Obra» (Work) in the interests of simplicity.

Lastly I want to express my gratitude to Lorna Close, constant friend and mentor; and to my parents, for reasons they well know.

Chapter I

POETRY AS INSTRUMENT OF SALVATION

Walter Pater, in the «Conclusion» (dated 1863) to his book on the Renaissance, claimed poetry as the ultimate means of redemption:

> We have an interval, and then our place knows us no more. Some spend this interval in listlessness, some in high passions, the wisest, at least among the «children of this world», in art and song. For our one chance lies in expanding that interval, in getting as many pulsations as possible into the given time. Great passions may give us this quickened sense of life, ecstasy and sorrow of love, the various forms of enthusiastic activity, disinterested or otherwise, which come naturally to many of us. Only be sure it is passion—that it does yield you this fruit of a quickened, multiplied consciousness. Of this wisdom, the poetic passion, the desire of beauty, the love of art for art's sake, has most; for art comes to you professing frankly to give nothing but the highest quality to your moments as they pass, and simply for those moments' sake.

The passage bears strict relevance to the aesthetics of JRJ, born just thirteen years before the death in 1894 of the English Victorian art critic and historian. It expresses that anguished sense of the destructiveness of Time; that need to arrest the transitory moment; that impassioned struggle for Eternity; and finally, that belief in the sanctity of Poetry as sole bulwark against temporality and instrument of Salvation, which are seminal to the Work of JRJ. But—and this is important—not solely to JRJ, but to that entire generation of poets in Europe who were writing at the turn of the century: the late nineteenth and early twentieth. For these were the prevalent preoccupations of the era, to which Pater gave early attention and crystallized in his impeccable prose. It is no mere accident therefore that JRJ should have admired his works, recognizing in them many of his own aesthetic precepts. We know from the testimony of his friend and apologist, Juan Guerrero Ruiz, that JRJ was well acquainted with Pater's writings and, indeed, that such was his esteem that he was capable of ranking Pater alongside no lesser critics than Goethe, Taine and Nietzsche. «España es un país donde no hay crítica, gran crítica; lo que han hecho Goethe, Taine, Walter Pater, Nietzsche», he declared.[1] Translations of Pater into Spanish were available

[1] **Juan Guerrero Ruiz, *JR de viva voz,* Insula, Madrid, 1961, p. 361. All future references to this work will be given under the name of the author only.**

at least from the early 1900s, one such example being P. Henríquez Ureña's *Estudios griegos* (Escalante, México, 1908) which was translated for the *Revista Moderna de México;* and Ricardo Gullón has corroborated the fact that Pater enjoyed a considerable readership among JRJ's contemporaries.[2] It is important to situate JRJ in the context of his own age, and one of the most radical features of his aesthetics is precisely the concern with temporality. This is of course a well-worn topic, already treated by a number of scholars and critics.[3] But my own interest here lies specifically in the aesthetic consequences of the consistent and continual endeavour to transcend Time itself: to attain timelessness and yet to reconcile this with the vision of endless recurrence—all within the Work, and through the medium of the Word. This goal, as has been seen in the passage cited from Pater, is formulated as a protest against the menace of Time. It is an ideal which, to take only a pair of examples, is to be found gripping the mind similarly of the contemporary French symbolist poet, Stéphane Mallarmé, and the Anglo-Irish poet, W. B. Yeats. I choose to refer in particular to these two, among many other possible examples, for two reasons: first, because they usefully serve to illustrate the way in which the same fundamental preoccupations prevailed not in any one given country, but throughout Europe generally; and secondly, because of their double relevance both to JRJ himself and to Walter Pater. Mallarmé, for whom «l'Oeuvre» was the crucible of all experience, as also was «la Obra» for JRJ, was highly esteemed by the latter. Indeed, Guerrero Ruiz records the following anecdote, on 26 April 1931, in which JRJ—somewhat astonishingly—rates Mallarmé thus: «Me explica», says Guerrero Ruiz, «cómo va a colocar los libros, manuscritos, cajas, etc., en los armarios de su despacho: en uno de ellos tendrá la poesía mejor universal: Shakespeare, la Biblia, los griegos, Mallarmé, y algunos de los libros nuevos».[4] In Paterian manner, Mallarmé placed his faith in art alone, as did JRJ. With this mutual ideal, it is easy to understand that JRJ, whose knowledge of the French language was virtually perfect, should have appreciated the esoteric style of the French aesthetician, and even have ventured to translate a number of his poems. Again, it is Guerrero Ruiz who documents the fact that JRJ recognized a further parallel between himself and Mallarmé, that is, between the «nihilismo» of Mallarmé and his own sense of nihilism. Regarding JRJ's project for writing six «novelas intelectuales», Guerrero Ruiz reports: «La primera de estas novelas se titula *Hijo y Obra;* está inspirada en el suicidio del hijo de Hofmannsthal. Dice [JRJ] que este gran poeta había llegado en su obra a una situación de nihilismo parecida a la de Mallarmé, a la suya».[5]

2 In a private interview given in Madrid in July 1977.

3 See for example R. Gullón, *Estudios sobre JRJ,* Losada, Buenos Aires, 1960, pp. 152-160; P. R. Olson, *Circle of Paradox: Time and Essence in the Poetry of JRJ,* The Johns Hopkins Press, Baltimore, Maryland, 1967; B. de Pablos, *El tiempo en la poesía de JRJ,* Gredos, Madrid, 1965; F. Verhesen, «Tiempo y espacio en la obra de JRJ», *La Torre,* Universidad de Puerto Rico, año V, núms. 19-20, July-December 1957.

4 Guerrero Ruiz, p. 161.

5 Guerrero Ruiz, p. 54.

It is significant that Mallarmé, like Pater a supreme aesthetician, and quester after that ideal Unity of Being which was the goal of Pater also, should have been acquainted with the latter's works and, indeed, with the man himself. In his introduction, «Déplacement avantageux», to the lecture entitled «La musique et les lettres» which he delivered first at the University of Oxford and then at Cambridge in 1894, Mallarmé referred to Walter Pater, albeit in characteristically oblique manner, as «le prosateur ouvragé par excellence de ce temps». Such superlative terms are proof of Mallarmé's high regard, and the choice of his adjective «ouvragé» is indicative of the grounds whereon Mallarmé based his admiration: Style. It is Pater's careful and contrived stylistic elegance, his exclusive reverence for art alone—art, artistry, artifice—that so appealed to the French symbolist whose poetry reflects those selfsame precepts. That is not, of course, to claim any direct influence of Pater upon Mallarmé, but merely to show the existence of kindred attitudes. It was in the course of this same visit to Oxford on 1 March 1894 that the two men met, at Brasenose College. Mallarmé presented Pater with a copy of one of his collections of poetry, *Vers et prose,* for which Pater wrote him a letter in gratitude.[6]

That the Paterian reflections on Time—its threatening nature, and the quest to halt it—are indeed representative of the anxiety of a whole European era, is borne out for example by Mallarmé's own poetic expression of it in his summary phrase: «un tremblement du voile du Temple trouble mon époque». Using the same metaphor, he again declares: «on assiste, comme finale d'un siècle, pas ainsi que ce fut dans le dernier, à des bouleversements: mais, hors de la place publique, à une inquiétude du voile dans le temple avec des plis significatifs et un peu sa déchirure».[7] These very words were to be taken up by Yeats to form the title of his book *The Trembling of the Veil,* incorporated in *Autobiographies.* In the «Preface», written in 1922, he explains the reason for his choice. It is because the selfsame sense of metaphysical anguish which Mallarmé thus conveyed in 1886 remained ever prevalent. «I have found in an old diary», Yeats writes, «a saying from Stéphane Mallarmé, that his epoch was troubled by the trembling of the veil of the Temple. As those words were still true, during the years of my life described in this book, I have chosen *The Trembling of the Veil* for its title». It is interesting to observe here also the influence which Mallarmé exerted indirectly upon Yeats through the intermediary, Arthur Symons, translator of a number of Mallarmé's poems including the famous «Hérodiade». In a tone that is markedly Paterian, Yeats reveals his admiration for this magnificent Mallarméan composition: «There was something in myself compelling me to attempt creation of an art as separate from everything heterogeneous and casual, from all character

[6] OLIVER ELTON, *Biography of F. Frederick York Powell,* 2 vols., Clarendon Press, Oxford, 1906, I, pp. 157-158.

[7] STÉPHANE MALLARMÉ, «Variations sur un sujet», *Oeuvres complètes,* Gallimard, Paris, 1945, p. 360.

and circumstance, as some Hérodiade of our theatre, dancing seemingly alone in her narrow moving luminous circle».[8]

In Yeats too we find corroborated that Paterian apprehension of the fragmented and fragmentary nature of life and that same quest for Unity. «A conviction that the world was now but a bundle of fragments possessed me without ceasing»,[9] declares Yeats, and later on: «I thought there could be no aim for poet or artist except expression of a "Unity of Being" like that of a "perfectly proportioned human body"».[10] These beliefs will later be seen to have their direct counterpart in those of JRJ. Like Pater, and like Mallarmé, Yeats too saw Art as the sole Way of Redemption, and the written Word as the ultimate sanctuary against the ravages of ephemeral Time, at which he roundly inveighs: «I spit into the face of Time / That has transfigured me».[11] It is not surprising to learn that a poet with concerns such as these should have found an admiring reader in JRJ, who is quoted as ranking Yeats as follows: «Los más grandes poetas—salvando a Dante—, son los ingleses: Yeats, Shelley, Browning»,[12] and whose sense of affinity with the Anglo-Irish poet led him to translate a number of his poems, some of which were submitted for publication by the Editorial Signo.[13] JRJ, adhering to the concept of the sacredness of the Word, could readily appreciate a poet whose very first collection, written in 1889 when Yeats was a mere twenty-four years old, is initiated with a lyric doubly affirming that «Words alone are certain good». Yeats's «The Song of the Happy Shepherd» from *Crossways* claims as sole bastion against all temporal changefulness, the eternal Logos:

> But O, sick children of the world,
> Of all the many changing things
> In dreary dancing past us whirled,
> To the cracked tune that Chronos sings,
> Words alone are certain good.

It is worth noting that that «children of the world» echoes the exact words of Pater in the passage with which I opened.

JRJ's intense and exaggerated sensitivity, indeed desperation, in the face of Time and temporality, was a factor largely responsible in the shaping of his aesthetics. But again, it is necessary to remind ourselves that he was not unique in this, as is demonstrated through the more or less contemporaneous examples of Pater, Mallarmé and now Yeats. The private suffering of one profoundly disturbed as was JRJ by the early death of his father,[14] should be seen not in isolation but rather as an adjunct to this

8 W. B. Yeats, *The Trembling of the Veil, Autobiographies,* Macmillan, London, 1955, p. 321.

9 *Ibid.,* p. 189.

10 *Ibid.,* p. 246.

11 W. B. Yeats, «The Lamentation of the Old Pensioner», «The Rose», *The Collected Poems of W. B. Yeats,* Macmillan, London, 1977, p. 52.

12 Guerrero Ruiz, p. 213.

13 Guerrero Ruiz, p. 88.

14 For references to this biographical background, see R. A. Cardwell, *JRJ, The Modernist Apprenticeship 1895-1900,* Colloquium Verlag, Berlin, 1977, p. 14; B. Gi-

acute form of Angst so peculiar to the entire «fin du siècle»—or «fin du globe», as Oscar Wilde caused Dorian Gray dismally to observe. It is interesting that as early as 1891, Gómez Carrillo gave a critical account of *The Picture of Dorian Gray* in an essay on Oscar Wilde.[15] The young JRJ grew up in the atmosphere of this all-pervading uncertainty, the death-throes of a century, which created a sense of «generation» unlike any other previous to it: a «modern» albeit moribund one. A return to Yeats, with whom JRJ felt a distinct fellowship, will illustrate this fact:

> Why are these strange souls born everywhere today, with hearts that Christianity, as shaped by history, cannot satisfy? Our love-letters wear out our love; no school of painting outlasts its founders, every stroke of the brush exhausts the impulse, Pre-Raphaelitism had some twenty years; Impressionism thirty perhaps. Why should we believe that religion can never bring round its antithesis? Is it true that our air is disturbed as Mallarmé said, by «the trembling of the veil of the Temple», or that «our whole age is seeking to bring forth a sacred book»? Some of us thought that book near towards the end of the last century, but the tide sank again.

Significantly, Yeats called the book (Book IV of *The Trembling of the Veil*) from which this passage comes, «The Tragic Generation». A little earlier on he refers to the works of Pater:

> The only great prose in modern English, and yet I began to wonder if it, or the attitude of mind of which it was the noblest expression, had not caused the disaster of my friends. It taught us to walk upon a rope, tightly stretched through serene air, and we were left to keep our feet upon a swaying rope in a storm.

The image perfectly captures and conveys the tension and insecurity so acutely experienced by a whole era and throughout Europe. Probably what Yeats had in mind when he chose this metaphor was that Pater, like many of the German Romantics also, often chose to express a vision of classical antiquity (as in Pater's *Marius the Epicurean,* for example) or artistically harmonious periods (as in his *The Renaissance*), rather than the volatile circumstances of the late nineteenth and early twentieth centuries. At all events, it was precisely this «tightrope» that JRJ himself was to tread. In further evidence of the kind of cross-pollination of contemporary aesthetic theory, it is interesting to observe that Yeats freely acknowledged his *Rosa Alchemica* to have been «shaped» by Pater, and a substantial number of his poems to have been «given elaborate form» by the influence of Mallarmé. In an era when «Things fall apart; the centre cannot hold»[16] the anguished

COVATE, *La poesía de JRJ,* Ediciones Ariel, Barcelona, 1973, pp. 39-40; G. PALAU DE NEMES, *Vida y obra de JRJ,* 2 vols., Gredos, Madrid, 1974, I, p. 158 et seq. JRJ's reaction to his father's death is also related in one of the poet's autobiographical notes, reproduced in E. DÍEZ-CANEDO's *JRJ en su obra,* El Colegio de México, México, 1944, pp. 38-39.

[15] See L. E. DAVIS, «Oscar Wilde in Spain», *Comparative Literature,* 25, 1973, pp. 136-152.

[16] W. B. YEATS, «The Second Coming», «Michael Robartes and the Dancer», *The Collected Poems of W. B. Yeats,* p. 210.

endeavour to immortalize the fleeting moment of the here and now was the prerogative not of JRJ alone but of many of the most acutely sensitive poets and aesthetes of the time. The sole available solution, the sole hope of achieving this «defeat» of Time, lay for JRJ—as for others too—in the power of the Word and in the Work. The struggle for perfect poetic expression was therefore of paramount importance.

The role of the Imagination

The poet's struggle with the Word, his struggle for expression, is essentially of a Romantic nature. This is a fact which it is important to bear in mind in any discussion of JRJ's own relationship with the Word, and one which therefore calls for consideration at this point. In conjunction with this, it is necessary to have a general appreciation of the role of the Imagination within the Romantic tradition, as exemplified for instance in Kant and in Coleridge. For it is the Imagination which provides the theatre of the battle. Without exception, the poets with whom we shall be concerned, accepted this Romantic sense of Imagination as a creative power, the finite counterpart—as Coleridge says in his *Biographia Literaria*—of the original creative act of God; significantly, of the act by which God created Himself, the divine «I Am»: the Logos.[17] It had been a commonplace from St Augustine and St Thomas Aquinas onward to find statements to the effect that man's rational activity comes near to mirroring the divine creative act. The Imagination was regarded as a much lower, mechanical and untrustworthy function of the mind, prone only to produce bizarre fancies. The great contribution of the Romantics lay precisely in their revaluation of Imagination. This re-appraisal, initiated in the eighteenth century, bore a continuing influence upon succeeding generations and is clearly apparent in Spanish literature of the nineteenth and twentieth centuries. As a result of the discovery—whether in philosophy, art or poetry—that there exists in the universe an infinity of things which reason alone is incapable of apprehending, the philosopher, the artist and the poet alike were thus to address themselves to the world of mystery: the rationally unknown and unknowable. In the words of Antonio Machado: «el alma del poeta / se orienta hacia el misterio». Through poetic intuition alone could any further advance henceforth be made:

> Sólo el poeta puede
> mirar lo que está lejos
> dentro del alma, en turbio
> y mago sol envuelto.[18]

[17] Samuel Taylor Coleridge, *Biographia Literaria,* edited by George Watson, Dent, London, 1975, p. 167.

[18] Antonio Machado, «Introducción» LXI, *Soledades, galerías y otros poemas, Obras: poesía y prosa,* edited by Aurora de Albornoz and Guillermo de Torre, Losada, Buenos Aires, 1964, pp. 103-104.

José Ferrater Mora, in his *Diccionario de filosofía,* succinctly lists the elements of Romanticism:

> (El romanticismo) sostiene con frecuencia el primado de la intuición y del sentimiento frente a la razón y al análisis; lo irracional le atrae indudablemente más que lo racional, lo imprevisible más que lo previsible, lo multiforme [...] más que lo uniforme [...] lo anónimo (o lo genial) más que lo nombrable, lo interno más que lo externo y lo dramático más que lo apacible.[19]

The problem of taming the unpredictable and unbridled products of the Romantic Imagination is especially explicit in the nineteenth century poet, Gustavo Adolfo Bécquer. His prose introduction to *Rimas* opens: «Por los tenebrosos rincones de mi cerebro, acurrucados y desnudos, duermen los extravagantes hijos de mi fantasía, esperando en silencio que el Arte los vista de la palabra para poderse presentar decentes en la escena del mundo». He is conscious of these fancies dwelling within him, «desnudos y deformes, revueltos y barajados en indescriptible confusión», seething about in an autonomous life: «una vida oscura y extraña, semejante a la de esas miríadas de gérmenes que hierven y se estremecen en una eterna incubación dentro de las entrañas de la tierra». He further acknowledges that formal expression alone can save, order and perpetuate them:

> Pero, ¡ay!, que entre el mundo de la idea y el de la forma existe un abismo que sólo puede salvar la palabra, y la palabra tímida y perezosa se niega a secundar sus esfuerzos. Mudos, sombríos e impotentes, después de la inútil lucha vuelven a caer en su antiguo marasmo [...] Estas sediciones de los rebeldes hijos de la imaginación explican alguna de mis fiebres: ellas son la causa desconocida para la ciencia de mis exaltaciones y mis abatimientos.

Again, in his prose introduction to Augusto Ferrán's *La soledad,* Bécquer treats the theme of Imagination and language; and in his *Cartas literarias a una mujer,* he makes the following definition of poetry: «La poesía es en el hombre una cualidad puramente del espíritu; reside en su alma, vive con la vida incorpórea de la idea, y para revelarla necesita darle una forma. Por eso la escribe». Bécquer's own relationship with poetic expression is the subject of the famous first «Rima», beginning «Yo sé un himno gigante y extraño», and whose second and middle stanza reads:

> Yo quisiera escribirlo, del hombre
> domando el rebelde, mezquino idioma,
> con palabras que fuesen a un tiempo
> suspiros y risas, colores y notas.

There follow the key words: «Pero en vano es luchar; que no hay cifra / capaz de encerrarlo» [al «himno gigante y extraño»]. Let us take this statement and see in what way it relates first to a poem by Rubén Darío and second, to a poem by JRJ.[20]

[19] José Ferrater Mora, *Diccionario de filosofía,* Editorial Sudamericana, Buenos Aires, 1958, p. 1175.

[20] The connexion between Bécquer and JRJ has been treated to some extent by

About two-thirds of the way through Darío's early and extensive poem entitled «El libro», we find the following echo of the Becquerian sentiment:

Mas es en vano cantar;
es muy grande mi flaqueza
y del libro la belleza
yo no podré retratar.

The stanza then continues to modify with somewhat more optimism its initial statement of the impossibility of finding expression:

Pero siento chispear
en mi cerebro algo intenso,
por lo cual conozco y pienso
y por eso al libro canto;
porque amo todo lo santo,
porque amo todo lo inmenso.

The procedure here is much like that of Bécquer. For the despairing negation of any hope of success in Bécquer's statement, «Pero en vano es luchar; que no hay cifra / capaz de encerrarle», is similarly mitigated by the phrase which immediately follows:

y apenas, ¡oh hermosa!,
si, teniendo en mis manos las tuyas,
pudiera al oído, cantártelo a solas.

It is an emendation which surely implies, as in Darío's stanza, a certain potentiality of achievement after all—no matter how tenuous. There is an inherent self-contradiction here too, of course. Bécquer is in fact employing within the «Rima» that very material (poetic diction) of which he is denying either possession or mastery. Indeed, he is employing it specifically for the paradoxical purpose of refuting his ability to do so.

These two examples of poets, each of whom is denying his own linguistic capability, only subsequently to add a kind of rider against such a negation, may appear to be dealing with nothing more than rather superficial modesty topoi of medieval tradition. However, this is not in fact the case. They are archetypal illustrations of the Romantic concept of the inadequacy of the Word to express the ineffable. A later stanza in that same epic poem of Darío will serve as confirmation. What is at stake is the struggle of the

critics, e.g. R. GULLÓN in his *Direcciones del modernismo,* Gredos, Madrid, 1971, pp. 11-16. Principally however it is to JRJ himself that we should look for acknowledgement of the connexion between the two poets. References to Bécquer abound in JRJ's *El modernismo: notas de un curso (1953)*, edited by R. Gullón and E. Fernández Méndez, Aguilar, México, 1962. Further, in the essay specifically dedicated to Bécquer in JRJ's *Españoles de tres mundos,* Afrodisio Aguado, Madrid, 1960, pp. 95-98, we find the following homage: «Són, Rima ya no podrán en muchos años usarse en España sin que vuelvan de Bécquer».

poet with his intractable material. Visited by the angel of Poetry, the poet says:

> Entonces yo le pedí
> que en mi pecho se anidara,
> que jamás me abandonara,
> que estuviese junto a mí.
> Mover los labios le vi
> y luego me dijo: «Escucha;
> entra al campo de la lucha,
> pero calma tu ansia loca.
> La vida es poca, muy poca.
> y la desventura es mucha».

These citations from so early a poem as «El libro» help to present a picture of the historical sequence of the Romantic struggle for «le mot juste». They have been chosen for this reason, despite the fact that the work is still patently immature and not of Darío's best. The poet was, after all, only sixteen years old at the time of its composition in 1882.

An essay by Eugenio Florit[21] further illustrates and examines the struggle of Darío with form: «a form», says Florit, «in pursuit of which he was endlessly engaged». In support of his argument, Florit cites the final poem of *Prosas profanas,* the title alone of which proves its relevance: «Yo persigo una forma».

> Yo persigo una forma que no encuentra mi estilo,
> botón de pensamiento que busca ser la rosa;
> se anuncia con un beso que en mis labios se posa
> al abrazo imposible de la Venus de Milo [...]
>
> Y no hallo sino la palabra que huye,
> la iniciación melódica que de la flauta fluye
> y la barca del sueño que en el espacio boga.

Out of the poem's total of four stanzas, it is these two (the first and the third) which most pertinently bear on the problem of the poet's struggle with his material.

Having thus clearly made his point with this example, Florit does not deem it necessary to expand upon it further. But for our own purposes it is nonetheless worth pausing to observe again the inherent self-paradox contained in the line «Y no hallo sino la palabra que huye». Its negation is a deceptive one, masking what is in fact a gesture toward achievement. The poet laments his inability to capture the Word—save that which flees. The paradox incorporated in that double negative, «no [...] sino», is evident: there is actually more of the possible than of the impossible, more of hope than of despair, in such a declaration. It is once more the same kind of

[21] The essay, entitled «The Modernist Prefigurement in the Early Work of Rubén Darío», was translated by John Wilcox and is to be found in *Rubén Darío: Centennial Studies,* edited by Miguel González-Gerth and George D. Schade, University of Texas at Austin, 1970, pp. 31-47.

intrinsic self-contradiction that we have noted above; the acknowledgement of an invincible impossibility—but in terms such as to vanquish it.

If we turn now to consider JRJ's own struggle for poetic expression, we shall find that as the Work develops, so the accent eventually shifts from that of despair, or at best merely tentative hopes, to confidence. Certainly JRJ was periodically beset by the same sense of anguished inability and paralysis as his poetic predecessors and contemporaries, when confronted with the task of expressing the ineffable. The early poetry betrays moments of deepest dismay and doubt, as in «Libertador» from *Poesía (en verso)* (1917-1923), with its opening lines: « ¡Con qué dificultad, tiempo, / te voy robando tus joyas...! »[22] The critic, Antonio Sánchez-Barbudo, has commented on the emphasis which this poem gives to the sheer effort involved in the realization of the poetic Work and to the «dolores de carpintero poético» which the second stanza suggests with its reference to the poet's «manos sangrientas / y aplastadas de las moles».[23] Another example is the poem beginning « ¡Espera, luz, espera! » from *Eternidades* (1916-1917) and ending with the desolate lines: «Y me echo al suelo, como un niño, / llorando para mí, sin verla ya» (*LP*, p. 557). Even as late as *La estación total* (1923-1936), we find poems such as «Mi reino» expressing the impossibility of the poet's task:

Sólo en lo eterno podría
yo realizar esta ansia
de la belleza completa. (*LP*, p. 1184)

Or again, «Dios primero» emphasizes the exasperating arbitrariness of poetic fulfilment:

Días nulos, cual los días
de parada indiferencia
de dios antecreador.

Only occasionally are these days of sterility punctuated by «de pronto, un día de gracia» (*LP*, p. 1185). Worse still, the poet may abdicate entirely before the unequal struggle, as in «El azul relativo» (*LP*, pp. 1150-1151).[24]

Nevertheless, it is the sense of the positive value of the struggle which ultimately predominates in JRJ's Work—the sense, indeed, of triumph. Thus in the late collection, *Dios deseado y deseante* of 1949, the theme is that of encounter and fulfilment. The long apprenticeship of struggle and perseverance since earliest childhood has found its reward:

Y yo poseedor, enmedio, ya,
de tu conciencia, dios, por esperarte

22 JRJ, *Libros de poesía,* compiled by Agustín Caballero, Aguilar, Madrid, 1972, p. 898. All future references to this edition are given after quotations in the text, in the abbreviated form, *LP*.

23 A. Sánchez-Barbudo, *La segunda época de JRJ (1916-1953)*, Gredos, Madrid, 1962, p. 93.

24 See commentary on this poem by A. Sánchez-Barbudo, *Cincuenta poemas comentados,* Gredos, Madrid, 1963, p. 107.

desde mi infancia destinada,
sin descanso ni tedio. (*LP,* p. 1306)

In «El nombre conseguido de los nombres» the second stanza rings with obvious triumph:

Yo he acumulado mi esperanza
en lengua, en nombre hablado, en nombre escrito;
a todo yo le había puesto nombre. (*LP,* p. 1291)

The affirmation could scarcely be more positive, more jubilant. Now, in the closing lines of «En lo mejor que tengo», JRJ can plainly assert his perfected grasp of poetic expression: «contento de ser tuyo [dios] y de ser mío / en lo mejor que tengo, mi espresión» (*LP,* pp. 1321-1322).[25]

That the artistic life is one of struggle and suffering is a familiar nineteenth and twentieth century topos. Edmund Wilson's *The Wound and the Bow* for example, or *Axel's Castle,* bear witness to this[26] and they were sufficiently well-known to be the subject of discussion between Ricardo Gullón and JRJ.[27] It might perhaps be tempting to construct a theory of this struggle concept as originating from the «agon» of Greek drama. But the idea that there either is or was any conscious, deliberate continuity between the two is too dubious to posit with much conviction. Nevertheless, the fact that the theme of struggle runs uninterruptedly through from Romanticism to «modernismo» and to that contemporary of JRJ who is the most lucid exegete of «agonía» with its essentially Greek etymology —Miguel de Unamuno—is of considerable interest.

The confluence of opinion with respect to the difficulty of achieving «le mot juste» has already been observed above in Bécquer, the great Spanish Romantic; in Darío, the founder of «modernismo»;[28] and in JRJ,

[25] For a full analysis, see A. SÁNCHEZ-BARBUDO, *La segunda época de JRJ (1916-1953),* pp. 186-187.

[26] For further analyses of the struggle concept in Romanticism see:

A. FARINELLI, *Il romanticismo nel mondo latino,* Fratelli Bocca, Turin, 1927. This deals with Italian, French and Spanish sources.

M. PRAZ, *The Romantic Agony,* translated from the Italian by Angus Davidson, Oxford University Press, London and New York, 1970.

H. G. SCHENK, *The Mind of the European Romantics,* F. Ungar, New York, 1967.

A. THORLBY, *The Romantic Movement,* Longmans, London, 1966.

P. VAN TIEGHEM, *Le romantisme dans la littérature européenne,* Michel, Paris, 1948.

[27] R. GULLÓN, *Conversaciones con JRJ,* Taurus, Madrid, 1958, p. 105.

[28] It is necessary to draw attention to the fact that this claim that Darío is the founder of «modernismo» is currently under much dispute. R. A. CARDWELL, for instance, in his book *JRJ, The Modernist Apprenticeship 1895-1900,* p. 127, seriously questions the validiy of such a claim:

> Although we should not minimise the importance of the Nicaraguan in the development of Spanish «modernismo» and Jiménez in particular, we must accept Gerald Brown's restrictions: the new poets may have owed more to Verlaine than to Darío; Darío's poetry liberated the young men from old inhibitions rather than provided models to be copied; the Spaniards turned inwards in a way that Darío rarely did.

the culminator of «modernismo». It follows therefore that the «modernistas» should be regarded as the inheritors of Romanticism and that it is above all this continued struggle to find expression for the inexpressible which is their Romantic patrimony and which unites the two schools. Certainly the «modernista» poets sought to disencumber themselves of all the Romantic excesses and superfluities—above all, of its tendency to false sentimentality—but they nonetheless retained the particular element with which we are here concerned and which was its quintessence. In the collection of notes taken from lectures by JRJ in his course entitled *El modernismo*[29] we find the poet recorded as defining the movement thus: «El modernismo fue para el romanticismo, lo que el Renacimiento para la Edad Media. [Edad Media exaltadora de mitos religiosos; fantástica. [...] El modernismo es un nuevo Renacimiento que une lo sensorial con lo metafísico, el dogma con el hombre]».[30] In associating «modernismo» with the Renaissance, JRJ coincides with his *Helios* contemporaries such as Cansinos Assens or Manuel Díaz-Rodríguez; and they, in turn, echo Ruskin and Pater. In his «Paréntesis modernista o ligero ensayo sobre el modernismo» in *Camino de perfección,* published in Paris in 1909, Díaz-Rodríguez detects two predominant tendencies in the new literary movement: a return to Nature; and a return to Mysticism—both of which, in his view, characterize the Renaissance. Thus he sees «modernismo» as a «segundo Renacimiento»:

> A la natural progresión de la doble tendencia en el segundo Renacimiento, corresponde una ascensión progresiva y luminosa del arte. Mientras la tendencia a volver a la naturaleza va, refinándose, a cumplirse en la perfección de la forma, la tendencia mística va, depurándose, a un misticismo lleno de gracia y fineza, como es al decir de Pater el misticismo de Leonardo.[31]

The notes from JRJ's lectures continue: «En poesía la forma es la mitad. Todo en la vida es una cadena. Nadie puede negar antecedencias ni consecuencias. Empieza poesía moderna española por Bécquer, Unamuno y Rubén Darío». The essence of what JRJ means when in a later lecture he states: «El modernismo, renacimiento contra romanticismo»[32] is that «modernismo» is an improvement on Romanticism, in the sense that it improves upon the best qualities of the Romantics whilst simultaneously waging war against its excesses and clichés. The statement is in perfect accord with the above quoted «todo en la vida es una cadena». To construe the word «contra»

However, I prefer to follow the opinion of E. Díez-Canedo who opens his book, *JRJ en su obra,* with the affirmation that «La escuela que en literatura se conoce con la denominación de "modernismo" tiene, como se sabe, por figura principal, a [...] Rubén Darío».

29 It is important to remember that *El modernismo* is a collection of the lectures verbally delivered by JRJ, not written by his own hand. The text is derived from the notes taken by members of his audience, and chiefly Gloria Arjona de Muñoz Lee.

30 JRJ, *El modernismo,* p. 80.

31 Manuel Díaz-Rodríguez, *Camino de perfección,* Editorial Cecilio Acosta, Caracas, 1942, p. 97.

32 JRJ, *El modernismo,* p. 109.

in this context as an indication of the categorical opposition of «modernismo» to Romanticism would be entirely mistaken.

We should now return to the essay by Eugenio Florit in order to substantiate further the consistency of the links between Rubén Darío and JRJ, which Florit admirably points out. He refers to the admiration and enthusiasm which the name alone of Rubén Darío inspired in JRJ even prior to their personal encounter in April of 1900. Florit then offers some convincing textual examples in evidence of a real resemblance both of tone and vocabulary between the two great poets. Whether such resemblance is indeed the result of influence or is attributable only to coincidence is of course always open to argument. Even so, it would in any case seem to corroborate JRJ's view of the chain-like unity of life and literature.

Florit's first comparison is between the poem «La niña de los ojos azules» written by Darío when still only adolescent and the poem by JRJ entitled «Adolescencia». The Darío poem is placed by Méndez Plancarte somewhere between 1882 and 1884; the JRJ poem, which appears in *Rimas de sombra,* was composed some two decades later.

> Cuando la hablé de mi amor
> inclinó la frente tímida;
> y como perlas, dos lágrimas
> rodaron por sus mejillas. (Rubén Darío)
>
> No se atrevía a mirarme;
> le dije que éramos novios,
> ... y sus lágrimas rodaron
> de sus ojos melancólicos. (JRJ)

The similarities speak for themselves.[33]

A further two poems of Darío are then adduced by Florit in support of his theory of resemblances. They are both «romances» which clearly prefigure and find their echo in the early JRJ ballads of *Rimas de sombra* and *Arias tristes,* written between 1898 and 1903. The existence of close textual affinities between Darío and the early JRJ are thus plainly established, which makes the coincidence of their views on aesthetic topics highly probable.

To sum up, it is Bécquer who is established by the «modernistas» and especially by Rubén Darío and JRJ as the poet acknowledged to be the principal forerunner of the «modernista» movement. From San Juan de la Cruz to Bécquer and Rosalía de Castro, the chain of affinities extends forward to Darío, Unamuno, JRJ and their «modernista» confrères. Out of this network we may perceive the existence of an inter-relationship and unity in these literary developments.

[33] This same comparison is adduced by BERNARDO GICOVATE, *La poesía de JRJ,* p. 52.

Chapter II

THE POWER OF THE WORD

The generation of 1914 (usually denoted by the dates 1911 to 1925 and centred upon the year 1914 in which Ortega's *Meditaciones del Quijote* was published)[1] found itself of necessity linked with Europe and with European intellectual movements, not only because it sought possible salvation for the problems of Spain in that quarter, but also because it suddenly discovered Europe to be in a state of crisis with the initiation of World War I. As a result of circumstance therefore, and also due especially to the influence of José Ortega y Gasset, the philosophers and thinking of the international vanguard came to be known in Spain: Dilthey, Freud, Simmel, Husserl, Bergson, Blondel, Scheler, Heidegger, and so on. The works of Nietzsche, already influential in Spain, were interpreted in a new light as a consequence of the War and, as shall be seen, new editions and translations appeared. In 1923 Ortega founded the *Revista de Occidente* which continued to be published until 1936 and this, together with its book publishing programme, the *Biblioteca,* kept its Spanish readers fully informed on contemporary philosophical and aesthetic matters. By means of editions and translations, Ortega incorporated into Spanish thought the most important parts of European, and particularly German, learning. Due to this and to his own philosophical endeavours a full school of philosophy, La Escuela de Madrid, was founded. Its membership included, and still does, such scholars as Manuel García Morente, Fernando Vela, Xavier Zubiri, José Gaos, Manuel Granell, Julián Marías and many more, all of whom helped to disseminate new philosophical thought in Spain.

One of the predominant preoccupations of the new current of philosophy was precisely the problem of language: the impossibility of putting objects into words directly, or of capturing reality linguistically. It was a problem close to the heart of JRJ. Nietzsche himself had written upon the subject of the arbitrariness of language.[2] We have ample testimony that JRJ read Nietzsche. Graciela Palau de Nemes in her biography of JRJ affirms that

[1] For an analysis and justification of the term «generation» see Julián Marías, *Introducción a la filosofía,* Revista de Occidente, Madrid, 1963, pp. 398-404. Also, J. Marías, *El método histórico de las generaciones,* Revista de Occidente, Madrid, 1949. See too José Ortega y Gasset, «El método de las generaciones en Historia», *Obras completas,* Revista de Occidente, Madrid, 1958, p. 50.

[2] See S. Kofman, *Nietzsche et la métaphore,* Payot, Paris, 1972.

«viviendo con Simarro y por mediación de Achúcarro, Juan Ramón leyó a Nietzsche»;[3] and this is corroborated by a conversation between JRJ and Gullón in which JRJ stated that it was there that he discovered «los libros de Nietzsche en traducciones francesas», and that this occurred «hacia 1905 o 1906».[4] The most compact source of information as to JRJ's knowledge of Nietzsche is to be found in Gonzalo Sobejano's *Nietzsche en España,*[5] for it adduces references not only from Gullón's *Conversaciones con JRJ* but also from the diary of Juan Guerrero Ruiz and from the notes taken from JRJ's own lectures, compiled in *El modernismo.*

The increasing philosophical concern with the function of language and its insufficiencies would not have escaped the attention of JRJ. Important work on the subject was being published by, for instance, the major phenomenologist Edmund Husserl. *Ideen zu einer reinen Phänomenologie und phänomenologische Philosophie* came out in 1913, and was translated into Spanish by José Gaos in 1949. Following upon Husserl's *Vorlesungen zur Phänomenologie des inneren Zeitbewusstseins,* edited by M. Heidegger and published in 1929, came the *Méditations cartésiennes. Introduction à la phénoménologie* in 1931. This too became available in Spanish in 1942, translated by J. Gaos. In 1936 Husserl published «Die Krisis der europäischen Wissenschaften und die transzendentale Phänomenologie» in *Philosophia,* edited by A. Liebert. Access to Husserl's work was early available to Spanish men of letters. It is probable that JRJ, like Antonio Machado, first read extensively of Husserl's theories in Georges Gurvitch's *Les tendances actuelles de la philosophie allemande* published in Paris in 1930 and subsequently translated into Spanish in 1933. As early as 1931, the analytical work by Theodor Celms entitled *Der phänomenologische Idealismus Husserls* (1928), became available in Spanish translation; and in 1936 Carlos Astrada wrote his *Idealismo fenomenológico y metafísico existencial.* Francisco Romero and Joaquín Xirau followed later with additional contributions to the understanding of Husserl's theories. In his recent book, *Ortega as Phenomenologist* (Columbia University Press, New York, 1978), Philip Silver stresses Ortega's unusual familiarity—pre-1914—with the early writings of Husserl. This, Silver argues, together with Ortega's other readings of German experimental phenomenological psychologists, helped to bring about the evolution by Ortega of a phenomenology of origins by the time he had finished his *Meditaciones del Quijote.* Thus Ortega's first book is placed squarely in the context of the phenomenological movement. Its influence on JRJ is well known.

The philosophical enquiry into the value of language conducted by Husserl, Scheler and later Wittgenstein and the so-called Vienna Circle, is significant as part of the background culture of JRJ. The point is that these philosophers and phenomenologists were all concerned in varying degree and manner with the insufficiency of language to capture or convey reality, and that JRJ was very much alive to this climate of thinking. He,

[3] G. Palau de Nemes, *Vida y obra de JRJ,* I, p. 313.
[4] R. Gullón, *Conversaciones con JRJ,* p. 58.
[5] Gonzalo Sobejano, *Nietzsche en España,* Gredos, Madrid, 1967, pp. 604-607.

no less than they, was undoubtedly aware of the appalling and at times seemingly insuperable difficulty of reconciling language with reality, of embodying reality in words. And yet this was the very goal at which he aimed. For him the Word represented not only, nor merely, an instrument for the stark naming of things, but a tool of sacred and creative significance. The Word, as conceived by JRJ, was the repository of just that reality which, as we shall see in the following pages, Wittgenstein denies it; of the irreducible essence of things, of emotions—in short, of all experience. Unlike Wittgenstein's negation of the possibility, it was precisely here, in the embrace of reality in language, that JRJ placed the faith of a lifetime. To embrace it, but further, to create it. The naming process for JRJ was more than a mere equation «let x=y+z»; it was a veritable act of creation with something of the ceremony of taumaturgy about it: «Nombrar las cosas ¿no es crearlas? En realidad, el poeta es un nombrador a la manera de Dios: "Hágase, y hágase porque yo lo digo".»[6] This is a concept which of course brings in its train the whole knotty problematic of «Reality», of existent fact. For how are we to construe reality if, as JRJ affirms, the poet's function is to *create?* And to create, moreover, out of that which is not. He offers us the following clarification: «El poeta es un creador. Lo que aparentemente no existe, lo crea, y si lo crea es porque sus elementos existen. Si un científico inventa [...] ¿por qué no ha de inventar un poeta, que puede hacerlo, un mundo o parte de él?»[7] Thus the function of the Word, in the hands of the poet, is to draw forth potentialities from their raw state of mere possibility and to realize them as actuality fulfilled: that which is «not-yet» thereby arriving at a state of Being, or permanence, in the poem. In this way, the process of poetic naming appears as a kind of religious «actus purus» of fulfilment; a creative elicitation. It is clear then that JRJ—for all his obsessive pursuit after linguistic precision, as will be seen—in no way regarded the Word as mere classifiable dictionary-material. In his conception, the Word was instinct with holiness. Rejecting the invitation, in 1934, to become a member of the coveted Real Academia Española, he roundly declared to Gregorio Marañón, spokesman for the Academy: «Yo no soy un filólogo; no estudio las palabras, las invento, que no es lo mismo; soy un creador que se debe a su obra».[8] It is the proud, not to say arrogant, affirmation of one who would have no part in the dusty pedantry, as he saw it, of philology or lexicography. For JRJ the Word was the crucible of all that is alive and variable. If he conceived of himself as «un dios sin espada, sin nada de lo que hacen los hombres con su ciencia; sólo con lo que es producto de lo vivo, lo que se cambia todo; sí, de fuego o de luz, luz»,[9] it is the Word, living and vital, which will be for the poet that weapon which he lacks, in his fight to seek out the quintessence of things.

[6] JRJ, «Lo "fable" y lo "inefable"», «Poesía cerrada y poesía abierta», *Pájinas escojidas; prosa,* selected by R. Gullón, Gredos, Madrid, 1970, p. 189.
[7] *Ibid.,* pp. 188-189.
[8] Guerrero Ruiz, p. 403.
[9] JRJ, «Fragmento primero», «Espacio», *Tercera antolojía poética,* compiled by

The success or failure of that struggle, as JRJ well knew, depended on the degree to which the poet could attain identity of word with object and thereby cause his *expression* of things to *become* that which they express. In his student copy of the *Manual de retórica y poética* (1890), JRJ had already shown his early preoccupation with the conformity of word with idea, underlining the following sentence: «Llámanse propias las palabras que enuncian exactamente la idea que intentamos expresar».[10] The question of essences, which the pursuit of Truth and of Reality indicates, must be reserved for later discussion. It is a wide philosophical problem and one which will necessitate enquiry into the concomitant issue of the Idea, in Platonic or neo-Platonic mode. For «essence» and «Idea» are concepts which must logically be consequent upon the view that language can indeed enfold the perfect reality of things.

JRJ's claim for the poet is momentous: he is the living witness of the universe, to which he testifies. But his implicit claim for the power of the Word is equally—perhaps more—ambitious; for it is by virtue of the Word alone that the poet can fulfil the stated function. The recreation of the World in the Word. Such, according to JRJ, is the capacity of language for the poet. This conception is not openly apparent in his earliest poetry, however. It is first formulated—in terms that transcend merely routine nineteenth century Romantic cliché, that is—only with the initiation of his so-called «Second Epoch» and specifically in the famous poem beginning « ¡Intelijencia, dame / el nombre exacto de las cosas! », written in 1918. Thereafter, JRJ does not waver from his tenet regarding the potency of the Word. It is important to recognize, however, that there do exist *some* earlier intimations of the 1918 statement. Graciela Palau de Nemes has pointed out that even as a schoolboy JRJ had marked in the margin of his *Manual de retórica y poética* passages explaining that «la verdad del pensamiento consistía "en su conformidad con las cosas a que se refiere" y que, de faltar esta conformidad, el pensamiento se llamaba *falso, inexacto*».[11] Evidently, the young JRJ paid close attention to those lessons which recommended clarity as the prime quality of language. Furthermore, in *Estío* written in 1915 shortly after *Sonetos espirituales,* the concept of «desnudez» is already increasingly developed and a predominantly intellectual strain appears in the evocation of emotion. The poem «Otoño» (*LP,* p. 193) heralds, for example, the 1918 statement in its exhortation to «burn the old leaves» of past poetic adornment and embellishment in order to free «el diamante puro, para incorporarlo al recuerdo». From now on his sole concern will be with « ¡lo ardiente, lo claro, lo áureo, / lo definido, lo neto! ». Clarity, definition, precision: the attributes of the intellect. On his return with Zenobia from the States to Spain in 1916, JRJ discovered the so-called «imaginista» movement. *Some Imagist Poets,* edited by Amy Lowell, proclaimed the need for linguistic exactitude (as manifested for

Eugenio Florit, Editorial Biblioteca Nueva, Madrid, 1970, p. 870. All future references to this anthology are given after quotations in the text, in the abbreviated form *TAP.*

[10] G. Palau de Nemes, *Vida y obra de JRJ,* I, pp. 26-27.

[11] *Ibid.,* pp. 54-55.

example in Lowell's own poem «Patterns»). This discovery both coincided and corresponded with JRJ's own increasing abandonment of «molde» and «adorno» in favour of a «poesía natural, libre de toda sujeción, sostenida levemente por palabras exactas e imágenes precisas».[12]

Nevertheless as I have said earlier, it would be mistaken to think that JRJ did not suffer from moments of doubt as to the efficacy of language. A few lines taken from the «Fragmento primero», written between 1941 and 1942,[13] of his prose poem «Espacio» serve to show his awareness of the problems language poses, the opacity of meaning: «Y el idioma, ¡qué confusión!, qué cosas nos decimos sin saber lo que nos decimos»; and immediately there follows on: «Amor, amor, amor (lo cantó Yeats), "amor en el lugar del escremento". ¿Asco de nuestro ser, nuestro principio y nuestro fin; asco de aquello que más nos vive y más nos muere?» Here, JRJ has chosen to cite a line from Yeats[14] to indicate the way in which the idea at times defies adequate expression, the shortcoming of language. He is obliged to inspect this elliptical line of Yeats and offer some exegetical rendering of it, albeit in a tentatively interrogative form, in order to clarify its enigma. It is the double question posited by JRJ which fully elicits the sense: that of the paradoxical duality of love, sublime and spiritual on one hand; scatalogical on the other, and the two forever conjoined, inseparable.[15] The curious thing to note here however is not merely JRJ's exegesis of the paradoxes of sex and by extension man's physical being, but the linking of this with «el idioma». Nor is this the only example of doubt about the expressive power of language.[16]

Certainly, then, it is true that JRJ was by no means unaware of the possible insufficiency of the Word; but what is important to observe is that no note of scepticism as such, is discernible. Of course, as has been pointed out, this is only to be expected in conformity with his aesthetic concept of the Word. To it, as the medium whereby the poetic act is consummated, he renders up his whole self. This mysterious metamorphosis through which he is subsumed into the Word, *becomes* the Word, he describes as follows: «Cuando yo escribo, desaparezco por completo; no me siento siquiera, soy todo idea o todo sentimiento, todo palabra, nom-

[12] *Ibid.*, II, p. 607.

[13] For the dates of composition and publication of «Espacio» in its various stages, see AURORA DE ALBORNOZ's edition JRJ's *En el otro costado,* Ediciones Júcar, Madrid, 1974, Appendix I.

[14] W. B. YEATS, «Crazy Jane Talks with the Bishop», «Words for Music Perhaps», *The Collected Poems of W. B. Yeats,* p. 294.

[15] For further analysis, see MARÍA TERESA FONT, *Espacio: autobiografía lírica de JRJ,* Insula, Madrid, 1972, pp. 82-83.

[16] For further examples see the *Tercera antolojía poética:*

«En la frescura de la tarde melancólica», p. 305.
«Lloro porque no eres mi sueño... Lloras», p. 416.
«Hasta hoy la palabra», p. 499.
«No sé con qué decirlo», p. 527.
«Me respondió en lo que no dijo», p. 565.
«¡Confusión de acentos...!», p. 584.
«¿Dónde está la palabra, corazón, ...?», p. 760.

bre».[17] Such loss of identity[18] and such a perfect oneness with the «Verbum» invites parallel with the divine mystic union of the soul with God, of the kind experienced by San Juan de la Cruz. It is of course a profane analogy; but although not explicit, it does appear that JRJ is deliberately calling comparison with religious concepts, and this was common «modernista» practice. This clearly indicates the sacred nature of the poetic act as JRJ conceived it, and the divine holiness of the Word. The reason for JRJ's capitalization of «Palabra» (Word) is therefore apparent: it is a veritable transcript into Castilian of the Latin «Verbum» of theology. My comparison with San Juan de la Cruz is based on the loss of conscious identity mutually experienced by the two poets. Where the parallel can not be said to be exact, however, is that in the case of the mystic rapture of San Juan there is exclusion of *idea* which, on the contrary, is ever-present in JRJ.

In the «Fragmento tercero» of «Espacio» JRJ playfully adapts the words of the first verse of the first chapter of *The Gospel According to St John*, «In the beginning was the Word, and the Word was with God, and the Word was God», to read thus: «En el principio fue el Destino, padre de la Acción y abuelo o bisabuelo o algo más allá, del Verbo». The context does not matter here. What matters is simply the fact that the theological conception of the Word was quite evidently present in the mind of JRJ. From his readings of religious texts—San Juan de la Cruz; Santa Teresa de Avila; St Augustine; Fray Luis de León; St Thomas Aquinas; Thomas à Kempis[19]—JRJ would have found constant reminders of the divinity of the «Verbum». In parenthesis, however, it should be noted that such readings as these appealed to JRJ not so much for any orthodox religious reasons, as for their aesthetic value. Thomas à Kempis's *The Imitation of Christ*, for instance, was a work to which JRJ made constant reference. But almost certainly he read it less as a religious treatise than as the work of a kindred mind that had discovered in the exaltation of Christ a similar kind of ecstasy to that which JRJ himself experienced in the exaltation of his poetic godhead. These were not, then, devotional handbooks for JRJ in the strictly orthodox Christian sense; because JRJ's

[17] JRJ, *La Prensa*, New York, published 1 February 1953. From JRJ's reply to a questionnaire set him by Juan Bertolí Rangel, in honour of the Fiftieth Anniversary of the University of Puerto Rico. See R. GULLÓN, *El último JRJ*, Alfaguara, Madrid and Barcelona, 1968, p. 110.

[18] For further consideration, see MENÉNDEZ Y PELAYO, *Historia de las ideas estéticas en España*, 9 vols., Imprenta de los Hijos de Tello, Madrid, 1920, III, p. 31. In his exegesis of the *Diálogos de amor* of León Hebreo, Menéndez y Pelayo signals out the following:

> Antes de entrar en materia (i.e. the theme of «Del origen del amor»), el autor hace una digresión sobre el *éxtasis* [...] en el cual se sostiene que, «siendo la esencia del ánima su propio acto, si se une para contemplar íntimamente un objeto, se transportan en él su esencia, y *aquél es su propia sustancia...*» Y tan íntima puede ser la contemplación, que «del todo se desenlace y retire el ánima del cuerpo [...] de modo que, aferrándose el ánima afectuosamente con el deseado y contemplado objeto, deje al cuerpo desanimado del todo».

[19] G. PALAU DE NEMES's *Vida y obra de JRJ* affords one of the best sources of evidence of JRJ's readings of these religious authors.

religious sense was centred around the notion of transcendence as achieved not through Christianity but by virtue of Poetic Expression. That is to say, by the Word, which thus becomes for him the profane embodiment of «The Way, The Truth and The Life». Already, in *Cantos de vida y esperanza* (1905), Rubén Darío had formulated this same idea, modifying the words of *The Gospel According to St John:* «El Arte puro como Cristo exclama: / Ego sum lux et veritas et vita! ». This last line was to become, in fact, a commonplace of «modernismo» and its virtual motto.

Furthermore, JRJ was undoubtedly acquainted with the passage of St Thomas Aquinas entitled «Nature of God»,[20] where the question of God's identity with his own Name is discussed: «The sole word that perfectly utters God is the Eternal Word»;[21] and again:

> The essence of God is his existence. Moses was taught this sublime truth when he asked: «If the children of Israel say to me, what is his name; what shall I answer them?». The Lord replied: «I am who am; so shalt thou say to the children of Israel: he who is has sent me to you».[22]

Lastly:

> This name, He Who Is, is the most proper name for God, and for three reasons. First, for denotation; it does not signify a kind of form, but being in itself. Second, for universality; it determines no mode of being, but names the boundless sea of substance. Third, for connotation; it intimates being entirely present, free of past and future.[23]

This «free of past and future» will later be seen to apply with great relevance to the aesthetics of JRJ.

Let us pursue the readings of JRJ on the connection of God with the Word. In his treatise *De los nombres de Cristo*,[24] Fray Luis de León reaffirms

[20] MENÉNDEZ Y PELAYO's *Historia de las ideas estéticas en España,* I, pp. 242-286, treats of Aquinas, and it is certain that JRJ read the works of the literary historian. The following references give evidence:

In R. GULLÓN's *Conversaciones con JRJ,* p. 113, JRJ speaking of literary criticism, declares that «Después de Menéndez y Pelayo no tuvimos a nadie».

In R. GULLÓN's *Direcciones del modernismo,* p. 250, it is recorded that works of Menéndez y Pelayo were published in the review *Renacimiento* in which JRJ collaborated.

In G. PALAU DE NEMES's *Vida y obra de JRJ,* I, p. 156, JRJ is quoted as referring to Menéndez y Pelayo's theory of symbolism in San Juan de la Cruz.

In JRJ's *El modernismo,* p. 106, he refers to Menéndez y Pelayo's work on Boscán; and on p. 271, to his *Antología de poetas hispanoamericanos* (1893).

[21] ST. THOMAS AQUINAS, «Nature of God», *Summa Theologica,* 1a, xiii, II, from *St. Thomas Aquinas: Philosophical Texts,* edited by T. Gilby, p. 95, paragraph 286.

[22] *Ibid.,* p. 69, paragraph 186.

[23] *Ibid.,* p. 97, paragraph 288.

[24] See A. SÁNCHEZ-BARBUDO, *La segunda época de JRJ,* p. 158. Despite JRJ's emphatic rejection of any Christian interpretation of his poetry, Sánchez-Barbudo says that:

> sin embargo sus poemas recuerdan a menudo, por el tono y las imágenes, a los místicos cristianos españoles; y también, en el amoroso nombrar, al Fray Luis de *Los nombres de Cristo,* como cuando dice, en el mismo poema

the identity of God as Word: «Dios [...] que es el concepto y verbo divino»[25] and later on discusses the perfect propriety of the name «Verbum» or «Word» for Christ, «según la naturaleza divina en que nasce del Padre eternamente».[26] He then takes the original Hebrew name «Dabar» meaning «Word», which was the name revealed by God to the prophets who wrote it in their language, and gives an exegetical account of its significance, letter by letter. In its entirety, however, he says that:

> Lo primero, Dabar significa el verbo que concibe el entendimiento en sí mismo, que es una como imagen entera e igual de la cosa que entiende. Y Cristo, en esta manera, es Dabar, porque es la imagen que de sí concibe y produze cuando se entiende su Padre. Y Dabar significa también la palabra que se forma en la boca, que es imagen de lo que el ánimo esconde.[27]

A few lines further on he asserts the relation of the Word to existence and therefore to the state of being and the reality of things: «Y significa también [...] cualquiera cosa de ser, y por la misma razón el ser mismo y la realidad de las cosas».

Bearing in mind these examples of religious exegesis of the Word which is God, or Divine Reality, the parallel (though profane) conception which JRJ formed of the Word can more readily be understood. What the Divine «Verbum» is for the Christian believer, the poetic «verbum» was for JRJ: the repository of Reality, and therefore Truth. Yet not only repository, but indeed, the *creator* of that Reality and that Truth—just as the Word that is God, in Christian terms, is Creator, Maker and Artist of the Universe. One is reminded here of the often repeated statement of St Augustine in *De Civitate Dei,* that the universe is the poem of God.

Absolute terms, such as those it has been necessary to use above, pose a ferocious challenge. Nevertheless, the terms «Truth» and «Reality» as applied within the special context of JRJ and his conception of the Word, may perhaps be clarified by observing that the measure of their attainment is strictly related to the measure of fidelity of expression with which they bear testimony to personal experience. Let it be noted that it is not the documentation of objective, scientific «fact» that is here at stake, but the truth of experience. This confluence of form and matter is not concerned with the kind of ideal equation set forth in, say, Wittgenstein's logically perfect language, in which he would like to see one name for every «simple»

> primero: «Eres la gracia libre, / la gloria del gustar, la eterna simpatía, / el gozo del temblor, la luminaria / del clariver, el fondo del amor [...]».

In a footnote to this, Sánchez-Barbudo further refers to an article by Oreste Macrí («El segundo tiempo de la poesía de Jiménez» in *La Torre,* July-December 1957, p. 287) in which Macrí says that whilst it would be absurd to attribute to JRJ the traditional characteristics of Spanish mysticism, nevertheless in his poetry: «Los "nombres de Cristo" de Fray Luis de León parecen vueltos "a lo profano"».

25 Fray Luis de León, «De los nombres en general», *De los nombres de Cristo,* Clásicos Castellanos, Madrid, 1914, I, p. 47.

26 *Ibid.,* «Jesus», III, p. 151.

27 *Ibid.,* p. 159.

or «fact» in a pictured geometric form. Nor are the poetically experienced facts the kind of facts («Sachverhalte» and «Tatsache»)[28] for which Wittgenstein seeks his absolute expression. Scientific objectivity, even were it possible, is not the essence of the fidelity referred to above. Moreover, we know the opinion that JRJ held of the poetry of Paul Valéry which he found too cerebral, and which he considered a mere vehicle for «ciencia filosófica».[29] Truth, then, is attendant upon that perfect reconciliation or fusion of the Word and experienced «fact»; and in turn, it must depend on the poet's integrity in the handling of the Word.

Before turning to the poetry itself of JRJ to see in practice the manner in which he strove for this ideal, we should refer once more to the writings of Fray Luis de León. For his exposition of the name and the naming process anticipates JRJ's own conception, and his famous poem of exhortation, « ¡Intelijencia, dame / el nombre exacto de las cosas! » (*LP*, p. 553). The proposition of Luis de León's fictitious spokesman, Marcello, in the chapter entitled «De los nombres en general» from *De los nombres de Cristo,* is to ascertain «qué cosa es esto que llamamos nombre, y qué officio tiene, y por qué fin se introduxo, y en qué manera se suele poner'[30] —questions pertinent indeed to JRJ. The definition of the name is then given as follows:

> El nombre [...] es una palabra breve, que se sustituye por aquello de quien se dize, y se toma por ello mismo. O nombre es aquello mismo que se nombra, no en el ser real y verdadero que ello tiene, sino en el ser que le da nuestra boca y entendimiento.[31]

The name, then, is the perfect image of its object of reference. And this name-image enjoys a reality no less real than the reality of the object, but of a differing kind. This is an observation which would surely seem to confirm the impossibility and, more importantly, the undesirability of linguistic equation in the objective scientific method mentioned earlier, and repudiated by JRJ. Things «live» and «have being» not only in our intelligence, but both in and through their names. How imperative therefore it is that they should be justly represented. Fray Luis de León continues:

> Todas las cosas viven y tienen ser, en nuestro entendimiento, cuando las entendemos, y cuando las nombramos, en nuestras bocas y lenguas. Y lo que ellas son en sí mismas, essa misma razón de ser tienen en nosotros, si nuestras bocas y entendimientos son verdaderos.[32]

This final word, «verdaderos», deserves attention. The condition upon which depends the true transcript of the object's reality is once again

[28] LUDWIG WITTGENSTEIN, *Tractatus Logico-Philosophicus,* Routledge & Kegan Paul, London, 1961.
[29] GUERRERO RUIZ, p. 179.
[30] FRAY LUIS DE LEÓN, «De los nombres en general», *De los nombres de Cristo,* p. 25.
[31] *Ibid.,* p. 27.
[32] *Ibid.,* p. 30.

integrity; that same integrity which earlier has been seen as the prerequisite for the faithful correlation of word and experienced «fact».

The two realities of an object or fact[33]—the objective reality, and the transcribed reality—are further explained by the conception of the imagistic character of ideas and words:

> En sí [real objects] son la verdad, mas en el entendimiento y en la boca son imágenes de la verdad, esto es, de sí mismas, é imágenes que sustituyen y tienen la vez de sus mismas cosas para el effecto y fin que está dicho; y finalmente, en sí son ellas mismas, y en nuestra boca y entendimiento sus nombres [...] El nombre es como imagen de la cosa de quien se dize, ó la misma cosa disfraçada en otra manera, que sustituye por ella, y se toma por ella para el fin y propósito de perfección y comunidad que diximos.[34]

The name, then, is the image of the named. It possesses its own authentic reality. It is of this order of reality that the poetic naming of JRJ will consist.

Moreover, declares Marcello, names fall into two categories. The first kind are «soul-words» or images which the mind apprehends as ideas, and these derive from nature, and are therefore perfect in their correlation. On the other hand, the second kind consist of words which are fashioned by art and are of human invention.[35] Applied to the poetry of JRJ, it is of course the latter class of name with which the poet is concerned. By way of corroboration of this, one need only recall the tiny but diamantine-clear poem called «Acción» which inaugurates the collection *Eternidades:*

> No sé con qué decirlo,
> porque aún no está hecha
> mi palabra.

The word «hecha» and the possessive adjective «mi» suffice for proof. The Juanramonian Word is indeed a poetic artefact. It is «fabricated», in the meaning that Luis de León's Marcello employs; and it is invention. Invention in its fullest sense of search and discovery as well as the skill of artifice. JRJ himself has clearly acknowledged this inventive nature, this deliberate craftsmanship, of the poetic process of naming. The following quotation has been cited in part earlier on, but it is one which bears repetition here for its importance: «Si un científico inventa, y a todo el mundo le parece natural el invento, sea práctico o no, ¿por qué no ha de inventar un poeta, que puede hacerlo, un mundo o parte de él? Es lo que

[33] For information on Nominalism and Realism, see José Ferrater Mora, *Diccionario de filosofía.* Also, the *Dictionnaire de théologie catholique,* Vacant-Mangenot-Amman, Paris, 1931, and in particular the article by Paul Vignaux entitled «Nominalisme», XI, cols. 717-784. See too Gerald L. Bruns, *Modern Poetry and the Idea of Language,* Yale University Press, Newhaven and London, 1974, pp. 34-35.

[34] Fray Luis de León, «De los nombres en general», *De los nombres de Cristo,* pp. 30-31.

[35] *Ibid.,* p. 31.

le acerca al mito divino [...]; crear a imajen y semejanza».[36] The poet is an artificer; but his artefact possesses a reality directly linked with that other, objective reality. Such is the inference to be drawn from the analogy that JRJ makes between poet and scientist. For the discovery of the scientist is that of pre-existing facts, and so the poetic invention likewise concerns the revelation of a pre-existent reality or truth. On this basis, the reality of the poetic name is construed by JRJ along the very same lines as Fray Luis de León's conception of the Word as being perfectly correspondent with empirical reality. The significance of this conception in the Work of JRJ is of considerable magnitude. For, if he has indeed handled the Word in such a way as to preserve this twinning of different-but-identical realities, then any charge against his poetry of being divorced from life, removed from the real world, or starkly dehumanized (in Ortegan terminology), will be rendered wholly meaningless. And accusations such as these have indeed been advanced by his detractors. Nevertheless, JRJ's conception of the Word as the instrument of invention and creation, of invented reality (i.e. both *found,* objective reality; and *created* «artificial» reality) must logically give birth to a poetry that, on the contrary, is the very mirror of mankind's experience and that does indeed relate to the human condition. The image-reality of the Word and the Name may soar; but never so high that it divests itself of the original reality it reflects.

Furthermore, this conception (which may be seen as an extension of the Aristotelian theory of the language of «praxis» and the language of «poiesis») serves to affirm the existence of two worlds, paradoxically at once autonomous and confluent. The everyday world of reality, and the poetically real world. They are simultaneously separate and conjoined. But that is not the main point here. What chiefly matters is to observe that it is by virtue of this belief in the veritable reality of the poetic world—a belief engendered and made possible solely by his concept of the Word's naming power—which will permit JRJ to transcend within the Work time, space and differentiation of identity. These are matters which will be analyzed within the framework of the corpus of his poetry. But it is appropriate at this juncture to indicate the fundamental importance of JRJ's special understanding of the Word. It is this conception which permits a «different» world wherein alone JRJ can assume divine omnipotence, ignore terrestrial dimensions, and surpass all limitations. As an example of the kind of conjuration of a new poetic world and different order of reality, of which the Word is capable, the following early poem may be cited. It comes from the third section, «Jardines dolientes», of *Jardines lejanos* written between 1903 and 1904.

Cuando la mujer está,
todo es, tranquilo, lo que es
—la llama, la flor, la música—.
Cuando la mujer se fue

36 JRJ, «Lo "fable" y lo "inefable"», «Poesía cerrada y poesía abierta», *Pájinas escojidas; prosa,* p. 189.

—la luz, la canción, la llama—,
¡todo! es, loco, la mujer. (*TAP,* p. 102)[37]

The structure of the poem is bi-partite to convey two different orders of reality. The first three lines display the objectively real presence of the woman in her context of the objectively real world, whose «tranquillity» is clearly consequent upon her being there. But with her physical departure, it is in the last three lines that the magic potency of poetic diction comes into its own. Through the power of the Word, the return of the woman is effected, conjured home again into a new poetic reality: a kind of absent presence. With the investiture of this new order of being, and resurrected to poetic reality, so the world about likewise undergoes a transformation, made newly real and existent *within the frame of the poem,* its serenity changed to the poetic frenzy of ecstasy. Indeed, World and Woman are now one—through the alchemy of the Word.

Silence

The concern amongst contemporary philosophers about the problems and insufficiencies of language has been mentioned. Perhaps the most radical example of such doubt as to the basic value of words is expressed by Ludwig Wittgenstein (1889-1951) in the «Preface» to his *Tractatus Logico-Philosophicus.* There are times, he declares, when confronted with the sheer inadequacy of language, silence is our only recourse: «What we cannot speak about we must pass over in silence» («Wovon man nicht reden kann, darüber muss man schweigen»). Again: «Objects can only be *named.* Signs are their representatives. I can only speak *about* them: I cannot *put them into words.* Propositions can only say *how* things are, not *what* they are» («Die Gegenstände kann ich nur nennen. Zeichen vertreten sie. Ich kann nur von ihnen sprechen, sie aussprechen kann ich nicht. Ein Satz kann nur sagen, wie ein Ding ist, nicht was es ist»). (Translators' emphases).[38] It is quite possible, since Wittgenstein's dates closely coincide with those of JRJ, that JRJ was aware of these particular statements. The *Tractatus* was first published in 1921, and the fact that the following year it was republished in the original German together with an English translation increases the likelihood that JRJ may have known it, even at second hand through the offices of his wife, Zenobia Camprubí, whose mother tongue was English. Furthermore, José Ferrater Mora published an article entitled «Wittgenstein o la destrucción» in *Realidad,* núm. 13 (1949) 1-2. This review was published in Buenos Aires by Francisco Ayala which may well allow for the supposition that JRJ read the publication. It is of course true that

[37] Compare with this Antonio Machado's «Elegía de un madrigal», *Soledades,* XLIX: a statement of involuntary sensory association, whereby objects are charged, as by an unseen current, with the presence of the absent person transformed.

[38] L. Wittgenstein, *Tractatus Logico-Philosophicus,* German text with translation by D. F. Pears and B. F. McGuinness, and with Introduction by Bertrand Russell, Routledge & Kegan Paul, London, 1961, p. 151 and p. 23.

Wittgenstein changed his viewpoints radically in various articles which were collected in *Philosophische Untersuchungen (Philosophical Investigations),* but these did not appear until after his death.

Bearing in mind the above remarks of Wittgenstein, his scepticism and his recommendation of silence in the face of that about which we cannot speak, it is worth observing what JRJ has to say on the subject of silence. In a letter to Luis Cernuda, written from Washington, D.C. in July 1943, he said:

> Creo que en la escritura poética, como en la pintura o la música, el asunto es la retórica, «lo que queda», la poesía. Mi ilusión ha sido siempre ser más cada vez poeta de «lo que queda», hasta llegar un día a no escribir. Escribir no es sino preparación para no escribir, para el estado de gracia poético, intelectual o sensitivo. Ser uno poesía y no poeta.[39]

And from his *Diario poético:*

> Si yo hubiera podido desenvolver, conservar, imprimir mi obra poética, en la forma, en una de las formas soñadas y pensadas, durante tantos años, por mi fe

[39] JRJ, *La corriente infinita,* Aguilar, Madrid, 1961, pp. 171-179. It is worth noting the analogies between the theory behind this poetic concept and abstract art, especially around the 1920s period. «Suprematism», with its principal theorists in Malevicht and Kandinsky, as also the «De Stijl» group with Mondrian, had as one of its chief aims the promotion of an awareness of the absence of the object. In «Suprematism» from his book *The Non-Objective World,* Kasimir Malevicht stated: «I understand the supremacy of pure feeling in creative art. To the Suprematist the visual phenomena of the objective world are, in themselves, meaningless; the significant thing is feeling, as such». Further on, he calls for:

> No more «likenesses of reality», no idealistic images—nothing but a desert! But this desert is filled with the spirit of nonobjective sensation which pervades everything [...] But a blissful sense of liberating nonobjectivity drew me forth into the «desert», where nothing is real except feeling [...] and so feeling became the substance of my life.

The reader interested in pursuing these analogies should consult HERSCHEL B. CHIPP'S *Theories of Modern Art; a Source Book by Artists and Critics,* with contributions by P. Selz and J. C. Taylor, University of California Press, Berkeley, 1971. However, it must be borne in mind that JRJ himself may not have been directly aware of this similarity of attitude in the world of painting. As ANGEL CRESPO states in his book *JRJ y la pintura,* Universidad de Puerto Rico, San Juan, 1974, p. 219: «Del neoplasticismo, del dadaísmo, de pintores tan importantes como Malevicht, Kandinsky, Klee y tantos otros, Juan Ramón, que sepamos, nunca se ocupó. Quedaban completamente al margen de sus intereses pictóricos».

And yet the critic Fernand Verhesen, consciously or unconsciously, has also perceived the analogy between the poetry of JRJ and the abstract art of the time. In his article «Tiempo y espacio en la obra de JRJ», *La Torre,* año V, núms. 19-20, July-December 1957, p. 103, he says: «La experiencia cumplida demuestra que todo lo que existe no puede *manifestarse sino en la purificación de la ausencia*». And again:

> Por eso es que se debe ir hacia el espacio: no ya para cruzar la puerta entreabierta y descubrir y enunciar el mundo, sino para asumir plenamente *la realidad de una ausencia.* Porque ahora sabemos que el mundo real percibido por los sentidos, está ausente» (author's emphases).

y mi duda, hubiese regalado, a lo último, un libro en blanco, con el título *Poesía No Escrita.*[40]

In both passages it is the fact that JRJ conceives «silence»—the unwritten page or book—as a *goal,* as the desirable and proper culmination of the poetic process, that is of such signal importance. Here, there is none of that negative defeat suggested by Wittgenstein. On the contrary, the silence to which JRJ actually *aspires,* is situated at the far pole of that other silence of Wittgenstein's. They are—and the repetition is warranted—polar opposites: the one, positive; the other, negative. For the silence to which JRJ refers is the silence of Perfection, in its Latin sense of completion, of the achievement of a process. Where Wittgenstein's silence occurs *before* any attempt at expression, that of JRJ is attained as a result of and conclusion to a whole commitment to expression. His particular brand of silence will be that of the unending soundless reverberation and resonance of «la vibrante palabra muda, / la inmanente» («Poeta y palabra», *LP,* pp. 1171-1172). It is the kind of silence which Mallarmé likewise apprehended and to which he came as close to evoking as possible, within the poetic frame. Through a technique of abolition and of negation, silence alone remains in his sonnet «Une dentelle s'abolit». But it is a miraculous silence for, out of the vacant and dormant «mandore» issues a music whose very fabric is of silence. Again, it is this same silence, peculiar and precious and perfect, which pervades the poem «Sainte» and from which the image of the saint draws her unheard melodies, that enigmatic «musicienne du silence». It is appropriate here too to make further mention of Rubén Darío. In Darío's *Prosas profanas*—which is of all his works the one that bears closest affinity with the poetry of Mallarmé, being published in 1896—we find set forth in the poem entitled «La página blanca» the similar notions of silence and of the unwritten sheet: «Mis ojos miraban en hora de ensueños / la página blanca». Darío's concept is admittedly slightly modified here from that of JRJ and Mallarmé,[41] since the blank page in this context is a metaphor for Life. It is a page *in potentia;* whereas the blank page at which JRJ and Mallarmé arrive signifies the completed end to their efforts. In the closing poem to *Belleza (en verso)* entitled «La Obra» (*LP,* p. 1125) it is «el papel blanco» in which JRJ must be «interred» by the «duro azadón de luz» which is the wing of Poetry; and it is from this grave of the blank page that he will rise, purified and transfigured: «volaré refigurado».

[40] JRJ, *Diario poético,* 1936-1937 (fragmentos), *Poética,* I (number dedicated to JRJ), La Plata, 1943.

In parenthesis it may be noted here that JRJ is in accordance with the sentiment of Plato, who said that anyone who wanted to return to the world of words after he had attained knowledge of what is real, cannot have understood the significance of his journey: «No sensible man will venture to express his deepest thoughts in words, especially in a form which is unchangeable». PLATO, *Seventh Epistle,* 343a. See GERALD L. BRUNS, *Modern Poetry and the Idea of Language,* Yale University Press, New Haven and London, 1974, p. 16.

[41] For further comparison, see E. K. MAPES, *La influencia francesa en la obra de Rubén Darío,* Managua, Nicaragua, 1966.

Despite their different handling of the theme, it is striking that the image of the blank sheet should be thus held in common by all three poets.

In an article called «Tiempo y espacio en la obra de JRJ», Fernand Verhesen examines the further dimension of the internal spatial quality of the Word in relation not only with universal external space but with silence:

> Se trata, pues, del espacio interior de la palabra acordada a las dimensiones del cosmos [...] Más que las palabras dichas, las cuales pudieran cerrar sobre ellas mismas el mundo del poeta, importa ese rumor de caravanas que ensancha el espacio en que la palabra no pertenece realmente sino al silencio expresado, al puente sonoro que se tiende entre un alma y otra alma situada en algún sitio del mundo donde nada *que no sea este canje de resonancias interiores* puede encontrar sitio.[42]

The ideal realm is the one in which the voice of man is «más desnuda, más despojada de significación práctica»—in short, the realm of the ineffable.[43]

It may be that JRJ's desire to attain the «silence» of a blank book —expressed in the beautiful metaphor of his Work as a «Casa de silencio y de tiempo»[44]—is none other than a recognition of the finite nature of the printed word and the voicing of his fear of the destructive interference of worldly temporality and the dangers of misinterpretation by posterity. Or indeed it may be that he is contemplating the inevitable destruction of Thought itself, symbolized in the intuition of the death of his Work:

> Tú, así labrada con mi vida ardiente
> hecha diamante para ti;
> tú, con tanto soñar perfeccionada,
> como una estrella por los siglos...
> ¡Qué pálido pensar que tú, obra bella,
> te has de morir, lo mismo
> que se muere de siglos una estrella...![45]

But even if such fears are the case, some kind of answer to them is nevertheless possible. Let us consider, for example, one way in which T. S. Eliot, the American-British poet, handles this very issue. The fact that JRJ not only read T. S. Eliot and made frequent reference to him in the course of his lectures on «modernismo», but that he also went as far as to translate passages of Eliot, in 1930, for publication in *La gaceta literaria,* provides sufficient justification to address ourselves at this point to the author of *Four Quartets.* The following extract is taken from the first of these *Quartets, Burnt Norton,* originally published in *Collected Poems 1909-*

42 F. VERHESEN, «Tiempo y espacio en la obra de JRJ», p. 103.

43 *Ibid.,* p. 104.

44 JRJ, «Estética y ética estética», «Ideolojía lírica», *Pájinas escojidas; prosa,* selected by R. Gullón, p. 147.

45 JRJ, «De siglos», *Rueca,* México, V, 1954, p. 3.

1935 (New York: Harcourt, Brace & C.°) in 1936: It is concerned precisely with the same problematic «silence» of JRJ:

Words move, music moves
Only in time; but that which is only living
Can only die. Words, after speech, reach
Into the silence. Only by the form, the pattern,
Can words or music reach
The stillness, as a Chinese jar still
Moves perpetually in its stillness.
Not the stillness of the violin, while the note lasts,
Not that only, but the co-existence,
Or say that the end precedes the beginning,
And the end and the beginning were always there
Before the beginning and after the end.
And all is always now.

Form, and pattern, remain the sole and indispensable means by which word or music shall reach ultimate stillness: the stillness of silence, of the blank page, of Eternity itself, to which JRJ so anxiously aspires.

Ultimately, silence is for JRJ a transcendence of language, a triumphant state, attained only after apprenticeship and mastery of the Word. It is that «langue sans paroles» sought by Mallarmé, and that «all is now» of T. S. Eliot. Not silence itself, but the articulation of silence in Eternity.

The following poem, the first of the collection called *Belleza,* answers the poet's own fears of the finite character of the Work and is a reassuring affirmation that, veritably, the Work is that «Casa de silencio y de tiempo» which JRJ desired. I shall quote the poem in full:

Sé que mi Obra es lo mismo
que una pintura en el aire;
que el vendaval de los tiempos
la borrará toda, como
si fuese perfume o música;
que quedará sólo de ella
—sí arruinado en nóes—
al gran silencio solar,
la ignorancia de la luna.

—No, no; ella, un día, será
=borrada=existencia inmensa,
desveladora virtud;
será, como el antesol,
imposible norma bella;
sinfín de angustioso afán,
mina de escelso secreto...—
¡Mortal flor mía inmortal
reina del aire de hoy! (*LP,* p. 985)

That «hoy» is the today of Eternity. We may apply to the Work of JRJ the words of Thomas Carlyle (with whose writings JRJ was well acquainted)[46]

[46] THOMAS CARLYLE's *On Heroes, Hero-Worship and the Heroic in History* was

about the Book of Dante. It «burns as a pure star, fixed there in the firmament [...] Let us honour the great empire of *Silence*, once more! ».[47]

«Eloquence of Silence» might indeed be an adequate title for the following untitled poem from JRJ's *Eternidades:*

Me respondió en lo que no dijo,
a lo que, sin decirlo, dije,
afirmando en un no lo no pedido
por mi pregunta falsa.

¡Sentí que lo más puro
se me cuajaba en su alegría,
cual si esa rosa que el rocío yerto
hace en la rosa suave,
la suplantara para siempre! (*LP*, p. 660)

The first stanza is precisely concerned with the speech of silence, which is perfect communication far transcending ordinary language. How, we may ask, has JRJ been able to convey such a silence when words alone, indicative of sound and utterance, are at his disposal for the task? He has achieved it by that same process of abolition through negation which already we have noticed in passing allusion to Mallarmé. Each of the first two lines embraces a dual assertion-within-negation; and the third line does so in duplicate, so that its sheer complexity renders it, superficially at least, a conundrum of the most perplexing self-contradiction and paradox within paradox. But the not-ness of the reply («me respondió en lo que *no* dijo»); the not-ness of the ensuing response («a lo que, *sin* decirlo, dije»); the not-ness of the affirmative («afirmando en un *no*») to the not-ness of the request («lo *no* pedido»):—all these are positive communicating strands interwoven and comprehended by the two interlocutors (if such they may be called), and they are authentic. In fact they are more perfectly so than their vocal utterance could ever be. The full realization of this truth is brought out only at the very end of the stanza, with the brilliant introduction and positioning of the adjective «falsa». The significance of this word is that it throws into relief the fact that throughout the entire non-conversation, the sole pronouncement lacking in authenticity is the one which has actually been given utterance: the verbally articulated «pregunta» which evidently initiated this silent intercourse. Thus the falsity of language as communication is denounced, by contrast with the absolute integrity and truth of the speech of silence. The perfect eloquence of the unsaid is then, in the second stanza, translated on to the plane of pure aesthetics and sensorial Beauty, incarnate in the symbol of the rose.

well known in Spain and influential in «modernismo». Numerous references to Carlyle in the collected notes of JRJ's own lecture course of that same name, *El modernismo,* bear witness to the poet's knowledge of his work. See *El modernismo,* p. 96; p. 100; p. 114; p. 180; p. 181. Further reference to Carlyle occurs in Guerrero Ruiz, *JR de viva voz,* p. 75. See also my note 28 to chapter IV for the interest in Carlyle in Spain.

47 Thomas Carlyle, *On Heroes, Hero-Worship and the Heroic in History,* 30 vols., Ams Press, New York, 1974, V, pp. 100-101.

The poem as a whole stands in adequate defence of JRJ from any accusation to the effect that he is blind to the possibilities of duplicity in language, in his optimistic pursuit of the «nombre exacto». It clearly, although subtly, reveals an inherent questioning of the worth of human utterance. Questioning. Precisely is it in question form that we find another, very brief, poem whose theme again is one of dubitative speculation on language itself:

¿Dónde está la palabra, corazón,
que embellezca de amor el mundo feo;
que le dé para siempre—y sólo ya—
fortaleza de niño
y defensa de rosa? (*LP*, p. 1080)

The doubt and the query are there. Where is one to find such a word? Does it—(the question is implicit)—even exist? A word, against the squalor of a universe! Surely it is too much to hope for? But the marvel of the poem is that even as it questions, it achieves exactly the miracle it both seeks and doubts. The last two exquisite lines are the consummation of that miracle, fulfilling in the act of their expression, the desire named. Unwittingly, as it were, the poem has in the very process of its own self-expression answered its own doubtings and given glorious solution to its own interrogation. The great talent of JRJ shows in this seeming unselfconsciousness of the poem. He has succeeded in practising his own theory of the need to «someter lo espontáneo a lo consciente». The poem, apparently so self-effacing, is daringly contrived and manipulated so as to weld in one inextricable unit both the question it posits and the solution it «unconsciously» bodies forth. The power of the Word is here fully, and most cunningly indirectly, restated.

With this realization of the potency of the Word and the feeling that he is the master of it, JRJ the poet is on his way to Salvation.

Chapter III

THE THEORY OF THE WORD PUT INTO PRACTICE

It is with the collection of poems called *Eternidades* that JRJ first clearly articulates his preoccupation with the Word. The collection was written between 1916 and 1917, at just about the same time as the composition (1916) and publication (1917) of *Diario de un poeta reciencasado,* which was hailed by the critics as marking the beginning of a «second epoch» in the poetry of JRJ. Eugenio Florit quotes JRJ himself triumphantly declaring that «la crítica mayor y mejor está de acuerdo en que con él comenzó una nueva vida en la poesía española (un gran "incendio poético", dijo uno)»; and going on to stress the fact that in his own judgement too, it is indeed «un punto de *partidas*».[1] The hinge upon which turns this new development is precisely the revised conception of the Word and its function in the poem», crystallized in the two renowned poems which go to serve almost as as an «Ars Poetica»: namely, the one beginning « ¡Intelijencia, dame / el nombre exacto de las cosas! »; and the one beginning «Vino, primero, pura, / vestida de inocencia». It is important however to emphasize my previous remarks pointing out the error of the assumption that the year 1916 saw the inauguration of an aesthetic so entirely novel as to be quite divorced and distinct from the earlier poetry. Such is not the case. Even *Diario de un poeta reciencasado* had, according to the poet himself, been present in embryonic imaginative form as early on as the composition of *Ninfeas.* «Era», he declares, «el libro que yo soñaba cuando escribía *Ninfeas*». It was the product not only of «el amor, el alta mar, el alto cielo, el verso libre, las Américas distintas» but notably also of «mi largo recorrido anterior».[2] Still more directly to the point in question—JRJ's concern with the Word and the Name—is the fact that as much as five years before he was to make his famous invocation to « ¡Intelijencia! », he was already manifesting the seeds of that very concern in «A un poeta», which appeared in the collection *Poemas impersonales,* dated 1911. The passionate accent, as of a credo, and the tone of almost religious exaltation, foreshadow those of the later poem, « ¡Intelijencia! ». «Creemos los nombres», he declares:

[1] JRJ, quoted by E. Florit, «Nota preliminar», *TAP,* p. 19.
[2] *Ibid.*

Creemos los nombres.

Derivarán los hombres.
Luego, derivarán las cosas.
Y sólo quedará el mundo de los nombres,
letra del amor de los hombres,
del olor de las rosas.

Del amor y las rosas,
no ha de quedar sino los nombres.
¡Creemos los nombres! (*TAP*, p. 274)

Already evident in this poem are the two major interrelated tendencies that mark the Second Epoch of JRJ. That is to say, the idea of «poesía pura»; and the aim toward nouns rather than adjectives. The «nombre», in its sense both of name and of noun, is sought by JRJ because it goes most directly to the «cosa». It is not merely a «signo», as Ortega y Gasset would have it. The view of JRJ coincides with that of Rubén Darío in this matter. In Darío's *El canto errante,* we find the Nicaraguan poet taking to task the following opinion of Ortega—although in fairness it should be added that Darío's understanding of Ortega is here only partial and incomplete, as later shall be seen.

> «Las palabras»—escribe el señor Ortega y Gasset [...]—«las palabras son logaritmos de las cosas, imágenes, ideas y sentimientos, y por tanto, sólo pueden emplearse como signos de valores, nunca como valores». De acuerdo. Mas la palabra nace juntamente con la idea, o coexiste con la idea, pues no podemos darnos cuenta de la una sin la otra [...]
>
> En el principio está la palabra como única representación. No simplemente como signo, puesto que no hay antes nada que representar. En el principio está la palabra como manifestación de la unidad infinita, pero ya conteniéndola. Et verbum erat Deus.[3]

For JRJ likewise, the Word and the name are no longer signs or signals. Furthermore, his emphasis on «el nombre» bears the aesthetic value of aiding the process of «depuración», that is, the exclusion of all that is superfluous. In connection with this pre-eminent concern with the name and the noun which JRJ manifests in the poem that has just been quoted, it is of considerable interest to recall for a moment the analysis carried out by Dámaso Alonso of the poetry of San Juan de la Cruz. Dámaso Alonso describes the function of the noun as primarily that of «sintetismo de las nociones». «Función predominante del sustantivo a expensas del adjetivo, a expensas de la función verbal».[4] This definition of the noun initiates his discussion of linguistic usage in the work of San Juan, in which he calls to attention the preponderance of single unit nouns, divested of verbal or adjectival decoration, and the resultant density, velocity and intensity of

[3] RUBÉN DARÍO, «Dilucidaciones», *El canto errante, Poesías completas,* Aguilar, Madrid, 1967, p. 699.

[4] DÁMASO ALONSO, *La poesía de San Juan de la Cruz,* Consejo Superior de Investigaciones Científicas, Madrid, 1942, p. 182.

poetic expression. The heightened concentration and cohesion which this emphasis on the purely nominal and substantive resources of language produces—as Dámaso Alonso convincingly proves—is similarly featured, and for the same reasons, in the poetry of the Second Epoch of JRJ. The following words of the Spanish critic are applicable as much to the later work of JRJ as to the poetry of the sixteenth century saint:

> Resulta resaltada la función del nombre. Resaltada en dos sentidos: porque los sustantivos se adensan, se suceden con una mayor rapidez, y, aún más importante, porque el nombre aislado, desnudo, tiene que multiplicar sus valencias afectivas, recargándose al mismo tiempo de su original fuerza intuitiva, que había sido cómodamente abandonada a la función adjetival.

It is not necessary here to relate the way in which Dámaso Alonso goes on to investigate the effect this purified nominalistic diction produces upon the adjective: its «refreshment» brought about by the new discretionary usage of it. It is enough to have observed the parallel between JRJ and San Juan de la Cruz, with regard to the role of the noun.[5] I have not been able to ascertain whether JRJ himself ever openly acknowledged a specifically stylistic debt to San Juan de la Cruz, but it is clear from references made to him in his course entitled *El modernismo* that JRJ held him to be the model par excellence of symbolism and of the ability to «precisar en una imagen muy bella lo impreciso, por medio de símbolos, de relaciones, de correspondencias entre unas cosas y otras».[6] A little further on he states: «En literatura un dogma es San Juan de la Cruz, un modelo; es una norma, una tradición. ¿Por qué San Juan de la Cruz está olvidado? Y los modernistas lo vuelven a poner de modelo, vuelven a ocuparse de él».[7] It may reasonably be deduced therefore that JRJ did indeed study and learn from the stylistic approach to the poetry of the ineffable of San Juan. Moreover, Donald L. Fogelquist has demonstrated the stylistic similarity between JRJ and San Juan de la Cruz. Citing the second stanza of the poem «Conciencia plena» from *Animal de fondo* as his example, he draws attention to the fact that it begins with a verse of seven syllables and ends with one of eleven syllables—both traditional verses used frequently in that same combination by San Juan. The stanza used in San Juan's «Canciones del alma» also begins with a seven syllable verse and ends with one of eleven. Fogelquist then shows the corresponding use of sound values between JRJ and San Juan. In the second and the two final verses of the stanza, JRJ uses e—o assonance (c*ie*l*o*, n*e*gr*o*, d*e*ntr*o*), identical with the rhyme in the second and two final verses of the «Canciones del alma». Whether such resemblances were the product of a conscious effort on the part of JRJ to follow the style of San Juan, Fogelquist also is unsure. «It is possible», he says, «that

[5] For further general discussion on the stylistic function of the various parts of speech, see: Carlos Bousoño, *Teoría de la expresión poética,* Gredos, Madrid, 1970; R. A. Sayce, *Style in French Prose,* Clarendon Press, Oxford, 1965; S. Ullman, *Style in the French Novel,* Barnes and Noble, New York, 1964.

[6] JRJ, *El modernismo,* p. 259.

[7] *Ibid.,* p. 261.

in this case Jiménez did not consciously imitate San Juan de la Cruz, but very likely he had so thoroughly assimilated the poetry of the mystic that he frequently, even though at times perhaps unwittingly, followed his example, in versification as well as in emotive imagery».[8] This would seem an accurate summation.

Further evidence of JRJ's early esteem for the absoluteness of the Word —long before its formulation in *Eternidades*—is to be found in a poem included in the collection called «La frente pensativa», written between 1911 and 1912:

Una bella palabra
es toda la palabra.
                    Todo velo
cubre un secreto sólo.

Si cojo todo el cielo,
aunque todos lo cojan, seré yo sólo Apolo. (*TAP*, p. 348)

The Word, self-sufficient and requiring no accessory support, is unique to the essence that it enfolds. Once grasped, it will render up absolutely and uniquely that reality. The poem is a brief one. But the three statements of which it is composed strongly body forth convictions often erroneously supposed to belong solely to JRJ's Second Epoch.

Let us now examine the two «poemas claves» of this Second Epoch. The first one reads:

¡Intelijencia, dame
el nombre exacto de las cosas!
... Que mi palabra sea
la cosa misma,
creada por mi alma nuevamente.
Que por mí vayan todos
los que no las conocen, a las cosas;
que por mí vayan todos
los que ya las olvidan, a las cosas;
que por mí vayan todos
los mismos que las aman, a las cosas;
¡Intelijencia, dame
el nombre exacto, y tuyo,
y suyo, y mío, de las cosas! (*LP*, p. 553)

[8] D. L. Fogelquist, *Juan Ramón Jiménez,* Twayne Publishers, Boston, 1976, pp. 111-112. Bernardo Gicovate, however, is of a different opinion. He sees a radical difference between San Juan with his «sacrificio total de la transfiguración» and JRJ with his «contemplación a la posesión total del pensamiento dominante», and argues that it is therefore a gross error to suppose any «parentesco o deuda intelectual». For Gicovate, «tanto los símbolos, forma de pensamiento, como la dicción, formas o fórmulas lingüísticas, son patrimonio común». Any possible resemblance in internal form or external structure is hence, in his argument, a simple historical fact, common to any writer in the language. (B. Gicovate, *La poesía de JRJ,* Ediciones Ariel, Barcelona, 1973, pp. 172-173).

Implicit in the poem is the expression of a whole poetic theory. Furthermore, it is precisely because it is suggestive and not explicit that the poem is a successful one in its own right. Rather than a stated manifesto, it is a sustained invocation and so retains its value as a poem *per se.* One source of inspiration for this poem may well be that of Ortega y Gasset. Ortega was a close friend of JRJ, who was perfectly familiar with all his work and held it in great esteem. Ortega initiates his first book, *Meditaciones del Quijote* (published in 1914) with words that undoubtedly bore a rich influence upon JRJ's *Eternidades* (published 1916-1917):

> Hay dentro de toda cosa la indicación de una posible plenitud. Un alma abierta y noble sentirá la ambición de perfeccionarla, de auxiliarla, para que logre esa su plenitud. Esto es amor—el amor a la perfección de lo amado [...] ¡Santificadas sean las cosas! ¡Amadlas, amadlas! Cada cosa es un hada que reviste de miseria y vulgaridad sus tesoros interiores, y es una virgen que ha de ser enamorada para hacerse fecunda.

Relevant here too is Ortega's article on Ernest Renan of April 1909, in which he treats «la manera renaniana de acercarse a las cosas» and states that «alojado en el órgano material, cada alma es una hilandera de ideal productora de hilos sutilísimos que traspasan otras almas hermanas».[9] Again, a little further on he says: «cada cosa está impregnada de Dios, cada cosa se brinda a servirnos de Eucaristía [...] Renan ha estudiado todas las creencias, ha hecho sonar todos los mitos [...] pero no contento con eso le sorprendemos a veces buscando a Dios por los rincones, en las cosas humildes, en lo que aparentemente se halla más lejos de la santidad».[10] The theme is a recurrent one in Ortega. It reappears, for instance, in his essay «Adán en el Paraíso»[11] in which he insists on the need for recognition of the soul of things, their essential «ser»—maintaining, in short, that «cosas» should not be regarded as «casos».

The topic of discovering the «alma de las cosas» by means of loving meditation is also a basically «krausista-institucionista» one, as expressed for example in Manuel B. Cossío's «El arte de saber ver» published in the *Boletín de la Institución Libre de Enseñanza* in 1879.[12]

In his review of JRJ's *Arias tristes* in *Renacimiento* (vol. I, 1907), Salvador Rueda describes JRJ as especially skilled in evoking «*el alma de las cosas*» (Rueda's own emphasis). He goes on to speak of the «crepúsculos, paisajes, jardines», declaring that «hay una *media luz* espiritual en toda la obra, mezclada con otra *media luz* de naturaleza, que, unidas, nos alumbran por dentro de un modo discreto y sugestivo». In the same issue, J. Martínez Ruiz (Azorín) sees JRJ as a poet of «delicadezas» with a special capacity for conveying «alma»: « ¡El alma de las cosas! Sólo los poetas y los filósofos poseen el secreto de encontrarla en el caos ruidoso y

9 JOSÉ ORTEGA Y GASSET, «Renan», *Obras completas,* 11 vols., Revista de Occidente, Madrid, 1957, I, p. 457.

10 *Ibid.,* p. 466.

11 ORTEGA Y GASSET, «Adán en el Paraíso» (May-August 1910), *OC,* I, pp. 473-493.

12 MANUEL B. COSSÍO, «El arte de saber ver», *Boletín de la Institución Libre de Enseñanza,* año III, Madrid, October 1879, núm. 65, pp. 153-154.

frívolo de la vida, y de mostrarnos como una partícula de ella en sus ensueños». Here, then, we find applied to JRJ's first published collection this much reiterated theme, in both Generation of '98 and «modernista» articles. There is yet a further interesting similarity in the views expressed by the Venezuelan «modernista» writer, Manuel Díaz-Rodríguez, in his *Camino de perfección.* For him, mysticism in literature is composed of this same «clara visión de las cosas y los seres». In support of his theory he quotes a passage from Lope de Vega's *Los locos de Valencia,* pronounced by the supposed madman to the doctor:

> Oh, señor licenciado, y cuanto huelgo
> de ver su reverendo personaje;
> que soy amigo de hombres virtuosos
> y que *sepan el alma de las cosas.*

Italicizing this last line, Díaz-Rodríguez goes on to contend that it is neither doctor nor sage «sino el poeta o el artista quien sabe el alma de las cosas. Cuanto más alto el poeta o el artista, es tanto mayor la adivinación con que él penetra en el alma de las cosas en apariencia inanimadas».[13]

Let us return to the poem under discussion. That enigmatic «Intelijencia» to which the poet addresses his petition may indeed be the light of intelligence which permits this insight into the soul of things. Yet it lends itself to varying possibilities of interpretation: as the intellectual powers of the poet's own mind; as intelligence, in the sense of intellectual perception, in the abstract; or even as the Divine Intelligence, the «Primum Mobile». It is, however, difficult to concur with the view of the majority of critics that this invocation renders the entire poem an «intellectual» one, that is, purely conceptual and cerebral. Eugenio Florit, for example, describes the poem as of intellectual concern, on the sole grounds of his interpretation of that initial appeal. Such is the inference that must be drawn from his juxtaposition of the epithet «intelectualista» with the quotation «¡Intelijencia, dame» etc., which follows in immediate parenthesis by way of qualification.[14] The fact is that the poetry of JRJ is never wholly «intellectual». Certainly, it is only fair to recognize that Florit does make a gesture towards modifying his epithet: «sin embargo, no es (the intellectual concern) bastante a oscurecer la vena sencilla de sus octosílabos de raíz popular y tradicional».[15] But the gesture is a weak and ineffectual one. Moreover, it is in almost identical terms that the poet and critic Angel González speaks of «el intelectualismo—intelijencia, dame el nombre exacto de las cosas—» permeating JRJ's later works. Again he stresses his point: «El impresionismo del poeta deja paso a un agudo intelectualismo. El poeta pide a la intelijencia el "nombre exacto de las cosas"».[16] The approach too of the excellent interpreter and exegete of JRJ's poetry, Antonio Sánchez-Barbudo, is a predominantly intellectual one, for which he himself finds it necessary on

13 M. Díaz-Rodríguez, *Camino de perfección,* pp. 101-102.
14 E. Florit, «Nota preliminar», *TAP,* p. 21.
15 *Ibid.*
16 Angel González, *JRJ: Estudio,* Ediciones Júcar, Madrid, 1973, p. 220.

occasion to make apology and to justify.[17] And yet JRJ himself repeatedly testified to his own abhorrence of intellectual poetry, including philosophical poetry in this same category. His disapproval of the works of Paul Valéry was founded—rightly or wrongly—on these very grounds, and his remarks thereon go to confirm his adamantly anti-intellectual stance. Presented with a copy of the newly published «Cahier, B. 1910» of Valéry, JRJ announced that the French poet appeared to write from the grave: «Es un muerto muy inteligente que escribe».[18] Six months later, in April 1931, he is reported as dismissing a gift of personally dedicated poems from Valéry, made to him through the offices of Matilde Pomés, with the following peremptory —not to say crude—words: «Claro ella (Matilde Pomés) no sabe que a mí las poesías de Valéry me estomagan y que este librito con sus 21 poesías antiguas primero, sus 21 poesías modernas luego, y la *Parca Joven* en medio, no me importa nada».[19] In more measured tone we find him clarifying the aesthetic views upon which was based his dislike of the French poet. A further three years have elapsed, but his opinion remains unchanged. Guerrero Ruiz records:

> Dice [JRJ] cuánto tiene la obra de arte de sorpresa para el que tiene facultades para saber sorprenderla, estimando superior lo que brota así del rapto espontáneo, depurado luego conscientemente, a lo que sólo es producto de un trabajo intelectual; en esto difiere de la opinión de Valéry, creyéndolo equivocado en su teoría.[20]

That «lo que brota así del rapto espontáneo, depurado luego conscientemente» will prove fundamental in the aesthetics of JRJ. Elsewhere, JRJ further affirms that poetry is an art—the only one, in fact—which manages to escape the purely rational, whilst paradoxically managing to preserve it at the same time, by virtue of its superiority: «La poesía es lo único que se salva de la razón y que salva a la razón porque es más hermosa y superior que ella».[21] And whereas a purely intellectual poetry would be open to rational and logical explanation, for JRJ on the contrary: «la poesía no se explica; lo que dice, dice».[22] Again, in his «Invitación a un juicio sobre la poesía actual», JRJ declares: «para mí la poesía es algo divino, alado, gracioso, expresión del encanto y del misterio del mundo».[23] This basic difference between JRJ and Valéry is stressed by the critic Antonio Blanch, who concludes his «Comparación de la poesía pura española con la de Valéry» with the categorical statement that «hay que situar al poeta español

[17] A. Sánchez-Barbudo, *La segunda época de JRJ*, pp. 162-163. It is notable that Sánchez-Barbudo's at times overintellectual analysis of JRJ is picked up by the critic Leo R. Cole in his book *The Religious Instinct in the Poetry* of *JRJ*, The Dolphin Book Co. Ltd., Oxford, 1967, pp. 113-114.

[18] Guerrero Ruiz, p. 65.

[19] *Ibid.*, p. 141.

[20] *Ibid.*, p. 311.

[21] JRJ, «"Anjel" y "Duende"», «Poesía cerrada y poesía abierta», *Pájinas escojidas; prosa*, selected by R. Gullón, p. 183.

[22] R. Gullón, *El último JRJ*, p. 179.

[23] JRJ, *La corriente infinita*, p. 218.

en el extremo opuesto de Valéry».[24] Describing the poetic act itself, JRJ once more repudiates the notion of intellectualism in his Work: «Yo no sé cuándo voy a hacer una poesía; si no la hago en el acto, no la hago; no es cosa cerebral y pesada, sino al contrario».[25]

In the light of such an overtly non-intellectual attitude, it must surely be deemed a mistake to consider as belonging to the domain of the intellect alone that kind of absolute denotative exactitude and nominal perfection which «Intelijencia» is called upon to bestow. It is certainly perfection which is sought; but in the words of the poet himself; «"Perfección" quiere decir para mí "complemento", que no falte nada y que nada sobre por el instante, *sin esceso intelectualista.* Perfecta es una cosa que lo sea *por instinto*»[26] (my emphases). Reference has already been made to Ortega y Gasset, and it is interesting to observe that here again Ortega was saying much the same thing as this in his *Meditaciones del Quijote*—a copy of which, incidentally, he presented to JRJ in 1914 with the inscription to «el Bayardo de los poetas». Intellectualism without «amor» is for Ortega meaningless and hence the importance he ascribes to resurrecting «el lindo nombre que usó Spinoza», namely «amor intellectualis». Ortega's own concept of perfection—the fulfilling by means of loving persuasion of the potential plenitude of things—nicely complements and concurs with that of JRJ expressed above.[27]

It is perhaps Rubén Darío who, in his «Atrio» to *Ninfeas,* most accurately anticipates the balance of intellect and passion in JRJ. The two lines in his last stanza read: «¿Y las voces ocultas tu razón interpreta? / Sigue, entonces, tu rumbo de amor. Eres poeta». They reveal Darío's early intuition of the nature of JRJ's future Work. «Reason» will serve JRJ as interpreter, that is, the poet's approach will be of an intellectual kind; but at the same time Darío accurately recognizes that «love» will provide the poetic orientation.[28]

Clearly the need arises for a revision of the intellectualist interpretation of that outcry, « ¡Intelijencia, [...]». For a truer grasp of its meaning it may be helpful to refer again to Fray Luis de León. The appeal is rather to that «entendimiento» of which Luis de León speaks, in which idea and image are exactly congruent because God has so ordained it. The names that are conceived by the «entendimiento» are «imágenes por naturaleza», and are further described by Fray Luis as residing «en el alma»: «Quiero dezir, que la imágen y figura, que está *en el alma,* sustituye por aquellas cosas cuya figura es, por la semejança natural que tiene con ellas»[29] (my

[24] ANTONIO BLANCH, «Comparación de la poesía pura española con la de Valéry», *La poesía pura española,* Gredos, Madrid, 1976, pp. 276-278.
[25] GUERRERO RUIZ, p. 112.
[26] JRJ, «Lo "fable" y lo "inefable"», «Poesía cerrada y poesía abierta», *Pájinas escojidas; prosa,* selected by R. Gullón, p. 190.
[27] ORTEGA Y GASSET, *Meditaciones del Quijote, OC,* I, p. 311.
[28] For further analysis of the «Atrio», see G. PALAU DE NEMES, *Vida y obra de JRJ,* I, pp. 154-155.
[29] FRAY LUIS DE LEÓN, «De los nombres en general», *De los nombres de Cristo,* I, p. 31.

emphasis). I have stressed «the soul» in order to point out the analogical concept in JRJ's poem. He desires that his word fit precisely its object; but also that the object be «creada por *mi alma* nuevamente». Thus the «entendimiento» of Fray Luis de León's passage as creator and repository of «soul-images» would indeed seem to provide a parallel precedent to the Juanramonian «Intelijencia». At all events, the resonant and complex associations of JRJ's «Intelijencia» prohibit its confinement to some figurative abstraction of the purely cerebral. Mere intellect is for JRJ, in any case, nothing but auxiliary in the matter of writing poetry. An aphorism in his «Estética y ética estética» pronounces that «la intelijencia no sirve para guiar al instinto, sino para comprenderlo»;[30] whilst a subsequent pithy recommendation gives the following caveat: «Vigilemos con nuestra intelijencia nuestro instinto; pero dejémoslo suficiente libertad para que el niño haga un poco... ¡bastante! lo que quiera».[31] Final repudiation of the purely intellectual construction which critics have been apt to put upon not only the invoked «Intelijencia» but upon the whole poem, and upon whole subsequent collections of poems, must arise from the sheer irrationalism of the plea involved. No word, rationally, can ever *be* the thing it signifies. Moreover, if the «cosa» is to be «creada por mi alma nuevamente», that recreation patently entails a change of state from the original. The point to be made here is that the irrational character of the poet's aim in no way invalidates the poem. Rather, it inspires admiration for one prepared to devote his life to the pursuit of an impossible idea.

In the poem « ¡Intelijencia, dame», the germinal notion of the poet as creator is present. The liturgical repetition of «Que por mí vayan todos» suggests that having gained perfect mastery of reality through the Word, he will now be the instrument of universal salvation, offering the path to omniscience to all who would listen. Nevertheless, this is no cabbalistic kind of incantation, and neither should the names be construed as magical in themselves. The final lines of the poem rise on a crescendo of exaltation and broaden into a gesture of universal embrace: «y tuyo, / y suyo, y mío», which suggests one vast brotherhood. This unitive conception of the Word and its naming process is of such wide implication that it must be reserved for later analysis. We should first return to JRJ's desire: «Que mi palabra sea / la cosa misma».

It has already been seen that Walter Pater was a critic highly esteemed by JRJ, and this renders it all the more appropriate to consider now some aspects of his aesthetic principles which will illumine the nature of the desire expressed above: the desire that the Word shall *be* the thing it signifies. The first and major implication of any such perfected mutual identity must be the necessity to suppress the relations between things; for only then are they free to be properly apprehended. The corollary of this will be the dissolution of temporality, the abstraction from Time of the object's essential reality. The process of finding the ideal verbal correlative

30 JRJ, «Estética y ética estética I», «Ideolojía lírica», *Pájinas escojidas; prosa,* selected by R. Gullón, p. 143.

31 *Ibid.,* p. 145.

of the object will demand absolute economy and frugality of language. Let us examine the first requisite, in the light of the well-known Paterian dictum that «All art constantly aspires towards the condition of music». Near the end of the paragraph which leads up to this pronouncement we are told, by way of preparation for it, that all the arts in common aspire towards the principle of music, «music being the typical, or ideally consummate art, the object of the great «Anders-streben» of all art, of all that is artistic, or partakes of artistic qualities».[32] The point Pater is making is that music achieves precisely that suppression of relations between things with which we are here concerned. That is to say, it abolishes any distinction between matter and form: «For while in all other kinds of art it is possible to distinguish the matter from the form, and the understanding can always make this distinction, *yet it is the constant effort of art to obliterate it*»[33] (my emphasis). Pater then immediately illustrates his contention by way of reference to the poetic art:

> That the mere matter of a poem, for instance, its subject, namely, its given incidents or situation [...] should be nothing without the form, the spirit, of the handling, that this form, this mode of handling, should become an end in itself, should penetrate every part of the matter: this is what all art strives after, and achieves in different degrees.[34]

The «condition of music», then, is the condition wherein the rightness of the term permits it to *become* what it signifies. The coincidence of thought here with the French poet, Mallarmé, ought not to pass unnoticed. One need think only of Mallarmé's statement that «La Poésie, proche l'idée, est Musique, par excellence—ne consent pas d'infériorité» to appreciate the affinity. In very general terms moreover, it is important to remember the immense importance which the French symbolists and the «modernistas» likewise, attached to music.[35] To return to Pater's views on the relationship of art to the condition of music, the supposition which he makes of a so-called «preexistent adaptation» which has but to be discovered, must at first seem impossibly unrealistic. On the other hand, one may quite readily subscribe to the belief that in order for the idea of a thing or object to come into being and exist, it must first be endowed with form, and that form is its existential prerequisite. As the German modern poet, Stefan George, concludes in his poem called «The Word»: «Where word breaks off no thing may be».

[32] WALTER PATER, «The School of Giorgione», *The Renaissance,* Collins, Glasgow, 1961, p. 129.

[33] WALTER PATER, «Style», *Appreciations,* Macmillan, London and New York, 1889, p. 27.

[34] *Ibid.,* p. 129.

[35] For further discussion on the importance of music for the French symbolists and the «modernistas», see GUY MICHAUD, *La doctrine symboliste,* Nizet, Paris, 1947; GUY MICHAUD, *Mallarmé, l'homme et l'oeuvre,* Hatier-Boivin, Paris, 1953; GUY MICHAUD, *Mallarmé,* Hatier, Paris, 1971. Also, L. M. ROSENBLATT, *L'idée de l'art pour l'art dans la littérature anglaise pendant la période victorienne,* H. Champion, Paris, 1931.

As a slight digression, a curious rider may be noted to this necessity of name for the existence of thing, in the way in which JRJ in 1927 began to insist on the abolition of his own personal name in favour of mere initials: initials, that is, which were not even his. Juan Guerrero Ruiz records this behavioural eccentricity: «Iniciales. Deseo de ocultar el nombre».[36] It evinces, in the light of the foregoing analysis of JRJ's own conception of Word and name, a distressing inclination toward self-obliteration. Not the initials «J.R.J.» but «K.Q.X.» were chosen; and chosen because he considered them to be «las tres letras más feas del alfabeto», according to the testimony of Rafael Alberti.[37] If the name *is* its object, then indeed such a gesture denotes the severest withdrawal of the self from the world.

[36] Guerrero Ruiz, p. 71.
[37] Rafael Alberti, *La arboleda perdida,* Seix Barral, Barcelona, 1977, p. 248.

Chapter IV

THE WORD AS IDEA

In the foregoing discussion I have been using the word «idea», and it is one which serves as an appropriate transition to the important consideration of temporal suppression in the naming of things. For the «idea» of things belongs to the realm of an eternal present. It can be said neither to be of the past nor of the future. By «idea» is meant the essential quiddity of a thing.[1] And it is the eternal, the a-temporal Word in which alone that being can exist. It follows therefore that words «recognize» an entire class of entities—which I have here referred to as ideas and which may equally well be called universals—the true apprehension and «realization» of which involves their abstraction from Time. The Platonic principle of «Eidos» is clearly implicit here; the belief that representative terms consist not of mere name or «nomen» but actually *are* that which they express, the «res» itself which thereby is sustained forever in the present. The timelessness of the perfectly expressed «idea» is the goal of Mallarmé, no less than of JRJ: «A quoi bon la merveille de transposer un fait de nature en sa presque disparition vibratoire selon le jeu de la parole, cependant; si ce n'est pour qu'en émane, sans la gêne d'un proche ou concret rappel, la notion pure».[2] An elucidation of this temporal suppression is to be found in an essay by the German philosopher, Arthur Schopenhauer, called «On the Metaphysics of the Beautiful and Aesthetics». The perception of the Idea, he says, requires that when contemplating an object, the poet shall abstract its position in time and space, and thus abstract its individuality and secure its enduring element, freed from subjection to change. He illustrates this with a metaphor peculiarly appropriate to the Work of JRJ:

> Now as regards the *objective* element of such aesthetic intuitive perception, the [Platonic] *Idea,* this may be described as that which we should have before us if time, this formal and subjective condition of our knowledge, were withdrawn, like the glass from the kaleidoscope. For example, we see the development of the bud, blossom, and fruit and are astonished at the driving force that never wearies of again going through this cycle. Such astonishment would vanish if we could know that, in spite of all that change, we have

[1] For a comprehensive definition of «idea», see J. Ferrater Mora's *Diccionario de filosofía,* pp. 669-672.
[2] S. Mallarmé, *Oeuvres complètes,* p. 368.

> before us the one and unalterable Idea of the plant. However, we are unable intuitively to perceive this Idea as a unity of bud, blossom, and fruit, but are obliged to know it by means of the form of *time,* whereby it is laid out for our intellect in those successive states.[3]

It is rewarding to consider the famous «El poema» of JRJ in the light of this passage: « ¡No le toques ya más, / que así es la rosa! » (*LP,* p. 695). Here, the poem—seen as a rose—has arrived at its apogee, the culmination and fulfilment of its own Idea, and within this sense of achievement is also conveyed the sense of all the preceding growth stages of the rose's unity: seed, plant and bud—i.e., all the stages of poetic creation—telescopically present and included in the named «rosa» as metaphor for the Poem. The rose-poem, then, is more than «nomen»; it is actuality, «res». And it is in the Word that it has gained its being. The Word is what permits it to persist in its own presence, to perdure, to *be.*

This theme—that the name gives permission for existence—is one which, after JRJ, becomes well established in Spanish poetry. One good example would be Jorge Guillén's poem, «Los nombres» from *Cántico.* The last stanza ends with this categorical statement:

> ¿Y las rosas? Pestañas
> Cerradas: horizonte
> Final. ¿Acaso nada?
> Pero quedan los nombres.[4]

The act of naming, the condition of music, and the elicitation of the «idea», which are the three themes which we have been considering, are furthermore the subject of the French symbolist, Mallarmé: «Je dis: une fleur! et, hors de l'oubli où ma voix relègue aucun contour, en tant que quelque chose d'autre que les calices sus, musicalement se lève, l'idée même et suave, l'absente de tous bouquets».[5] JRJ's own admiring recognition of these Mallarméan qualities is evident: «El hecho concreto es que Mallarmé escribía una poesía de una gran profundidad formal, muy rica de sugestiones, muy rica de correspondencia, que era al mismo tiempo música, pintura, poesía, etc.», he states in *El modernismo* (p. 17).

Returning to the couplet poem of JRJ, « ¡No le toques ya más, / que así es la rosa! », the indication is clear that it is only after many and successive «toques» that the perfectly competent expression can be arrived at for the possession of the «idea». This brings us to consider the problem of the revisionary process of alteration and correction which the poet must practise in order to distinguish the inessential from what is essential, thereby to attain the «idea». A necessary economy of language must be the outcome. Transparency, a luminous clarity in the Word, is requisite if the

[3] A. SCHOPENHAUER, «On the Metaphysics of the Beautiful and Aesthetics», *Parerga and Paralipomena,* 2 vols., translated from the German by E. F. J. Payne, Clarendon Press, Oxford, 1974, II, p. 207.

[4] For a note on the influence of JRJ on Guillén, with special reference to this poem, see E. DÍEZ-CANEDO, *JRJ en su obra,* pp. 126-127.

[5] S. MALLARMÉ, *Oeuvres complètes,* p. 368.

«idea» is to shine forth. «Transparency» is the very title of one of JRJ's most consummate poems: «La Trasparencia, Dios, La Trasparencia»—a poem written towards the end of the poet's career (1949) almost, it would seem, as a summation of his poetic practice. It is an invocation to the divine Transparency of the Word—«el nombre conseguido de los nombres», as the ensuing sister-poem defines it—which is at one and the same time the godhead both of «conciencia» and «esencia». The closing three lines read:

la trasparencia, dios, la trasparencia,
el uno al fin, dios ahora sólito en lo uno mío,
en el mundo que yo por ti y para ti he creado.

The God of Transparency is the Word: «El Dios. El nombre conseguido de los nombres» (*LP,* pp. 1289-1290). In practical terms, the attainment of this perfect transparent Word meant the strict elimination of all superfluities. Thus we find JRJ declaring: «Cultivemos, ante todo, la voluntad de rechazar»[6]; and, in conversation with Ricardo Gullón, only three years before JRJ's death: «Yo, según voy haciéndome más viejo, siento mayor deseo de quitar al poema, a mis cosas, todo el virtuosismo».[7]

Possibly the earliest appearance of «depuración» comes with the rigorous sonnet form of the *Sonetos espirituales* (1914-1915), in which JRJ achieves a controlled equilibrium between the physical and the ideal image. Notably, this was one of the first collections written as a result of his love for Zenobia: adolescent erotic love is now tempered and purified with a certain spiritual love. *Estío,* which has earlier been mentioned in connection with this matter, continues this development. But it is the famous poem «Vino, primero, pura» of the later collection *Eternidades* (1916-1917) which most clearly formulates the urge for «depuración». Austerity is its tenor, and a certain moral and aesthetic asceticism. To what extreme this poetic concept will take him has already been indicated: it will be the path to his ultimate goal of Silence. And yet, paradoxical though it may seem, that austerity neither extinguishes nor annuls the very living sensuous and sensual element in much of the later poetry of JRJ, nor even quenches the linguistic profusion of the last two collections.

In order to understand this compatibility between the austerity of «depuración» and sheer sensuality—the equilibrium between idea and the senses—we should remember the control with which the young JRJ handled, for instance, synaesthesia in his earliest verse. This control, coupled with his emotional sensibility, was already much admired by his contemporaries as epitomizing «modernismo»: the union of the sensual with the metaphysical. The whole of the prose poem «Espacio» bears witness to the fact that the aesthetic concept of «depuración» is by no means the negation of sensuality. Its vibrant language is proof to the contrary: «Las flores nos rodean de voluptuosidad, olor, color y forma sensual; nos rodeamos de ellas, que son

[6] JRJ, «Estética y ética estética», «Ideolojía lírica», *Pájinas escojidas; prosa,* selected by R. Gullón, p. 149.

[7] R. GULLÓN, *Conversaciones con Juan Ramón,* p. 152.

sexos de colores, de formas, de colores diferentes» («Fragmento primero»). Or again: «Desnudez es la vida, y desnudez la sola eternidad... Y sin embargo, están, están, están, están llamándonos a comer, gong, gong, gong, gong, en este barco de este mar, y hay que vestirse en este mar, en esta eternidad de Adán y Eva, Adán de *smoking,* Eva... Eva se desnuda para comer como para bañarse» («Fragmento tercero»). A kind of tropical luxuriance, a revelry in the sheer abundance of things, manifests itself in the poet's response to colour and form in prolific Nature; and an erotic delight in Life itself.

Reaching the very peaks of sensual ecstasy and delight in the awareness of being alive, is the small poem called «Estoy viviendo», from *La estación total:*

Estoy viviendo. Mi sangre
está quemando belleza.

Viviendo. Mi doble sangre
está evaporando amor.

Estoy viviendo. Mi sangre
está fundiendo conciencia. (*LP,* p. 1175)

The equilibrium and compatibility is notable here between the senses and reason, between «sangre» and «conciencia»: a balance finely achieved by the precision and control of the poetic statement. As I have suggested, this control between physical image and ideal image, between body and spirit, first becomes apparent in the *Sonetos espirituales*—undoubtedly the result of the verbal economy which the rigour of the sonnet form imposes. Here, in «Estoy viviendo», the skeletal economy of language proves again in no way incompatible with a fiery, fleshy and full-blooded sensuality. Nor does the self-restraint of stylistic austerity deny the possibility of passion. In «Nostaljia», from the collection entitled *Piedra y cielo,* a minute green leaf is the very synthesis of the poet's desire:

¡Hojita verde con sol,
tú sintetizas mi afán;
afán de gozarlo todo,
de hacerme en todo inmortal! (*LP,* p. 819)

The vocabulary here («afán»; «gozar») is powerfully urgent, plainly suggestive of an overwhelming desire for mutual impregnation of poet and world, overtly sexual.

One may wonder whether, in reading Walter Pater's lectures on Plato, JRJ might not indeed have recognized himself in the following description by Pater of the Greek philosopher-poet: «Austere as he seems, and on well-considered principle really is, his temperance or austerity, aesthetically so winning, is attained only by the chastisement, the control, of a variously interested, a richly sensuous nature».[8]

[8] Walter Pater, *Plato and Platonism; a series of lectures,* Greenwood Press, New York, 1969, p. 113.

In this connection too, we do well to remember JRJ's admiration for the aesthetic philosophy of Nietzsche. (No less than sixteen works of Nietzsche are included in his personal library at Moguer alone). The progression of Nietzsche's views on art, from the need for cool impartiality to intense personal participation, is relevant here because of the consistently keen interest JRJ displays for the German philosopher. Whereas in *The Birth of Tragedy* Nietzsche had adhered to the principle of Kant and Schopenhauer that art is «disinterested contemplation», he finally dismissed this idea as the «emasculation» of art and openly asserted the physical and even sexual sources of art. The «peculiar sweetness and fullness» of the aesthetic state of mind had its source in «sensuality»: it was not cancelled but transfigured in art. From this, it is easy to conceive how an aesthetic understanding of such a kind should have found favour with JRJ, for whom it is peculiarly apposite. Moreover, the fact that Nietzsche's conclusion upon the nature of the artist (using an idea deriving from Heraclitus) was to see him as the prophet of the doctrine of Eternal Recurrence further strengthens the bonds between the Spanish poet and the German philosopher.

The increasing interest generally shown by the «new generation» of 1914 in Nietzsche's aesthetics from the year 1910 onward is pointed out by Gonzalo Sobejano in his book *Nietzsche en España:* «Si las personalidades europeas que fecundaron a modernistas y noventaiochistas fueron principalmente Zola, Tolstoy, Ibsen, Nietzsche y Verlaine, sólo el influjo de estos dos últimos pervive y pasa a la generación nueva».[9] It is above all with Nietzsche as aphorist and poet that JRJ is concerned, and it is in large part thanks to the translating abilities of two of his own literary confrères, Ricardo Baeza and Francisco A. de Icaza, that he was able to steep himself in Nietzschean thought and aesthetics. In Ricardo Baeza's anthology *Nietzsche, aforismos y sentencias* (in the «Colección Microcosmos»), JRJ had at his disposal a fine collection of aphorisms gathered from a variety of Nietzsche's works and grouped under general titles of Baeza's own choosing, such as «Del arte y de los artistas», «De la amistad y del amor», etc. This method was much in keeping with the contemporary Spanish taste for assimilating the concentrated essence of European thought.[10] As for Nietzsche the poet, it was Icaza who after first publishing fourteen of Nietzsche's poems in translation in *La Pluma* (1920), the following year in 1921 brought out a substantial poetic anthology entitled *Nietzsche, poeta (interpretaciones líricas),* drawing attention in his prologue not only to Nietzsche's fine lyricism but also to his excellence as philologist. In the same year there swiftly followed further and superior translations of Nietzsche's poetry, this time by the Catalan, Manuel de Montolíu. The ensuing lines from Montolíu's preface concerning Nietzsche's aesthetics are curiously applicable to JRJ himself who must have read them appreciatively, sensing the affinity:

> La poesía de Nietzsche nos la ha definido él mismo como una llama [...] irguiéndose anhelante al cielo en forma de un magno interrogante. Interrogación,

[9] GONZALO SOBEJANO, *Nietzsche en España,* Gredos, Madrid, p. 489.
[10] *Ibid.,* p. 497.

trágica interrogación, que llena el ambiente de toda una época, tal es la lírica de Nietzsche que él vertió en verso y prosa por toda la extensión de su obra.[11]

Since I have already spoken of certain affinities between JRJ and the Anglo-Irish poet W. B. Yeats, it is appropriate while mentioning Nietzsche to observe that they further share in common—and to a great extent—the influence of this extremely important philosopher. As Cleanth Brooks has shown in his essay on Yeats in *The Hidden God,*[12] a great deal of Nietzsche is to be found in Yeats, particularly in his later work, in the celebration of man's vitality and man's ability to do and to suffer. It was Nietzsche's contention that in beauty «contrasts are overcome, the highest sign of power thus manifesting itself in the conquest of opposites»; and according to Nietzsche, it is out of joy and strength, not out of weakness, that the artist creates and thereby causes «harmony to ring out of every discord». Further, the test of the artist is «the extent to which he can acknowledge the terrible and questionable character of things», while nevertheless still affirming the essential goodness of life. This mood of rapt exaltation, accompanied by the deliberate introduction of a discord which the poet then resolves, is characteristic no less of JRJ than of Yeats; and it is precisely this which is meant by the Nietzschean notion of harmony out of discord. The very concept of poetic creation itself is of a fundamentally Nietzschean character both in JRJ and in Yeats. An extract from the latter's «Under Ben Bulben» reads:

Even the wisest man grows tense
With some sort of violence
Before he can accomplish fate,
Know his work or choose his mate.

Out of constant striving, effortful activity, is born the Work of the poet. The true sense of completeness and wholeness does not come out of lassitude or timidity but must be wrested and won from a certain violence of action. It is this «violence» which is manifest in the relentless energy of the questing spirit of Yeats and of JRJ alike.

The continual practice of «depuración» which is demanded by the struggle to attain «le mot juste» is an important part of Mallarmé's aesthetics, just as it is for JRJ. «Un désir indéniable à mon temps», says Mallarmé, «est de séparer comme en vue d'attributions différentes le double état de la parole, brut ou immédiat ici, là essentiel».[13] But it is an aim not easily fulfilled. Not always does JRJ attain that «ajuste» which he seeks. If at times—as in the couplet « ¡No le toques ya más, / que así es la rosa! »—triumph is his, at other times his inadequacy is such that he can but acknowledge the enormity of the hardship involved. A telling poem therefore

[11] Gonzalo Sobejano, *Nietzsche en España,* p. 501.
[12] Cleanth Brooks, *The Hidden God,* Yale University Press, New Haven and London, 1963, pp. 52-53.
[13] S. Mallarmé, *Oeuvres complètes,* p. 368.

is the one that bears this very title, «Ajuste». Set beside the couplet just quoted, it both sheds light on this latter and in turn significantly gains from it:

> Qué difícil es unir
> el tiempo de frutecer
> con el tiempo de sembrar.
>
> (El mundo jira que jira,
> ruedas que nunca se unen
> en una rueda total.)
>
> Un solo día la vida,
> un día completo y todo,
> que no se acabe jamás. (*LP*, p. 1183)

No longer here is that fullness of satisfaction experienced in the achieved «idea» of the rose. On the contrary, the exclamation, negation, desideration reveal a helplessness and a hopelessness in the face of the challenge posed. The «rosa» couplet has, patently, in its own turn passed through this very stage—the stage of flagging poetic strength—but has endured it, winning through to that selfsame union, here so urgently and so despairingly sought, of the Many in the One: seed, blossom, fruit, perfectly fused in the Rose-Idea. It is interesting that this notion of a work of art as a vegetable cycle is also to be found in Schelling. José Ferrater Mora, in his *Diccionario de filosofía,* summarizes it thus:

> El carácter romántico de la filosofía del arte de Schelling se muestra no sólo en su estimación por la obra genial del artista como una creación inconsciente y, a la vez, profundamente reflexiva, sino, sobre todo, porque en el arte llega a quedar anulada toda aparente oposición y se revela de la manera más pura y más completa la identidad de los contrarios en el seno de lo Absoluto. Así ocurre, por ejemplo, en el organismo viviente, cuyo aspecto objetivo queda englobado en el aspecto subjetivo de su vitalidad; así ocurre también y muy especialmente en la creación artística, que hace de lo pasivo y de lo muerto lo que vive eternamente.[14]

The initial stanza of «Ajuste» is a notable reminder of the asperity of the poet's road to perfected expression, and if the perfection of the couplet poem appears simple, it is the momentously hard-won simplicity of the flawless transparent «ajuste» in which past, present and future unite in a transcendence of Time. This unitive power of the «nombre-exacto-de-las-cosas» will, as we shall see, have far-reaching consequences upon the Work as a whole.

However rebarbative may appear this word-surgery to expose nude bone, nevertheless there is a distinct aesthetic «frisson» to be had from the feeling of victory over difficulty, which this process alone can achieve. But if the «desnudez» of omission is the prime consequence of JRJ's

[14] For further discussion of the concept of organic unity in Schelling, see MANUEL GARCÍA MORENTE, *Lecciones preliminares de filosofía,* Losada, Buenos Aires, 1952, pp. 333-334.

conception of the Word's role to crystallize essences, the extraordinary phenomenon of his unceasing habit of retrospective correction ought not to be forgotten. «Corregir», «pulir», «limar», «retocar», «recrear»:—these are among the terms used by JRJ to describe his method. But by far his most significant description of correcting his poems is that of «revivirlos». The act of correction was for him, quite literally, the renewal of an experience. In his own words: «Para mí, correjir es revivir; revivo momentos de mi vida cuando corrijo los poemas escritos en el pasado».[15] It also is, in itself, an act of creation: «Crear es ser dominado para lo bello; correjir es crear dominando».[16]

There are two major implications here. The first is that the corrections themselves, no less than the original creations, stem from within the poet. They are not the product of a purely mechanical operation of the intellect. This is clear from a report by Ricardo Gullón of a conversation with JRJ in November 1952: «Yo—insiste [JRJ] en el *yo*—no corrijo. Las correcciones se hacen solas [...] A veces no recuerdo la línea original y al querer repetirla surge de otra manera y la corrección está hecha por sí misma».[17] There is a parallel here with Antonio Machado, for whom this theme of reliving the past and of creating the past is also of central importance, manifested notably in his *Juan de Mairena*[18] and *Abel Martín* and his notebooks. In *Juan de Mairena,* Machado further reveals his strong conception of the progressive *invention* of the past, citing Goethe as one of the «grandes videntes de lo pasado». He continues: «En verdad, lo poético es ver, y como toda visión requiere distancia [...] Es el viento en los ojos de Homero, la mar multisonora en sus oídos, lo que nosotros llamamos actualidad».[19] The second implication of this term «revivir» is that it embraces the fundamental concept of the unity of the Work: its cyclical unity. The retrospective «reliving» of past poems is a continual and succesive cycle of regenerative activity. Fixity, stasis, have no part in Juanramonian aesthetics. On the contrary, for him the Work is a living, breathing, growing organism, «un todo orgánico», composed of poetry which, he says, «no es sino aspiración constante a algo nuevo». It is important too to remember that correction does not consist exclusively of elimination but of alteration and, indeed, inclusion and insertion as well at times.

Notably, it was JRJ's early verse—*Ninfeas* (1900); *Almas de violeta* (1900); *Rimas* (1902); *Arias tristes* (1903)—which, incurring the poet's later dissatisfaction, most frequently underwent correction[20]—and even total

15 R. GULLÓN, *Conversaciones con Juan Ramón,* p. 119.

16 JRJ, «Estética y ética estética», «Ideolojía lírica», *Pájinas escojidas; prosa,* selected by R. Gullón, p. 154.

17 R. GULLÓN, *Conversaciones con Juan Ramón,* pp. 80-81.

18 See for example ANTONIO MACHADO, *Cancionero apócrifo,* CLXVIII, «El "arte poética" de Juan de Mairena», *Obras: poesía y prosa,* edited by Aurora de Albornoz and Guillermo de Torre, Losada, Buenos Aires, 1964, pp. 315-322.

19 *Ibid.,* XV, p. 397.

20 B. GICOVATE in his *La poesía de JRJ,* p. 140, prefers to specify that «En *Rimas de sombra* de 1902 comienza la constante reelaboración y corrección».

suppression. Enrique Díez-Canedo comments upon these alterations in his critical work, *JRJ en su obra,* and points out how the *Segunda antolojía poética* published in 1920 includes some of the verse from *Rimas* of 1902, but predictably not without changes. A line from «Recuerdos», for instance, is altered (successfully in the critic's opinion) from «en la inmundicia lóbrega del lago» to «en la verdina lóbrega del lago»; whilst the closing line, «(un ruiseñor despierto) / lanzó un dulce quejido epitalámico» suffers a less felicitous change from the adjective «epitalámico» to «desgarrado».[21] The main point here is that it should not be assumed that JRJ's corrections were always and infallibly better than the original. Certainly, as Díez-Canedo says, the change in title from *Rimas* to *Rimas de sombra,* although losing in simplicity, does gain in atmospheric evocation. But if we are thinking now of titular alterations, JRJ's decision to substitute his original *Diario de un poeta recién casado* (1916) with the heading *Diario de poeta y mar* —as it appeared in the new Losada edition of 1948 and again in the Afrodisio Aguado edition in Madrid, 1955—must surely be considered an error of judgement.[22] Proof of this is his eventual reversion, with the preparation in 1956 of *La tercera antolojía poética* under the collaboration of his wife Zenobia and Eugenio Florit, to the modified original: *Diario de un poeta reciencasado.* Another study of JRJ's poetry which takes into account such variants and which draws certain theoretical conclusions from them is Bernardo Gicovate's *La poesía de JRJ.* He notes for instance with approval an alteration in a poem in *Rimas:* «Los árboles no se mueven, / y es tan medrosa su calma» becomes, in the *Segunda antolojía poética,* «Los árboles no se mueven; / es tan humana su calma».[23] Less valuable however is the change in the title of the ballad «Los árboles» by the addition of what Gicovate deems a superfluous adjective: «Los árboles hombres».[24] Discussing this and a selection of other examples,[25] Gicovate notes a final marked dropping-off in the practice of «revivencia» and «rechazo» in the years drawing toward the death of JRJ.

The poetic integrity of JRJ in the unceasing self-restraint which he

[21] E. DÍEZ-CANEDO, *JRJ en su obra,* pp. 31-33.

[22] See R. GULLÓN, *Conversaciones con Juan Ramón,* p. 84.
Recorded here is an attempt by JRJ to defend his alteration: «Cambié el título porque quería destacar la importancia que en su gestación tuvo la presencia del mar, el contacto con el mar».

[23] B. GICOVATE, *La poesía de JRJ,* pp. 22-23.

[24] *Ibid.,* p. 28.

[25] Amongst others, the following alterations are also recorded by Gicovate: «Paisaje del corazón» in *Ninfeas* changes its adjective «fatigados» to «que se cansan» in the *Segunda antolojía poética* (*La poesía de JRJ,* p. 47).

The poem «El pájaro del agua» of *Canción* sustained successive radical changes from its 1907 original to its 1936 version (*ibid.,* pp. 59-61).

«Marina de ensueño» of *Poemas mágicos y dolientes* alters its line «El viento da, y atormentado y hondo» to become «Furioso el viento da, y atormentado y hondo» in the *Segunda antolojía poética*—thus enhancing with its impressionism the tortured, disordered effect of the moment (*La poesía de JRJ,* pp. 71-72).

For further discussion and examples of «revivencia», see G. PALAU DE NEMES, *Vida y obra de JRJ,* I, pp. 185-187 and pp. 284-288. Also, *Vida y obra de JRJ,* II, p. 620.

exercised by renouncing all that was not «poesía pura» is rivalled only by the Herculean labour of his re-appraisal of past work. Both were processes that imposed a maximum exertion. Witness to the «heroism» of JRJ's perpetual revision of the Work is Antonio Machado, who said of him:

> Lo que él hace es *heroico;* todos los que trabajamos en poesía sabemos que es mucho más difícil corregir un verso que hacer un poema nuevo; por esto no volvemos sobre la obra anterior, porque significa un trabajo enorme volver a situarse en el ambiente de una poesía para corregirla y mejorarla, ya que cuando no se ha hecho mejor ha sido porque se ha encontrado una limitación que no se ha podido vencer [...] Someter una obra como la suya a la depuración que él hace, tan perfecta, es verdaderamente heroico [...] Yo le admiro mucho.[26]

The quotation is a lengthy one, but it deserves to be included here as the valuable recognition by another great poet of the toil involved in the struggle for «poesía pura». Machado's emphatic and repeated use of the adjective «heroico»[27] calls to mind, moreover, the Nietzschean concept of the Hero and his glorification of the Will. It is also suggestive of the theme of heroism treated in Thomas Carlyle's *On Heroes and Hero-Worship and the Heroic in History* (1841), especially Lectures III and V entitled respectively «The Hero as Poet» and «The Hero as Man of Letters».[28]

26 GUERRERO RUIZ, pp. 339-340.

27 R. A. Cardwell notes that, in turn, «Jiménez saw Giner and his Krausist friends as «héroes españoles» in the sense given to the word by Krause, Sanz del Río and that group of confessional writers—Sénancour, Emerson, Carlyle, Ruskin, Nietzsche,—who so dominated Idealist thinking in the nineteenth century». R. A. CARDWELL, *JRJ, The Modernist Apprenticeship, 1895-1900,* p. 32.

28 In January 1896 Unamuno published his essay «La dignidad humana» in *Ciencia social* (Barcelona), in which he made reference to «el culto de los héroes de Carlyle»; and in May 1902 a further essay, defending the hero-worship of Carlyle against falsification and entitled «Maese Pedro. Notas sobre Carlyle», appeared in *La España moderna,* año XIV, núm. 161, Madrid. Both essays were included in UNAMUNO's *Ensayos,* 7 vols., Residencia de Estudiantes, Madrid, 1916-1918, III. It is interesting to note that according to Gonzalo Sobejano: «En líneas generales cabe decir [...] que la influencia de Nietzsche en Unamuno existe, pero que no es la más intensa que éste padeció, pues queda sobrepujada por la de otros europeos del mismo siglo XIX: Carlyle y Kierkegaard principalmente» (*Nietzsche en España,* p. 282). Further, in 1900, in *La revista blanca,* año III, p. 684, Pedro Corominas speaks of «el individualismo heroico de Emerson y Carlyle» and notes the vitalist affinity between Carlyle and Nietzsche. However, the most influential medium for disseminating new philosophical thought was *La España moderna* (1889-1914) organized by José Lázaro. Sobejano records a part of its impressive list of contributions and translations from foreign works, among which figures that of Carlyle: «[...] de V. Basch, sobre la obra de Nietzsche y sus períodos; A. Fouillée, sobre la mora (*sic*) aristocrática del superhombre [...]; de E. Faguet, sobre Goethe como predecesor de Nietzsche; de J. Ravenna, sobre el héroe en Carlyle y en Nietzsche» (*Nietzsche en España,* p. 90). The interest in Carlyle was a continuing one: in May 1905 Alvaro de Albornoz published an essay entitled «Aristocracia y democracia (Carlyle, Ruskin, Nietzsche)» in the review *Nuestro tiempo;* Ramón Gómez de la Serna cited Carlyle in his *Morbideces* published in Madrid in 1908; and Ramón Ledesma Miranda testified to Maeztu's possession of the works of Carlyle in his fine personal library, in his article «Maeztu en mi recuerdo», «Homenaje a Don Ramiro de Maeztu», *Cuadernos hispanoamericanos,* 33-34, September-October 1952, p. 22.

Let us turn to some examples of poems from JRJ's Second Epoch to consider the degree of success in the appropriation of reality that the Word can attain, in its role as «nombre-exacto-de-las-cosas». In so doing, it will become apparent too that the search for the «mot juste» is directly concerned with conveying «durée», that it is, in fact, related to Time. (See Appendix).

In the poem «Elejía» from *Diario de un poeta reciencasado,* it is the witnessing presence of the poet which «creates» and appropriates the reality of the sea. It is to the poet that the ocean owes its reappearance in the repertoire of the world's reality:

> Ahora parecerás ¡oh mar lejano!
> a los que por ti vayan,
> viendo tus encendidas hojas secas,
> al norte, al sur, al este o al oeste;
> ahora parecerás ¡oh mar distante!
> mar; ahora que yo te estoy creando
> con mi recuerdo vasto y vehemente. (*LP,* p. 502)

The poem deserves a close analysis because it is exemplary of JRJ as the «maker-witness» of a natural phenomenon which, embraced within the Work, he then endows with perpetuity. How does he achieve this «realization» of so massive a phenomenon as the very ocean itself and from there, render it eternal? The answer is, by means of a startlingly skilful use of two dimensions: spatial and temporal. To take the first: the sea is geographically evoked. It will «appear» to those who voyage on it, in all four points of the compass and in its totality—«al norte, al sur, al este o al oeste». Thus its physical presence will emerge, we are told, before our eyes. And yet the invocation « ¡oh mar lejano! » serves—paradoxically—to distance it once again, beyond our reach. The vocative mood of the poem is a brilliant coup, for the fact that the poet is able to address himself to the sea in this way implies a degree of intimacy, a certain proximity, again. Nevertheless, at the same time there is a tantalising and contradictory oscillation between an implied proximity and a declared unattainability of distance within each of the two vocative exclamations: « ¡oh mar lejano! » and « ¡oh mar distante! ». They are, moreover, all the more tantalising because each follows hot on the heels of its respective preceding, boldly categorical affirmation that Yes! the sea will indeed materialize, will indeed «realize» itself before us; an affirmation whose credibility this juxtaposed stress on the farawayness of the sea instantly undermines, brings into doubt. Herein lies the cunningly wrought tension of the poem. Will the poet prove competent to fulfil the claims of his Work? Will he indeed «realize» the sea for us, and for ever?

The poem is a drama; a drama of creation. And since the substance of drama is tension, JRJ is deliberately sustaining tensions, maintaining suspense, until the highest pitch is reached. Then, and only then, does the resolution follow and our question find its answer. This culminating point of tension occurs in the enjambement of lines 5 and 6. Line 5 ends with the adjective «distante», an adjective which even more than its equivalent

5**

predecessor «lejano», serves to remove the sea. The distancing of the sea to an impossible remoteness seems now a finality. The poet has failed. Irretrievably, the sea is a lost phenomenon. But then follows the startling enjambement of line 6: «mar; ...». The sea has «returned», in a sudden inrushing tide, with this sole syllable. The return is total and irreversible. Because this «mar», we realize, is the object of its own self, the object of its subject: «parecerás... mar; ». This «mar» is the quintessence of «sea-ness», of «sea-hood». The sea will appear in all its sea-ness, will resemble sea, will resemble its own reality. And so indeed it does, in the full impact of that isolated word, so brilliantly and appositely positioned. The «mar» of the penultimate line stands nude: an unashamed self-affirmation, a plenipotential reality. The accomplishment of the poem does not, however, rest here. We should now analyse it further in the light of its temporal dimension.

The poem embraces three tenses, present, future and an implied past —but each is used with differing temporal *effect* due to the proximity of the three main verbs to the radically important adverb, «Ahora».

> Ahora parecerás ¡oh mar lejano! [...]
> ahora parecerás ¡oh mar distante!
> mar; ahora que yo te estoy creando [...]

The futurity of the two «parecerás» is reduced to a strictly immanent present, by juxtaposition with the immediate now-ness of «ahora». This is a deliberate piece of strategy on the part of the poet for it occurs twice, each time in a key position within the space of so brief a poem (only seven lines altogether). The joint «ahora parecerás» is firstly the initiation to the poem; it is retrieved and repeated after the intervention of a three-line parenthesis; and then instantly a third «ahora» stakes its claim as pivot to the overall structure of the poem, this time linked not with a verb of the future but with the continuous present of «yo te estoy creando». The poet's intention is not solely that of creating or «realizing» the sea, but of eternalizing it. This he achieves by rendering a poetic a-temporality through the synthesis of immanence, actuality and resurrected past. It is from this fusion of the three tenses that JRJ magically creates an eternal present, the eternal presence, of the sea. To evoke this from the crucible of the implicit *past* of his *remembering* is a daring accomplishment indeed. The triple stress of «ahora» abbreviates the distance of futurity, and its cumulative effect, gaining speed in lines 5 and 6, arrests us in the here and now. But this here and now is no transient present but a perpetual instant, abstracted from world-temporality. The continuous present of the creating activity is precisely that: continuous. The fact that its catalyst and indeed very substance is the poet's memory («mi recuerdo») is in no way incompatible with the perpetuity of the creative action—for the one is as inexhaustible and fecund as the other. With supreme confidence, JRJ measures the faculty of his creative and creating memory against the sea itself. His «recuerdo» is «vasto y vehemente»: two attributes patently chosen for being mutually applicable to the sea. The parallel «recuerdo» / «mar» is thus drawn, and the equation of their respective power established. Both will perdure forever within the eternal present.

Lastly with regard to this poem, we should turn our attention to the technical virtuosity of JRJ whereby he fulfils the poem's intention. By this is meant not only the construction of the whole, the deliberate placing of each word, but the extraordinary instinct for what is generally called «la palabra justa» but which I prefer to call here «fatal», in the same sense that JRJ uses the word. For instance, in his second «Nota final» to the *Segunda antolojía poética* he speaks of «defectos esenciales o fatales», in which the conjunction «o» bears a unitive, not disjunctive, value—so that «essential» and «fatal» are synonymous. Thus we may say that there is a kind of fatal pre-destination, a pre-ordaining, behind the word «vehemente» for example. It ends the poem. But, in accord with JRJ's principle that a poem should never terminate, it has a peculiar quality of re-opening. Rationally analysed, it is clear why this is so. It is a four-syllabled word whose length has the effect of a long slow sighing away, rather than the snapped-shut noise of a monosyllable. Furthermore—and this is quite extraordinarily appropriate to the idea of wave upon monotonous wave of a rolling sea—each of those four syllables has the same sound value, the same sameness as the sameness of the sea. The exclusive choice of this adjective has therefore the quality of fatality about it. It is «fatal» in the strictly classical sense, for several reasons: it incorporates, phonically, the realized sea; and it perpetuates, with its undulating length and opening frontiers of its last vowel, the poetic experience, achieving that a-temporality which JRJ seeks: the eternal present. Its association, moreover, with «recuerdo» is a surprising one but again supremely apt, for it suggests an uncommon degree of activity and purposiveness. The poet's consciousness and the sea are further linked by the alliterative effect of the doubly applicable «vehemente».

Another example of accurate instinct for the perfect word is to be found in «tus encendidas hojas secas», a startlingly apposite metaphor to suggest the crisp curling outline of waves, whilst at the same time implying the subordinate association of autumn, and of loss, often linked in JRJ's early verse with evocation through recollection.

JRJ's preoccupation with temporality and a-temporality is clear from the analysis of this poem as well as the one about to be discussed. This preoccupation is a common element in the writing of many of JRJ's contemporaries also. Such is the breadth of the topic however that it has been necessary to consider it separately in an Appendix.

Meanwhile, let us turn to «Cielo» as a partner-poem to «Elejía». While the latter causes the redemption of the reality of the elemental sea, the former will redeem the elemental sky. «Cielo» appears in the same collection as «Elejía», namely *Diario de un poeta reciencasado,* although rather earlier on since it belongs to the opening subsection entitled «Hacia el mar».

> Te tenía olvidado,
> cielo, y no eras
> más que un vago existir de luz,

visto—sin nombre—
por mis cansados ojos indolentes.
Y aparecías, entre las palabras
perezosas y desesperanzadas del viajero,
como en breves lagunas repetidas
de un paisaje de agua visto en sueños...

Hoy te he mirado lentamente,
y te has ido elevando hasta tu nombre. (*LP*, p. 262)[29]

The remoteness of the sky is again invoked in terms both temporal and spatial. But with major differences from those seen in «Elejía». Its elusive insubstantiality in the spatial dimension is conveyed in negations of a more ambiguous character than before; for they do not serve entirely to annul the possible sky, but rather to admit of its possibility. Hence the ambiguously negative-permissive quality of that first tentative approach: «y no eras / más que», which both denies sky whilst nevertheless allowing it—albeit in embryonic state, *in potentia.* The sky *is* not; and yet, simultaneously, it *is*—although no more than a «vago existir de luz». That hiatus between the affirmative «eras» (affirmative despite the fact that it is preceded by «no») and the following «más que...» is no mere accident. It is a powerful piece of syntactic manipulation to convey suspension: the suspense between being and non-being. That non-existence of «sky» in space is, ambivalently, informed with potentiality. When this is properly understood, the entire poem will reveal itself to us as a processional of Becoming into Being. So tenuous, so merely virtual, is this hovering between absence and presence of the incipient sky that it can be defined only in the abstract noun-infinitive, «existir», quiveringly poised between the uncertain «vague» and the ephemeral «light». A hypothesis, no more. And devoid of name. That «sin nombre», in fact, relegates the sky again to the realms of non-being. It is rejected spatially. If the sky may be said to appear at all, or manifest itself in any way, it has done so only in terms of otherhood: only in terms of its sister element, the sea—«como en breves lagunas repetidas / de un paisaje de agua». The character of sky, subsumed into the nature of the sea, has thereby all the more forfeited its spatial actuality.

It is, however, the temporal aspects of this particular poem which must claim most attention. They fall into three main divisions. Firstly, we shall examine the way in which the poet has manipulated language itself to convey Time; secondly, the matter of the poem's own time-span, that is, the duration of the poem as related to its internal process; and thirdly, and most importantly, the subjective temporality internally experienced by the poetic voice in relation to forgetting, dreaming and remembering.

Linguistically, JRJ has again proved here his flair for perfect expression. The structure of the poem identifies precisely with the poetic experience: nine lines progressively describing a Becoming, concluded with a couplet

[29] This poem has been analyzed by A. SÁNCHEZ-BARBUDO, *La segunda época de JRJ*, pp. 52-54. Also by L. R. COLE, *The Religious Instinct in the Poetry of JRJ*, pp. 46-47.

that determines the completion of that process in Being. The change of tense from first to second part both tightens the construction and is a vital requisite for the meaning of the whole experience. The entire passage of «sky-incipient» is conducted in the imperfect tense, with the effect that even so mere and uncertain a virtuality as this, suffers yet further removal in time and space. With the couplet, however, we are swung sharply into the present. «Hoy»—explosively actual—not only initiates the final stage but represents the very axis of the poem as a whole. I have said «present»; and indeed, the force of the last two lines is veritably of the here and now. Why then, one may ask, has JRJ failed to carry through the present tense which «hoy» would appear logically to demand? Why has he not given us the equivalent of that penultimate line of «Elejía», namely: «ahora que yo te *estoy creando* / con mi recuerdo vasto y vehemente»? (my emphasis). Is not the «Hoy» of the poem «Cielo» of equal value to the «ahora» of «Elejía»? The answer is that there is a distinction in the intention of the two poems. It is precisely this which governs the need for a concluding present tense in «Elejía», but a perfect tense in «Cielo». What is fascinating is that verbal tense can so decisively alter a poem's total significance. For, whereas in «Elejía» we are invited to witness a creative experience *in continuum,* «Cielo» offers us that same experience *in completion.* The former, so to speak, is a doing; the latter, a thing done. That is why the transition in «Cielo» is not from the imperfect to the present, but from the imperfect to the closely immediate past of the perfect tense of accomplishment: «Hoy te he mirado lentamente, / y te has ido elevando hasta tu nombre». It is a choice logically consequent upon, and coherent with, the essential poetic intention.

Language conveys the sense of Time not only through verbal tense forms, of course. From the self-circumscribed past of «olvidado», the poem develops in a rhythmic series of rallentandos; a slow measured pace of lengthening lines, swelled with lazy adjectives, their lassitude expressed as much in the subtler monotone of their syllabic prolongation as in their primary meaning. To cite only two examples: «cansados ojos indolentes», or «palabras / perezosas y desesperanzadas». The particular adroitness of these unhurried phrases is not only due to the fact that they work within the temporal dimension, evoking the slow unfolding passage of Time, but that they do so jointly, within the spatial dimension. With the long slow swell of temporal development coincides the long slow expansion in space of sky in its Becoming. From «olvidado» to «vago existir de luz»; from «vago existir de luz» to those unending successions of «breves lagunas repetidas / de un paisaje visto en sueños», the potential sky progressively dilates in ratio and concurrence with the unfolding slownesses of Time. The very typography itself of the poem—those ever elongating lines—are suggestive of the tentative outreaching fingers of light of a sky as yet mere immanence. It is this correlation between developing Time and developing immanence-in-space which leads to a further consideration: that of the poem's own historical time, the duration of the poem *qua* poem.

Unlike the a-temporal lyricism elsewhere, in poems such as «Nocturno», «Convexidades» or «Ciudad del cielo» in which the purely objective duration of the poem bears little on its interior substance, on the contrary here in «Cielo» the two are strictly interrelated. For the textual structure of the poem as a whole is so timed as to permit, within the time it takes to read it, the internal time-realization of the experience. Thus we have two classes of time simultaneously at work, the one upon the other: the historical or external time involved in the reading of the poem, which is of course governed by the poem's organism; and the internal chronology of the poetic experience. The two are integrated perfectly. From oblivion, through the unfolding immanence of Becoming to the ultimate triumph of Being, the experience passes through its phases in perfect sequential conjugation with the poem's own chronology. If the duration of the poem were one whit longer, the impact of the culmination would be lost. If shorter, then that tardy uncertainty of a Becoming would suffer likewise.

This interrelationship of objective and subjective chronologies is not the sole one. The whole Time question here is one of considerable complexity. For within the poem itself is a yet further temporal connection: the connection between the poetic voice which is the witness, and the witnessed experience. It is this which brings us to the third matter, namely that of forgetting, dreaming and remembering.[30] As a very simple way in to the problem, let us observe the first and last two lines of the poem. They clearly indicate the direct interdependence of poet and sky. «Te tenía olvidado» cannot suggest other than that the absence of the sky is the result of oblivion on the poet's part. The sky cannot be construed as having «disappeared» in any objective, empirical sense. Its absence is subject to a single mind-state or mood of an individual, i.e. of the poet. Consequent upon this, it is evident that the slow and measured contemplation of the poet bears strict relationship with the equally slow and measured ascendance of sky to its own «nomen». The juxtaposition is no otiose quirk. If the sky can so depend on the poet as to lose identity in his forgetting of it, then by analogy we must infer that it is by virtue only of the poet's newly applied attention that the phenomenon of realization can take place. The «y» of the last line proves itself a positively unitive link.

This is by way of introduction to that further temporality hidden beneath the layers of these other time considerations we have discussed. It is the «soul-temporality» of the voice that speaks. And it is one which radically concerns the act of creation. The time required to attain that condition of active creative contemplation which is exemplified in «Hoy te he mirado lentamente» is the time that is first needed to convert memory and memories into a kind of limbo of forgetfulness. Only there, in those realms of semi-oblivion, can the imagination come into play. It is from this catalytic operation that memory is resurrected and made instinct with the power to create.

30 This topic has been treated by critics such as GEOFFREY RIBBANS in his article «Recaptured Memory in JRJ and Antonio Machado», *Studies in Modern Spanish Literature and Art presented to Helen F. Grant,* Tamesis, London, 1972; B. DE PABLOS in his book *El tiempo en la poesía de JRJ;* and P. OLSON, *Circle of Paradox* (notably chapter V).

THE IMPORTANCE OF «OLVIDO» IN THE CREATIVE PROCESS

The achievement of this particular poem, «Cielo», in its realization of the actuality of sky and in its very presentation of sky before us, is all the more remarkable in the light of one of JRJ's observations from his «Estética y ética estética». He notes the propensity of the elements toward sheer oblivion: «La tierra, el agua, el aire, el fuego—no lo olvidemos—son fuerzas más del olvido que de la memoria». But it is here precisely through and by way of «el olvido» that the transition is made to recreative and attentive memory. For Antonio Machado too «el olvido» is a necessary part of the process of poetic «depuración». In his *Juan de Mairena* he reveals his deep aesthetic interest in the mysterious faculty of memory and its fallibility in the perfect recreation of the objective past:

> Porque no está probado, ni mucho menos, que nuestro cerebro conserve huellas de las impresiones recibidas dotadas de la virtud milagrosa de reproducir o actualizar las imágenes pretéritas. Y aunque concediéramos la existencia de las tales huellas, dotadas de la antedicha virtud, siempre nos encontraríamos con que el recuerdo nos plantea el mismo problema que la percepción.[31]

Fascinated himself by «el olvido», Machado was quick to recognize the importance which JRJ also gave it. In his tribute, «Al libro *Ninfeas* del poeta Juan Ramón Jiménez», published in Paris in June 1901, Machado called it «Un libro de olvido divino». And in his own poetry this interest is manifest. In Machado's poem, «La tarde en el jardín», as a single example, so closely are oblivion and memory linked that it is precisely because the garden «era un rincón de olvido» that it allows for the resuscitation of «mil sueños de ayer», and eternalizes the present reality of «el alma de la tarde».[32]

If we compare the poem «Cielo» with that of «Elejía» once again, it becomes clear that in the latter the «chronology of creation» as it may be called, is lacking; or at the very least, is present only in elliptical form in the allusion of the last two lines to the creative «recuerdo vasto y vehemente». «Cielo» on the other hand traces that process throughout its full chronological development within the soul. The initial limbo of forgetting—«te tenía olvidado»—gradually mutates into a dreamscape—«visto en sueños»—and from this conjunction of oblivion with rêverie, the forgotten with the imagined, emerges finally that plenary and consummate memory through whose attentive concentration—«te he mirado lentamente»—reality is recreated. Temporal harmonies conveyed in the poem «Cielo» are therefore various in kind, and multiple. There is the chronological development of the process from non-Being, through Becoming, to final Being; the temporal co-extension of the poem *per se* with that of its contained experience; and finally the

[31] ANTONIO MACHADO, *Juan de Mairena*, XLII, *Obras: poesía y prosa*, pp. 492-493.
[32] A. MACHADO, *Soledades*, *Obras: poesía y prosa*, p. 37.

temporal co-ordination between successive moods and the correspondent phasing of a realization of a phenomenon upon which they prevail.

That same potency of forgetting, its ultimately positive character, is once again the esoteric message latent in the tiny and enigmatic poem from *Eternidades:*

Ante mí estás, sí.
Mas me olvido de ti
pensando en ti. (*LP,* p. 601)

Perhaps the secret of this little poem—which is almost an aphorism—lies in the allusions and elisions enclosed in it. The poet says: «Ante mí estás», from which we infer that she—the woman he loves or desires—is present before him: «... sí», and that the poet is rejoicing in the contemplation of her beauty. Suddenly, however, the poet is no longer able to see her, or else no longer wishes to see her, in the *here* and *now* of her existential presence. Immediately, he takes a radical new decision: «Mas me olvido de ti». He forgets her; but he does so «pensando en ti». It is in this «pensando»—a gerund which indicates a surprising activity of thinking which belongs both to the continuous present and to the imminent future—that the entire charge of the poem is concentrated. Its significance is this: from the contemplation of the woman physically before his eyes («estás»), the poet passes to the possession of her within himself, that is, within his thinking recreation of her—a thought which emanates from her essential being, her «ser». The woman has thus been translated from her state of «estar» to that of «ser», by virtue of the poet's deliberate action of forgetting.

It is interesting to note that the poem has an early antecedent in one that belongs to the collection of *Estío* of 1915:

Cuando ella se ha ido
es cuando yo la miro.
Luego, cuando ella viene,
ella desaparece. (*LP,* p. 106)

There is a parallel to be drawn once again here with Antonio Machado. In his «La imagen emotiva» of *Juan de Mairena* he corroborates the idea that to forget the objective reality of the loved one, i.e. through physical absence, positively strengthens her essential imagistic being: «Los verdaderos amantes se huyen tanto como se buscan; porque la presencia pone entre ellos un algo irreductible a la imagen erótica, y la ausencia, en cambio, puede reforzar esta imagen con todo el bloque psíquico influido por ella».[33]

The curious importance of «el olvido» in the creative process is one which merits a still closer look. The significance, for example, of the very deliberately chosen title, *Olvidos de Granada,* for a collection which is patently one of memories and reminiscences, should not be either overlooked or misconstrued. The choice is not an aberration. On the contrary, it corroborates and affirms the idea that things, if they are to be resurrected

[33] A. Machado, *Obras: poesía y prosa,* p. 555.

—i.e. recreated—must first be banished from the memory. Only then can imagination come into operation and restore them to their fresh and newly vigorous reality. A brief passage from the prose poem «El cielo bajo» of *Olvidos de Granada* serves as a useful adjunct to the poem «Cielo»:

> El olvido del cielo bajo y el alto es, un instante, inmenso, distanciado por un yerto abismo sin vallados, en el que no hay existencia posible; pero ahora el cielo bajo sube más y el cielo alto baja y se unicielan en maravilloso fundimiento blanco. Y los que miran y ven, contra el balcón de los suicidios, se van quedando prendidos entre los dos barrios, entre los dos cielos, habitantes ya irretirables de la dejada y perenne telaraña del decisivo ensimismamiento.[34]

In brief digression from the matter of «el olvido» we should note here an interesting parity of function between the neologism «se unicielan» in this passage, and the last line of «Cielo»: «y te has ido elevando hasta tu nombre». Both express the coming into selfhood, so to speak, of the sky; and both are inseparably conjoined with the act of «mirar». There is however a difference between the two experiences, in spatial terms. Or at least, so it would at first appear. That midway fusion of «cielo bajo» with «cielo alto», the former ascending to «unisky» itself in the descension of the latter, seems to afford a compromise in distance. The realized sky is neither near nor far; it is a kind of halfway-house. By contrast, the sky of the poem «Cielo» mounts in ever-increasing distance, to great heights. Yet what the poem is stressing is not so much this remoteness as a problem of semantics. That is to say, not *where* realization may occur (here, there; near, far), but *how*. This «how» of realization is the «how» of language. Considered in this light, it becomes evident that the struggle ever upward, to higher and remoter spheres, has less to do with purely physical distance-in-space than it has to do with characterizing, through metaphor, the sheer asperity of the act of self-realization. The concept of ascent has immemorial connections with difficulty and danger, *askesis* and asceticism.[35] The «nombre», which embodies the desired self-realization, is therefore imaged in the poem as perched aloft in almost unreachable domains. The aspiration towards it will acquire all the greater virtue precisely due to the near impossibility involved. The attainment of the «nombre» will be all the more glorious in direct proportion to the hardship entailed. Thus the significance of the poet's emphasis on height and distance sheds its primary physical sense, to reveal itself as the metaphorical expression of the dignity of language. From the dignification of the «nombre», through its metaphorical

[34] JRJ, *Cuadernos,* edited by Francisco Garfias, Taurus, Madrid, 1971, pp. 142-143.

[35] Ortega y Gasset uses this concept of *askesis* in his analysis of the «minorías excelentes» in *La rebelión de las masas,* notably in chapter VII entitled «Vida noble y vida vulgar, o esfuerzo e inercia»: «Son los hombres selectos, los nobles, los únicos activos [...] para quienes vivir es una perpetua tensión, un incesante entrenamiento. Entrenamiento=*áskesis.* Son los ascetas». *La rebelión de las masas, OC,* IV, p. 183.

It is interesting to note here too an evident parallel between JRJ's private philosophy of the daily need to «superarse a sí mismo» and Ortega's affirmation that «el hombre selecto o excelente está constituido por una íntima necesidad de apelar de sí mismo a una norma más allá de él, superior a él» (*ibid.,* p. 181).

elevation, we ought plainly to infer that precisely upon that linguistic dignity is dependent our own. Finally, this metaphorical struggle to distant heights bears with it the concept of appropriation: the appropriation by which realities can linguistically be mastered. Just as the incipient sky must go forth to meet its destiny—the destiny of its «nombre»—so all language likewise must be appropriated. In fact, within the very term of the «naming process» lies the clue to the proper understanding of appropriation. It is a «process» in its original meaning of «procession», a proceeding forth. It is thus a positive and active effort. Hence the struggle, as of parturition, in the nascent «Cielo»; and hence its effortfully slow procedure up to lay claim finally to that which is its own. Immanence and emanation: these are the two faces of named reality.[36]

The foregoing joint consideration of the poem «Cielo» and the prose poem «El cielo bajo» illumines therefore certain features of the way in which JRJ manages the concept of space and of distance. It may be that the poetic medium lends itself more favourably to the theme; certainly the poem «Cielo» is particularly rich in complexity of meaning.

As has already been suggested, the words «se unicielan» in «El cielo bajo» bear the same meaning-value as the words «y te has ido elevando hasta tu nombre» in «Cielo». This is of some consequence: for JRJ has chosen deliberately to use neologism at the very crux and centre of the prose piece. The invented verb is here admirably adjusted to its idea. A verbal creation itself, it expresses the creation of a phenomenon; itself a conjunction of two verbs, it tells of the conjoining of two essences. The impact of its freshness images the impact of sky-union. Semantic creativity has, therefore, mirrored to perfection the experiential creation which it describes. The conclusion is that at certain times it is neologism which affords JRJ the unique «nombre-exacto-de-las-cosas». It is however worth noting the difference between the pure suggestiveness of the name in the poem «Cielo», in which the reader is allowed to form the word for himself, and the quality of personal assertiveness that the neologism in the prose passage bears.

The function of neologism in the Work of JRJ is indeed important. Unlike its use in other avant-garde poets—(«creacionistas», «tremendistas», etc.)—it is not introduced for mere shock value. In fact the neologisms of JRJ are formulated usually out of the most commonplace terms. Yet even though calling upon the canon of everyday vocabulary, they bring fresh vision to his poetry. Notable too is the absence of any etymological scholarly sources in Greek or Latin, as are to be found in the neologisms of philosophers, scientists or theologians. The neologisms of JRJ integrate perfectly within their poetic context. Furthermore, they are never mere adornments. On the contrary, their economy—and often their synthetic formulae—serve

[36] This notion of procession, linked with «Logos», is further apparent in the four-line poem «Fiesta» from *Poesía (en verso)* (*LP*, p. 879). Here, «las cosas» first proceed from and then return «cantando» to the poet's inner being. For an analysis of this poem, see A. SÁNCHEZ-BARBUDO, *Cincuenta poemas comentados*, pp. 70-71. See also my chapter VI, p. 149.

JRJ's demands of linguistic «depuración». Paradoxically they at once «purify» and enrich, with their contribution of new possibilities of meanings. It is significant that JRJ's use of neologism is by no means uniform throughout the Work. It is not entirely absent from his early poetry, but at that period it is of a more fortuitous, occasional kind than that of the later. It is not until the Second Epoch that the use of neologism becomes systematic and abundant. Indeed, it is not even with the beginning of *Eternidades* that the neologism comes into its own. It is, in effect, not until 1949 with his book *Dios deseado y deseante* that we find its frequent use. The fact that it is above all in this collection, where JRJ is drawing most closely to the expression of mystical experience, that he seeks the linguistic inventiveness of neologism, can surely be no mere arbitrary coincidence. One solution may be posited. In «Despierto a mediodía» (*LP,* pp. 1308-1309) the poet ascribes to the sea his imminent encounter with «dios deseado y deseante». In his heightened state of consciousness, he must find a way of conveying poetically the distinction between things as seen from a normal point of view and as they are seen now, in the fullness of ecstasy. Thus the neologism «pleacielo» arises, modelled on the precedent of «pleamar», and in turn gives rise to «pleadios», in the poem's closing couplet which reads: «Conciencia en pleamar y pleacielo, / en pleadios, en éstasis obrante universal». The invention also of that active participle «obrante» confers a dynamism which is in the literal sense extra-ordinary; but it is even more so for its juxtaposition with the implicit *stasis* of ecstasy. Mystical experience, and the encounter with the divine, bring with them a sense of unification, of fusion. Here too, it is to linguistic inventiveness that JRJ must turn if he is to express the inexpressible. The composite of «riomardesierto», with its variants of «riomar» and «desiertoriomar», is a good example. Again, fusion with the deity may imply a reconciliation of opposites, as expressed in «cuerpialma» («En país de países», *LP,* pp. 1333-1334); or «niñodiós» («Con la Cruz del Sur», *LP,* pp. 1312-1313). Neologism can be effective in other ways too. It may produce the subtle ambiguity of «sonllorante» («El todo interno», *LP,* pp. 1323-1324) or the impressionistic colouring of «verdemar», «amarillomar» («Para que yo te oiga», *LP,* pp. 1319-1320). But it would seem from the above observations of linguistic innovation specifically evident in *Dios deseado y deseante* that one of the major functions of the neologism in JRJ is that of transfiguration, of dealing with the ineffable. The poet's heightened state of consciousness demands a new language to convey paranormal perceptions.[37]

From this digression, we shall return now to our study of «el olvido» as

[37] For further commentary on the use of neologism in JRJ, see D. L. Fogelquist, *JRJ,* pp. 114-115; Concha Zardoya, *Poesía española contemporánea,* Ediciones Guadarrama, Madrid, 1961, p. 238; R. Gullón, *Estudios sobre JRJ,* p. 140.

The following defence of neologism, written by Manuel Díaz-Rodríguez who was one of JRJ's *Helios* contemporaries, may fittingly be applied to JRJ: «El neologismo viene siempre o casi siempre a la luz, no solicitado por el capricho del escritor, sino extraído por el tosco anzuelo del hierro de la necesidad; [...] puede en general decirse que todo neologismo [...] surge a designar una cosa nueva, o una relación nueva de las cosas». (*Camino de perfección,* pp. 61-62).

the crucible of potential creation of the Word. Further testimony to this special function of «el olvido» is the poem from *Piedra y cielo* which bears that very title: «El olvido». Here too the additional attributes of aesthetic beauty and power to liberate are found:

> ¡Olvido, hermoso olvido,
> libertador final
> de nuestro nombre puro,
> en la imajinación del tiempo feo! (*LP*, p. 823)

To forget is to be master of ignoble mundane Time. It empowers us to transcend the calendar of the world and, furthermore, to rise above our own poor limitations, expressed in the metaphor of the «nombre» which denotes, defines and pins the self to self. «El olvido» is the gateway to the past, and the door to the future, for the fruit of forgetting is remembrance itself.[38] In parenthesis we may recall in connection with this the words of Yeats, that all joyous or creative life is a «rebirth as something not oneself, something which has no memory and is created in a moment and perpetually renewed».[39]

Thus JRJ can claim in another poem, « ¡Presente, porvenir, llama en que solo», the following polyvalence of «el recuerdo»:

> ¡Todo lo vivo y por vivir en mí; yo
> todo en lo vivo y por vivir; con los recuerdos nada más,
> de lo que no ha pasado todavía,
> de lo que va a venir seguramente! (*LP*, p. 824)

The complexion of memory is evidently, for JRJ, multi-faceted. The poem unequivocally displays the potency of memory to bear upon not «lo vivo» alone, not just the present—(a present derived of course from the past)—but upon what has not yet come about, the uncertainly immanent; and finally, upon a dependable and determinate future.[40] Such are the memories invoked in the poem called «El recuerdo» from the collection *Piedra y cielo:*

[38] For further comment on this poem, see F. VERHESEN, «Tiempo y espacio en la obra de JRJ», *La Torre*, Universidad de Puerto Rico, año V, núms. 19-20, July-December 1957, p. 115.

[39] W. B. YEATS, *The Death of Synge, Extracts from a Diary kept in 1909, Autobiographies*, p. 503.

[40] M. P. PREDMORE in his book *La poesía hermética de JRJ*, Gredos, Madrid, 1973, pp. 219-220, places a specifically autobiographical emphasis on the importance of «el olvido» in this poem: the obsessive memories that haunt JRJ of his past and of his confined and solitary youth must be committed to oblivion, for only through their relegation to oblivion will the way to aesthetic creativity be opened up to him. It is in this connection that Predmore makes his own point about the inversion in the normal meaning of the word «recuerdo» as used here by JRJ. He says:

> Tan ansioso está el poeta por librarse y por no experimentar más las imágenes y recuerdos obsesionantes del pasado, que invierte el sentido normal de la palabra «recuerdo». Si ha de haber recuerdos en su vida, que sean los del presente y del futuro «nada más», de lo que aún no ha acabado de pasar y de lo que está por venir.

¡Recuerdos, que una noche,
de pronto, resurjís,
como una rosa en un desierto,
como una estrella al mediodía
—pasión mayor del frío olvidado—,
jalones de la vida
mejor de uno,
que casi no se vive!

¡Senda
diariamente árida;
maravilla, de pronto,
de primavera única,
de los recuerdos olvidados! (*LP*, p. 707)

Twice within the text comes confirmation of the enigmatic parentage of memory, born of «el olvido». For «el recuerdo» is the «pasión mayor» of chill oblivion; and like any offspring, bears the character of its begetter, as implied in the epithet of «los recuerdos olvidados». The last stanza speaks of the peculiarly regenerative, recreative and rejuvenating power of memory. The arid path of life is, through memory and recollection, miraculously transformed into a unique, vernal springtime.

Not only does memory rejuvenate, however. It also positively redeems and saves. In a life insidiously undermined and on the very brink of dissolution, when the poet seems to have lost all point of supportive reference, it is to «el recuerdo» that he looks for redemption. Let us consider the poem which immediately succeeds the one we have just cited. It bears the selfsame title: «El recuerdo».

El río pasa por debajo
de mi alma, socavándome.
Apenas me mantengo
en mí. No me sostiene
el cielo. Las estrellas
me engañan; no, no están
arriba, sino abajo, allá en el fondo...

¿Soy? ¡Seré!
Seré, hecho onda
del río del recuerdo...

¡Contigo, agua corriente! (*LP*, p. 708)

In a footnote the critic also adds his interpretation of JRJ's frequent use of the word «nada», particularly in *Piedra y cielo.* It signifies, says Predmore, the realm of «no-ser» in which all memories are obliterated by «el olvido», this being—according to him—the sole state to allow for the potentiality of a future «increado», situated beyond the limits of consciousness. This theory, although valid to a point, seems nevertheless questionably one-sided. The sheerly negative value of «el olvido» which is posited here, fails to admit its other facet: that of its inherently creative potency. It is this positive quality of «el olvido» in the Work of JRJ—the poetic *stimulus* which it affords him—that is so intriguingly original and which I have tried to demonstrate.

The first seven-line stanza is the powerful expression of a critical breakdown; a Yeatsian falling apart of things, in which the crumbling of the elemental cosmos partners and reflects the crumbling psyche of the poet. «Apenas me mantengo / en mí», the poet cries. It is the Juanramonian centre, now, which cannot hold. And yet there does remain something, amid all this shapeless chaos of collapse, to afford the possible—the veritable certainty, in fact—of persisting selfhood. For in striking apposition to the initially destructive river metaphor: «El río pasa por debajo / de mi alma, socavándome», appears its concluding redemptive and recreative partner-metaphor: «Seré, hecho onda / del río del recuerdo».[41] The poem is one of metaphysical anguish. Its existential queryings, reflections and ultimate response are curiously reminiscent of Quevedo. Where memory, for JRJ, will afford the power to rescue and prolong beyond the threshold of the grave his essential Being, so love will override, for Quevedo, his not dissimilar anguish and perform much the same life-prolonging function. His defunct limbs «serán ceniza, mas tendrá sentido; / polvo serán, mas polvo enamorado».[42]

It may seem perhaps extravagant to discover in the poet's clutching at the hopeful straw of memory an indication of immortality to be gained thereby. But the justification lies in the futurity of the twice stressed «Seré»—a futurity which is further implicit in the final rallying cry, « ¡Contigo, agua corriente! ». The same significantly future tense is observable in Quevedo's couplet above, affirming immortality in the beyond. The doubtful question posed by JRJ, «¿Soy?», is annulled in the victorious affirmation of « ¡Seré! ». Paradoxically enough, it is precisely memory—with its implicit historicity or pastness—that will sweep the poet forward in the living current of perpetuity. Again, it is that juxtaposition of «¿Soy? ¡Seré! » which denotes the dismissal of the present, with all its concomitant anguish,

[41] There is an interesting parallel here with the couplet which closes the *Polifemo* of Góngora: «a Doris llega (Acis), que, con llanto pío, / yerno lo saludó, lo aclamó río».

[42] FRANCISCO DE QUEVEDO, Soneto XLV, *Canta sola a Lisi, Poesías amorosas, Obras en verso, OC,* 2 vols., edited by Luis Astrana Martín, Aguilar, Madrid, 1952, II, p. 72.

Cerrar podrá mis ojos la postrera
sombra que me llevare el blanco día,
y podrá desatar esta alma mía
hora a su afán ansioso lisonjera;

mas no, de esotra parte en la ribera,
dejará la memoria, en donde ardía;
nadar sabe mi llama la agua fría,
y perder el respeto a ley severa.

Alma a quien todo un Dios prisión ha sido,
venas que humor a tanto fuego han dado,
medulas que han gloriosamente ardido,

su cuerpo dejarán, no su cuidado;
serán ceniza, mas tendrá sentido;
polvo serán, mas polvo enamorado.

in favour of a glorious future. The special conception of memory which JRJ is expressing in this poem raises him to a peak of optimism and induces in him a state of ecstatic dynamism. The reason is evident. It is because of the inseparable co-operation of «el recuerdo» with the act of poetic creation. The Word and the Work itself lie nascent in «el recuerdo». It is memory which—with the aid of the midwife, imagination—will give birth to the Word. And in the Work, here metaphorically described as «el río del recuerdo», will persist and perdure the essential JRJ. The Word, created out of recollection, stands surety for everlasting life.[43]

As a rider, it is intriguing to note the twist of meaning that lies embedded in those watery metaphors of memory. The «river» most usually construed as separating the present from the Beyond (the «Soy» from the «Seré»), is the Styx; and that watery wave, that «agua corriente» of JRJ's poem, would in any other context rather signify the Lethean Waters of Oblivion than those of Memory, as here they do. The Juanramonian waters are a far cry from that «agua fría» which Quevedo's burning passion must learn to swim, in the sonnet from which I have quoted.

The interrelationship of memory, sky and the Work itself forms a thematic network in the Second Epoch of JRJ. In the poem «A la vejez amada» from *Piedra y cielo,* the poet expresses the longing that he be remembered in the manner of the azure sky. Or rather, more accurate is it to say that his wish is that the ideal «recuerdo» *be* that blue May sky, suppressing all equivalence, all «as if»:

> ¡Ay, si el recuerdo
> tuyo de mí, fuese este cielo azul
> de mayo, lleno todo
> de las estrellas puras de mis actos!
>
> ¡De mis actos iguales, como ellas: todos puros,
> limpios, buenos, tranquilos, igual que las estrellas!
>
> —¡Debajo, tu sonrisa en sueños
> =sueños de tus recuerdos de mi vida!— (*LP,* p. 715)

Memory and sky are fused in the one identity, through the yoking adjective «lleno», applicable to both. «El recuerdo», no less than «el cielo», is thus filled with the «estrellas puras de mis actos». Born of the indulgent smile of dream, memory shall be woven out of the transparent sky. For it is at night that original purity, the truth of that dazzling «limpieza primera» which is described elsewhere in the poem entitled «Ciudad del cielo» from *La estación total,* perfectly manifests itself and which the poet ideally requires of «el recuerdo». The central stanza of this poem, moreover, eloquently captures those limpidly precise and pellucid qualities of the

[43] There is an evident connection here too with the famous dictum of William Wordsworth (1770-1850): «Poetry is the spontaneous overflow of powerful feelings: it takes its origin from emotion *recollected in tranquillity*» (my emphasis). From the «Preface» to *Lyrical Ballads.*

tranquil night sky which likewise are the essential attributes of «el recuerdo»:

En la noche brillante
de limpieza primera,
Ciudad del Cielo, arriba,
sobre un detrás de luz de hora que viene,
alza la línea de la tierra hermosa.

(Todo es pleno en un valle azul de exacta
temperatura trasparente,
que fija con su nítida quietud
la belleza completa.

Alamos agrupados
en la fuente de agua elemental,
determinan confiado paraíso,
total murmullo verdeoscuro,
alrededor de la inmortal ausencia.) (*LP*, p. 1145)

The Citadel of the Sky, synonymous with memory in its «inmortal ausencia», is the Mecca to which the Work itself must strive, for the attainment of these same qualities:

¡Quisiera que mi libro
fuese, como es el cielo por la noche,
todo verdad presente, sin historia.

Que, como él, se diera en cada instante,
todo, con todas sus estrellas; sin
que niñez, juventud, vejez, quitaran
ni pusieran encanto a su hermosura inmensa.

¡Temblor, relumbre, música
presentes y totales!
¡Temblor, relumbre, música en la frente
—cielo del corazón—del libro puro! (*LP*, p. 828)

Composed of memory perfect as the starry sky and equally pure of historicity, the Book will be the lustrous Sky of the soul. That Book which is the eternal living Word, «nutrida, por la luz, con mi memoria».

The response has here been found to that self-doubting poem which opens the collection *Eternidades*. Aptly enough, it is entitled «Acción». It is the dubitative curtain-raiser upon the stage whereon the struggle for the «palabra justa» is played out before us:

No sé con qué decirlo,
porque aún no está hecha
mi palabra. (*LP*, p. 551)

The curtain falls, completing the cycle of *Eternidades,* with the victorious mood of the closing poem. The initial doubtings are dissolved, in the course of the Work:

¡Palabra mía eterna!
¡Oh, qué vivir supremo
—ya en la nada la lengua de mi boca—,
oh, qué vivir divino
de flor sin tallo y sin raíz,
nutrida, por la luz, con mi memoria,
sola y fresca en el aire de la vida! (*LP*, p. 688)

It is the use of that possessive adjective in, first, «mi palabra» of the poem «Acción», and secondly «palabra mía» of this last quoted poem, which must dispel any purely objective understanding of the «nombre-exacto-de-las-cosas». That perfectly adjusted Word is compositely fashioned from the subjective world of «olvido», «sueño», and «recuerdo». In short, the affirmation—pronounced by JRJ himself—remains true: that «la poesía es traducirse el poeta a sí mismo».[44] For indeed, the «palabra justa y viva» (of the poem thus entitled) is precisely «la del alma»:

¡Palabra justa y viva,
que la vida interior brota, lo mismo
que una rosa vaciada en un lucero;
cúmulo, cima del sereno monte
del corazón, contra el cénit exacto;
final estrella del surtidor recto
de la fuente más honda
—la del alma—! (*LP*, p. 887)

The Word bursts from its source: the «vida interior».

The question of memory recall in the poetry of JRJ has drawn the attention of Geoffrey Ribbans in his interesting comparative article, «Recaptured Memory in JRJ and Antonio Machado».[45] He detects a fundamental difference between the two poets and finds that whereas Machado is concerned with evoking specific past events and experiences, the kind of memories with which JRJ deals have little or none such referential particularity. He says of Machado that his «heightened feeling for things in themselves is one of the features of his poetry which separate him most decisively from JRJ. In Jiménez it is only rarely, in fact, that we can relate a memory very closely with an actual lived experience».[46] Ribbans then proceeds to select, for his purpose of comparison, one of these «rareties», «Retorno fugaz», which he subjects to an admirable analysis. Certainly we may agree with the argument that, in general, the poetry of JRJ regards not

[44] Guerrero Ruiz, p. 264.

[45] Geoffrey Ribbans, «Recaptured Memory in JRJ and Antonio Machado», *Studies in Modern Spanish Literature and Art presented to Helen F. Grant*, pp. 149-161.

[46] To what extent critical opinion may differ can be seen from the fact that on the contrary, G. Palau de Nemes, for instance, makes a point of insisting on JRJ's need for actual lived experiences as the direct source of his poetic inspiration. She sustains this thesis throughout her work, *Vida y obra de JRJ*, relating the poems she analyzes specifically to JRJ's biographical data.

so much the particular experience as the urge to reach out «towards an aesthetic abstraction in which whatever "anécdota" or "historia" was involved is spirited away». Nor is it my intention here to discuss whether this is a defect—as some critics maintain—or not. What does seem necessary is to explore the reasons why such an observation may validly be made.

The chief distinction between the process of recall in JRJ's poetry and that of others, is the difference between an act of volition and a purely involuntary one. The latter, as Proust so definitively revealed, is more often than not the outcome of some sensorial ignition: unexpected, uncalled for, spontaneous and above all, effortless. It results in an evocation of the specific. The action of memory in JRJ, however, is quite the opposite. It is a veritable effort of the creative will, a synthesis of imagination and intellect, the result of which is not simply evocation, but a fresh and different creation. Not the resurrection of a past «fact», but the recomposition of a universal. This voluntary nature of memory in JRJ is indicated, as has already been observed, in the close accompaniment of that intellectual speculation of «mirar», the intense scrutiny of the «seeing» mind, brought to bear upon the act of creative remembering. The senses are not, for JRJ, the springboard to recollective creativity. If they were, then his poetry would indeed manifest that kind of subjectivity to be found in Antonio Machado. What JRJ conveys is an elusive psychological state that is almost impossible to define (and herein lie further affinities with Bécquer). The reader is directed to the *immediacy* of the state experienced. Many of JRJ's early poems, such as «Crepúsculo» from *Olvidanzas* (1906-1907), seem concerned with exploring the psychological complexities of memory. The focus is sharply on the *state,* the phenomenon, rather than the thing recollected itself, as in Machado.

JRJ, then, treats the process of memory recall rather from the standpoint of a universal, omniscient «dios», than from the limitations of a private world. If he deals in «abstractions» it is because he wishes to remove that veil of habitual names whose very familiarity blocks our true vision and true understanding. Therefore the language itself through which he conveys memory assumes a universal character unlike the individual and subjective diction of poets concerned with special reference to special events. What saves JRJ from the accusation of strict cerebrality in the matter of memory recall—and what is, in fact, its most distinguishing feature of all—is the role of «el olvido», that vital collaborator with «el recuerdo». It is, as it were, the negative to the final positive of the colour-photograph; its antithesis, and yet necessary complement. The period of gestation which «el olvido» affords its converse, «el recuerdo», is nowhere invested with more importance than in JRJ. This firm conviction of the radical value of forgetting in relation with remembering, patently reveals that for JRJ the role of the unconscious is of no lesser moment than that of strictly intellectual volition, in the process of memory recall.

The remarks in Ribbans's article have far-reaching implications inasmuch as the poetry which recalls the specific, the actually lived experience, appears to find favour. The reader's satisfaction in being able to trace the real event in its poetically recollected counterpart may indeed make the poem more readily enjoyable because more understandable. Bereft of reference, the reader feels discountenanced. But it is surely precisely here that JRJ shows most truly his «modernity». For memory, with him, is not an achieved act but a process; and those poems of his which are concerned with recollection reveal it not as meaning, but as a non-referential process. Any sense of disorientation that the reader may experience in the face of this must be attributed to a failure to understand the nature of language itself as it is now understood, that is: language as defiant of finality, as Process.

Lastly, it serves only as counter-productive to judge a poet according to standards from which he himself has deliberately sought to disencumber himself. JRJ's concern for «la palabra justa» is an aesthetic concern, not an ethical preoccupation nor one of communication. Thus it is only conformant with his aesthetic philosophy that his particular process of memory recall should have but the most tenuous referent, and that the poetic recreation should thereby be released from its actual moorings to be as free as possible to exist in its own right, self-sufficient and unregarding of communication. The trajectory of JRJ's poetry certainly reveals an ever-increasing remoteness from human reality. But it is from an aesthetic norm, not a moral one and above all not one of communication, that it must be evaluated. If the memory of a seascape, a sky or a loved one, is transcribed into a poem virtually divorced from such starting-points, and whose substance has become the almost immaterial substance of the poet's own pulsations—a kind of sounding of his own heartbeat—then it is the logical outcome of one for whom referential language, communication, was a very inferior subordinate to the primacy of aesthetic perfection; of one who could declare: «Para mí, no hay otras razones en la vida—ni en la muerte—que las razones estéticas».[47]

I opened this discussion of the Word and Work in JRJ with a quotation from the historical literary criticism of Walter Pater. It is fitting to close the present chapter with a passage taken this time from his one piece of fictional writing, the novel *Marius the Epicurean.* Its relevance to JRJ's own concept of the Word, with its special potency to arrest Time and to perpetuate, will be self-evident:

> And yet, with a kind of inconsistency in one who had taken for his philosophic ideal [...] the pleasure of the ideal present, of the mystic *now*—there would come, together with that precipitate sinking of things into the past, a desire after all to retain «what was so transitive». Could he but arrest for others also, certain clauses of experience, as the imaginative memory presented them to himself! In those grand, hot summers, he would have imprisoned the very perfume of the flowers. To create, to live perhaps a little while beyond the allotted hours, if it were but in a fragment of perfect expression:—it was thus

[47] JRJ, «Estética y ética estética», «Ideolojía lírica», *Pájinas escojidas; prosa,* selected by R. Gullón, p. 145.

his longing defined itself for something to hold by amid the «perpetual flux». With men of his vocation, people were apt to say, words were things. Well! with him, words should be indeed things,—the word, the phrase, valuable in exact proportion to the transparency with which it conveyed to others the apprehension, the emotion, the mood, so vividly real within himself. *Verbaque provisam rem non invita sequentur:* Virile apprehension of the true nature of things, of the true nature of one's own self being ever the first condition of genuine style.

CHAPTER V

TOWARDS THE PERFECTED WORK

What Pater calls the «apprehension of the true nature of one's own self' will be central to our investigation of the significance of JRJ's Work as a whole. JRJ himself expresses this same sentiment in his affirmation that «la poesía es traducirse el poeta a sí mismo», a self-translation which is self-revelation. It is in his Work that JRJ enacts the search for his essential self. The Work represents a journey not without parallel in the great journey of Dante's *La Divina Commedia.* Both literary works are a Book of the Universe, and both the *Commedia* and JRJ's *opus* describe a spiritual quest for the self and an arduous passage toward Perfection.[1] To what extent did JRJ succeed in his endeavours? It seems on the whole safe to say that, even if at the very last he felt that he had been defeated by a task which in itself must ultimately prove unrealizable, nevertheless he had certainly succeeded in wrenching forth and discovering the supreme poet that all along he knew to be contained within him. Poetry is the «animal» which he believed that we all have buried within us, and which must be extricated from the «fondo» as if in childbirth. His book *Animal de fondo* represents the culmination of his journey; and it is the manifestation of precisely this achievement.

That brief, explosive exclamation of JRJ's: « ¡Qué espectáculo el de mi imajinación en movimiento! » is the expression of a man discovering

[1] There is a fundamental difference to be noted, of course, between the *Commedia* and the JRJ corpus. The quest in Dante is for a goal which is already pre-established and known to exist; the problem is one of attainment of a specific, pre-ordained and unquestionable Truth. In JRJ, on the other hand, the journey of search is conducted in the obscurity of ignorance as to the thing sought. A closer parallel is perhaps to be drawn between JRJ and Yeats. The consistent handling, inspecting, analyzing and criticizing of religions throughout Yeats's work lends it the unified character of a quest. But the poet-questor has, in common with JRJ and unlike Dante, no initially clear idea of the direction nor the goal. Cleanth Brooks has written, in an essay on W. B. Yeats entitled «Search for a New Myth», words which might equally apply to JRJ at least until his final encounter with the god of Poetry:

> The importance of religion is something which Yeats never doubts for a moment. As to which or what is the true religion, he is often in doubt and he plays with the notion that all religions are merely variants of one religion. But the abiding importance of religion itself never comes into question. (*The Hidden God,* p. 55)

and watching the poet within him at work: the Paterian apprehension of the true nature of his own self.

The fact that «Palabra» (Word) and «Obra» (Work) are given capital letters by JRJ is an immediate indication that they signify much more than their usual everyday counterparts, in the lower case. The capital letters operate as typographical signposts to a deeper and more mysterious meaning, a richer currency, than that normally ascribed to such familiar terms. In one sense, the present study may be seen as an attempt to justify those capital letters; to show why and in what way the claim to transcendental values which they make is valid. It is necessary first to establish at what point in his career JRJ began to speak of his Work as a total entity and to lend it this capital letter. Such an action was no mere idiosyncrasy. There is ample proof of the rigour and scrupulousness with which JRJ attended to such matters of typography, print, format and the like. That capitalization of the Work coincided with the growth and fruition of his vision of the Work as a total Book, a *Summa.* It is the visual symbol of a whole concept.

Eternidades saw the initiation of the Work. But its roots were there from the very first. On 20 July 1931, JRJ acknowledged this fact to his friend, Juan Guerrero Ruiz, who records him thus: «Cuando habla de su Obra es después de treinta y cinco años de meditar sobre ella». The long slow gestation of the Work does not rest there. Its realization is one of unceasing process for, in continuation, Guerrero Ruiz reports: «por eso cuando escribe no sólo está escribiendo versos, sino que está realizando su estética, y cuando deja de trabajar y se recuesta en el sofá es para seguir meditando sobre lo mismo». It was in August of this same year, 1931, that JRJ contracted with the publishing-house, Signo, for the preparation of his Work under the title *Obra poética* which he by then was publicly employing. The decade extending approximately between 1925 and 1935 saw the most crucial period in which JRJ sifted and selected from the entire corpus of his poetry thus far, the material which he considered most worthy, for its aesthetic value, of inclusion in the definitive Work. Just prior to this, in 1924, he wrote to E. R. Curtius: «A mis 42 años—y después de 25 de incesante trabajo con la Belleza—siento, pienso, veo claramente que ahora es cuando comienzo; y si vivo 15 o 20 años más, creo que podré ver realizada mi Obra—que, de modo informe, existe ya toda».[2] Possibly the first public declaration of this conception of his Work as a whole, organic unit, came in 1928 with the publication of a booklet bearing the title *Obra en marcha (Diario poético) de JRJ* and supplemented thus: «España. 1928. Sin día. Cuarenta y seis años de vida; treinta de poesía. Empiezo mi Obra terminante». Nonetheless, it is considerably earlier, from 1916 onwards, that the Work began to formulate itself in his mind as something other, far more profound, than simply a collection of poems. Our study must begin here, then, with the turning-point of *Eternidades.*

The evolution of the Work as a Unity is reflected in the evolution of

[2] See ANTONIO CAMPOAMOR GONZÁLEZ, *Vida y poesía de JRJ,* Ediciones Sedmay, Madrid, 1976, p. 179.

the poetry itself. From *Eternidades* onward, JRJ's poetry was to have for its sole true «subject», poetry itself. The poetic Word was to become the instrument of its own meditation. This self-regarding nature of the Work was, in large part, the logical development from the manner in which JRJ conceived the special relationship between himself as poet and the Work created. «Yo concibo el libro como un todo orgánico», he stated, and indeed it was for him something very much akin to a living breathing creature. He believed, moreover, in the organic one-ness of the poet with his Work, the latter being born of the rhythm of heart- and blood-beat and of the very pulsations of the lung. In his lecture course on «modernismo» he described the French poet, Paul Claudel («primer poeta de Francia actualmente», according to JRJ),[3] as composing his free verse out of the alternating tempo of inhalation and exhalation, and he went on to add: «Mucho más humorístico, Goethe dice que su verso le salía según el pulso de su novia». Certain it is that JRJ himself identified Language, Life and Poem in one. «El verso», he declared, «es como un río de agua de la tierra, río de la sangre de nuestra carne, nuestro barro; el río de esta sangre que respiramos del mar del aire y la echamos con el ritmo del corazón y del pulmón nuestros, al aire de la tierra y del mar».[4] This conception of the organic nature of the Work is again testified by Guerrero Ruiz:

> Dice que un poeta verdadero debe contener en sí toda la historia de la poesía; volver a crearla con su obra, y ser romántica en su primera juventud hasta recorrer el ciclo completo. Es—aunque sea una comparación demasiado naturalista—como el feto en el vientre de su madre, que experimenta una evolución total.[5]

A perfect illustration of this conception is to be found in the poem «La menuda floración» from *Dios deseado y deseante* (*LP*, pp. 1347-1348). JRJ is in communion with his Obra daily, and throughout his lifetime. This anthropomorphic concept is reinforced by a further description of «cohabitation» between JRJ and the Obra: «Yo tengo escondida en mi casa, por su gusto y por el mío, a la Poesía, como una mujer hermosa; y nuestra relación es la de los apasionados». In this physical, sensual, amorous «convivencia», the Work assumes the shape of woman; and in Juanramonian terms, Woman is Beauty. The anatomy of a poem is therefore rendered by him thus: «La décima tiene que ser esbelta como lo es una palmera o un cuerpo bello femenino, igual que el soneto es también un cuerpo bello de mujer, y tiene sus brazos, sus caderas, sus piernas».[6] Such an analogy

[3] Guerrero Ruiz, p. 75.

[4] JRJ, «El romance, río de la lengua española», *El trabajo gustoso,* Aguilar, México, 1961: a lecture delivered in Río Piedras in 1954 at the invitation of Jaime Benítez, the Chancellor of the University of Puerto Rico.

[5] Guerrero Ruiz, p. 92.

[6] It is conceivable that to some extent these remarks of JRJ may have been playful. Antonio Machado, for instance, has his Juan de Mairena make some skittish comments on the same theme: «El culto a la mujer desnuda es propio del poeta. Con el desnudo femenino simboliza el poeta, a veces, la misma perfección de su arte». And he goes on to admonish the reader that, nevertheless, the really sensual man never makes the mistake of forgetting the female attire! (*Juan de Mairena,*

between poem and woman is not of course without antecedent. Above all, it is Bécquer who comes to mind in this respect. In Bécquer's «Prólogo» to *La soledad* of Augusto Ferrán, (about which JRJ himself said that «en ello hay todo lo que se puede decir sobre poesía moderna»), we read the following appraisal of the «cantares» of Ferrán:

> Seguramente los suyos se distinguen de los originales del pueblo; la forma del poeta, como la de una mujer aristocrática, se revela, aun bajo el traje más humilde, por sus movimientos elegantes y cadenciosos; pero en la concisión de la frase, en la sencillez de los conceptos, en la valentía y la ligereza de los toques, [...] rivalizan, cuando no vencen, a los que se ha propuesto por norma.

Bécquer's own work, moreover, is the very embodiment of this preeminently Romantic analogy. One has only to recall his *Cartas literarias a una mujer;* or the daringly extravagant closing couplet of his fourth «Rima»: «mientras exista una mujer hermosa, / ¡habrá poesía! »; or again, his «Rima» XXI:

> «¿Qué es poesía?», dices mientras clavas
> en mí tu pupila azul.
> «¿Qué es poesía? ¿Y tú me lo preguntas?
> Poesía eres tú.»

From the foregoing, it would appear that JRJ is in love with his poetic Work as if with a beautiful woman, his love being of the teleological kind aroused and inspired by the prospect of Perfection, to which it is drawn like a magnet. It is a love analogical with that expatiated upon by León Hebreo in his *Diálogos de amor:*[7]

> El tal amor es deseo de unión perfecta del amante con la persona amada, la cual no puede ser sino con la total penetración del uno con el otro [...] Por-

Obras: poesía y prosa, p. 508). My own feeling, however, is that these impassioned statements and beliefs of JRJ should be taken seriously and at face-value.

[7] JRJ would have known of the importance of León Hebreo from his readings of Menéndez y Pelayo's *Historia de las ideas estéticas en España* (and probably gained much of his knowledge of the neo-Platonists from this source also). Menéndez y Pelayo dedicates considerable space to his discussion of Hebreo (*OC,* 9 vols., Imprenta de los Hijos de Tello, Madrid, 1920, III, pp. 11-62). He concludes with an apology for his lengthy quoting from what he says is

> un libro apenas leído hoy de nadie, pero que no deja por eso de ser el monumento más notable de la filosofía platónica en el siglo XVI, y aun lo más bello que esa filosofía produjo desde Plotino acá [...] Nunca, antes de Hegel, ha sido desarrollada con más amplitud la estética idealista [...] La *idea* única, engendrando de su seno toda forma, la forma lidiando con la materia, y señoreándola, vivificándola y hermoseándola [...], tales son los fundamentos de esta síntesis deslumbradora. (p. 60)

Menéndez y Pelayo regards the *Diálogos* as a «poema cosmogónico en prosa» written by one who «quiere arrancar a las cosas el secreto de la razón universal»; one who «*destila* de los seres creados las formas latentes» (p. 62). On the basis alone of this exegesis of an aesthetic so attuned to his own, it is safe to assume that JRJ would have been encouraged to read—had he not already done so—the Spanish translation by Garcilaso de la Vega (El Inca) of Hebreo's *Dialoghi d'amore* published in Madrid in 1590.

> que, como dice el filósofo, el amado tiene razón de más perfecto que el amante, porque, siendo fin del amante, el fin es más noble que lo que es para el fin.[8]

Again, León Hebreo points out the teleological nature of love that seeks to transcend itself in the superiority of its object:

> Asimismo, el mundo espiritual se hace uno con el mundo corporal mediante el amor [...] Asimismo, los inferiores se unen con sus superiores, el mundo corporal con el espiritual, y el corruptible con el eterno, y el universo con su Creador, mediante el amor que les tiene y el deseo suyo que les da de unirse con El y de beatificarse en su divinidad.[9]

In the Work, JRJ sought the superior goal of Perfect Beauty and, ultimately, his own «dios». His untiring loving meditation thereon corresponds with Hebreo's analysis of the lover:

> Del todo es ajeno de sí mismo y propio del que ama y contempla, en el cual se convierte totalmente, que la esencia del ánima es su propio acto, y si se une para contemplar íntimamente un objeto, se transporta en él su esencia y aquél es su propia sustancia, y no es más ánima y esencia del que ama, sino sola especie actual de la persona amada.[10]

Such is the one-ness of the poet with his Work, for the Work is simultaneously both the object of his contemplation and the subject of it since it is integral with its author. This fusion is particularly true in the case of free verse, above all other forms of poetry, according to JRJ. For, as he says:

> En el poema en verso libre, todo es del poeta. No así en otro género de composiciones, donde es la rima quien dirige y tuerce el desarrollo natural del poema: las ideas vienen de la mano del consonante, en tanto que cuando éste falta, como sucede en el verso libre, no hay bastón en que apoyarse y la poesía debe sostenerse sola.[11]

Free verse, in other words, is self-generating, independent of the exigencies of rhyme. The question of cause and effect with regard to poetry is a complicated one. Does the thought precede the word? Or the word engender the thought? José María Valverde, in his book entitled *Estudios sobre la palabra poética,* points out the error of the belief that a poetic work is the product simply of an anterior attitude of mind: «De hecho, la mente y sus producciones se dan enlazadas, reobrando recíprocamente: no sabemos bien [...] cuándo es el pensamiento el que engendra la palabra y cuándo es la palabra la que ocasiona el pensamiento, ni aun si tiene pleno sentido plantearse esa disyuntiva». Even, he says, it may be that the spiritual state

[8] LEÓN HEBREO, *Diálogos de amor,* Espasa-Calpe Argentina, Buenos Aires, 1947, p. 60.
[9] *Ibid.,* p. 153.
[10] *Ibid.,* pp. 161-162.
[11] R. GULLÓN, *Conversaciones con Juan Ramón,* p. 116.

is the product, rather than the premise, of the poetic creation. Valverde sums up the interaction of the poet with his Work, and vice versa, in the following words: «Incluso en los poetas que parten de una fe, sin salir de ella en su vida, la poesía reobra sobre su creencia, ahondándola y enriqueciéndola humanamente».[12]

If we turn to the text itself of JRJ, we will find evidence of this kind of mutual integration. The poem called «Poeta y palabra» from *La estación total* is an excellent illustration. It also exemplifies that poetry of self-reflection which has been mentioned earlier. It is a poem upon poem-making, in which poet and Work are fused, both physically and spiritually. It concludes thus:

La carne, el alma una de él, en su aire,
son entonces palabra:
principio y fin,
presente sin más vuelta de cabeza,
destino, llama, olor, piedra, ala, valederos,
vida y muerte,
nada o eternidad: palabra entonces.

Y él es el dios absorto en el principio,
completo y sin haber hablado nada;
el embriagado dios del suceder,
inagotable en su nombrar preciso;
el dios unánime en el fin,
feliz de repetirlo cada día todo.

As the opening to this poem shows, it is when the poet is left in solitude, away from all social commerce, that he can be transubstantiated into the Word and become himself the Work:[13]

Cuando el aire, suprema compañía,
ocupa el sitio de los que se fueron,
disipa sus olores, sus jestos, sus sonidos
y vuelve único a llenar
el orden natural de su silencio,
él [...]
se queda con el aire en su lugar, [...]

Puede olvidar, callar, gritar entonces dentro
la palabra que llega del redondo todo,
redondo todo solo; [...]
la vibrante palabra muda,
la inmanente. (*LP*, pp. 1171-1172)

[12] JOSÉ MARÍA VALVERDE, *Estudios sobre la palabra poética*, Ediciones Rialp, Madrid, 1958, pp. 100-101.

[13] See also ANTONIO MACHADO, *Juan de Mairena, Obras: poesía y prosa*, p. 526: «Sólo en el silencio, que es, como decía mi maestro, *el aspecto sonoro de la nada*, puede el poeta gozar plenamente del gran regalo que le hizo la divinidad, para que fuese cantor, descubridor de un mundo de armonías».

The narcissism implicit in this special conception of the Work was something of which JRJ was aware. His transposition of the classical myth into theological terms in no way masks the analogy with his own situation: «En la doctrina cristiana encontramos que Dios crea el hombre a su imagen y semejanza: narcisismo. El misterio de la Trinidad es narcisista, porque reúne en un mismo ser y al tiempo al amor, al amante y al amado».[14] The poet's task is to create a whole poetic universe. It is this which «lo acerca al mito divino, que es el del Narciso verdadero [...]; crear a imajen y semejanza. Todo dios es narcisista». In these words (from «Lo "fable" y lo "inefable"»), JRJ was undoubtedly including himself. He continues: «El misterio católico de la Trinidad ¿qué es sino narcisismo? El Padre se contempla en el Hijo, la creación, como en un espejo, y el Espíritu Santo es el amor entre los dos [...] Y ¿qué más da que lo divino sea un mito, si es belleza que tiene un nombre?». For «Padre» we may understand the poet-progenitor, JRJ himself; for «Hijo», his progeny, the poetic Work; and for «Espíritu Santo», the sacred breath of poetic inspiration. Nevertheless, the analogy is absolved of blasphemy, since it operates on the plane of pure aesthetics and because the reward of the Narcissus myth is none other than Beauty itself. Moreover, JRJ saw theology and mythology as synonymous and interchangeable. «No hay que olvidar», he declared in a conversation with Ricardo Gullón, «que teología es mitología y mitología es teología». His own further self-identification with the Narcissus theme is evident in his appraisal of it under its other aspect, that of pantheism: «Narciso es el hombre que se encuentra con la naturaleza; el Dios que quiere ser y hacerse naturaleza. Es el gran mito del creador que desea metamorfosearse en la naturaleza, convertirse en naturaleza».[15] When he pronounces that «el hombre Narciso es el panteísta que quiere reintegrarse en la naturaleza»,[16] he is in effect once again speaking of himself.

The pantheism of JRJ is close to that of the «krausismo» of the «institucionistas», as originated in Spain by Julián Sanz del Río. This pantheism is, more properly speaking, panentheism, that is, the presence of God in all things—panentheism being the word adopted by Sanz del Río and, as Guillermo de Torre affirms, the «clave del credo krausista».[17] From Gullón's «Preface» to *El modernismo,* we have the following information on JRJ's

[14] R. Gullón, *Conversaciones con Juan Ramón,* p. 121.

[15] *Ibid.*

[16] *Ibid.*

[17] Guillermo de Torre, «Cuatro etapas de JRJ», *La Torre,* Universidad de Puerto Rico, año V, núms. 19-20, July-December, 1957, p. 61. See also Juan López Morillas, *El krausismo español,* Fondo de cultura económica, México, 1956, pp. 38-39. That pantheism was an important part of the doctrines of Krause can be verified, for example, in Wilhelm Windelband's now classic manual, *Historia de la filosofía:*

> Krause [...] trata de aunar con el concepto de *personalidad* divina la concepción panteísta del mundo del idealismo; [...] ve en el mundo el desarrollo de la «esencia» divina que se exhibe en las Ideas: mas estas Ideas son la *autocontemplación de la más alta personalidad.* La Esencia—así llama Krause a Dios—no es la razón indiferenciada, sino el principio orgánico y personal del mundo.

connections with «krausismo»: «No sabemos si Juan Ramón lo leyó (el *Compendio de estética* de Krause), pero sí que convivió con los krausistas y fue influido por ellos [...] Juan Ramón hablaba de "krausismo español" y, para decirlo más exactamente, de "krausistas españoles", cuya relación con los modernistas es un hecho y no una opinión».[18] JRJ's view of the interchangeability of theology with mythology allows for an intermingling, in his poetry, of his panentheistic beliefs with Orphism. If God is omnipresent and all things therefore animate, then the poet JRJ shows himself possessed with the Orphic power to listen to and interpret the hidden voice of tree, river, bird—indeed, all natural phenomena. The «Fragmento primero» of the prose poem «Espacio» expresses a communion and understanding of natural things far deeper and far fuller than any the poet can attain in ordinary human society:

> Yo puedo acariciar como yo quiera a un perro, un animal cualquiera, y nadie dice nada; pero a mis semejantes no; [...] Vida animal, ¿hermosa vida? ¡Las marismas llenas de bellos seres libres, que me esperan en un árbol, un agua o una nube, con su color, su forma, su canción, su jesto, su ojo, su comprensión hermosa, dispuestos para mí que las entiendo!

He is the elect to the brotherhood of Nature, and capable of metamorphosis such as to discard even his own humanity: «Tú y yo, pájaro, somos uno». His ear can detect the secret harmonies of Nature and apprehend the meaning of a birdsong: «canta tú, que yo te oigo, que mi oído es tan justo por tu canto». Even the unselfconscious utterings of the ocean are for him intelligible, as the poem «Para que yo te oiga» from *Dios deseado y deseante* tells:

> Rumor del mar que no te oyes
> tú mismo, mar, pero que te oigo yo
> con este oír a que he llegado
> en mi dios deseante y deseado
> y que, con él, escucho como él [...]
>
> Para que yo te oiga, mi conciencia
> en dios me abre tu ser todo para mí,
> y tú me entras en tu gran rumor,
> la infinita rapsodia de tu amor
> que yo sé que es de amor, pues es tan bella. (*LP*, pp. 1319-1320)

Animate Nature imparts her secrets to the poet alone. In the poem «Arboles hombres» from *En el otro costado,* the Orphic privilege of the poet to commune with the trees surpasses even that of a bird, which is put to flight: «solo yo podía estar / entre las rosas finales». The trees are not only articulate; they also have «eyes» to see and «minds» whereby to understand:

> Cuando yo ya me salía
> vi a los árboles mirarme.

[18] R. Gullón, «Preface» to *El modernismo,* p. 26.

Se daban cuenta de todo,
y me apenaba dejarles. (*TAP*, pp. 919-920)[19]

So perfect is the human-arboreal intercourse that, in measure with the divestment of the poet's own bodily shape, merging with the trees, so they in their turn appear to adopt human form. The animation of JRJ's natural world is a sympathetic one, with no trace of the nascent hostility in the sensible world of, for instance, Gérard de Nerval—a poet, incidentally, whom JRJ greatly admired. Ricardo Gullón records the following praise of Nerval by JRJ: «El caso de Nerval es claro: es un poeta de lo mejor; un gran poeta. Esos sonetos suyos son magníficos».[20] A sense of exhilaration reigns here in Nerval, it is true, but it is accompanied by a certain subtle and pervasive malevolence:

Crains dans le mur aveugle, un regard que t'épie:
A la matière même un verbe est attaché [...]

Souvent dans l'être obscur habite un Dieu caché;
Et comme un oeil naissant couvert par ses paupières,
Un pur esprit s'accroît sous l'écorce des pierres.[21]

This conviction of the poet as visionary alone capable of penetrating and acting as channel for the elemental and contradictory forces of Nature is shared alike by Victor Hugo and by Rubén Darío. In Hugo, for example, we read:

Tout parle. Et maintenant, homme, sais-tu pourquoi
Tout parle? Ecoute bien. C'est que vents, ondes, flammes,
Arbres, roseaux, rochers, tout vit.
Tout est plein d'âme.
Mais comment? Oh! voilà le mystère inouï.[22]

Rubén Darío's «Coloquio de los centauros» in *Prosas profanas* is an important statement of his aesthetic; and worthy too of note here is his poem « ¡Torres de Dios! ¡Poetas! / ¡Pararrayos celestes! », n.º IX in *Cantos de vida y esperanza,* which may indeed derive from sources in Hugo. Nor should Bécquer be overlooked in connection with this belief in the poet's special insight into the mysteries of Nature.

Miguel de Unamuno also has some interesting things to say in connection with the impulse to «concientizar» even the very stones:

[19] The poem may at times appear almost to read as a parody of the pathetic fallacy. Nevertheless, it is a serious poem and not intended as ironic. JRJ was, both as man and poet, a person of extremes and this poem, for all its exaggeration, should be taken at its serious face-value. In connection with this poem, it is interesting to know that the first reviewers of *Arias tristes* in *Renacimiento* compared JRJ with Góngora, among other reasons because of his feeling for Nature.

[20] R. Gullón, *Conversaciones con JRJ,* p. 138.

[21] Gérard de Nerval, «Vers dorés», *Les chimères, Oeuvres,* Garnier, Paris, 1966, p. 709.

[22] Victor Hugo, «Ce que dit la bouche d'ombre», XXVI, *Les contemplations,* Garnier, Paris, 1969, p. 434.

> Descendiendo desde nosotros mismos, desde la propia conciencia humana [...], suponemos que tienen alguna conciencia, más o menos oscura, todos los vivientes y las rocas mismas, que también viven. Y la evolución de los seres orgánicos no es sino una lucha por la plenitud de conciencia a través del dolor, una constante aspiración a ser otros sin dejar de ser lo que son, a romper sus límites limitándose. Y este proceso de personalización o de subjetivación de todo lo exterior fenoménico u objetivo, constituye el proceso mismo vital de la filosofía en la lucha de la vida contra la razón y de ésta contra aquélla.[23]

It is valuable to read as an extension of the «Arboles hombres» poem the later one called «Los mármoles seréis árboles» from *Una colina meridiana* (*TAP,* pp. 961-963). Here, the metamorphic interpretation of the trees lends itself ideally to JRJ's conception of the role of Time and Eternity in poetry. It is the expression of that statement that «el mito del retorno, de la eterna juventud, primavera, es el de la poesía misma». The «death» of these trees is not death, but a period of waiting before regeneration: «Vosotros sois de vosotros / perpetuidad retornable». In this, they resemble the gods, in an unceasing, undying succession of eternal metamorphoses. A triple layer of analogies emerges out of this: for if trees and gods share this perpetuity in common, so also does the true poet. In «La razón heróica» we read that: «el poeta tiene que ser siempre nuevo, porque la novedad es continuación; y es difícil concebir la permanencia sin presente [...] El poeta es sucesión interior y esterior, a través del tiempo y el espacio dados [...] Y si la vida no fuera aspiración de permanencia, moriría en el acto, el realismo mataría la vida verdadera». This vision of the cyclical regeneration of Nature affords the perfect illustration therefore of the cyclical concept of poetry itself and indeed of the poet himself as its instrument. Trees, gods and the true poet all identically «refuse» to die, through their unyielding aspiration toward self-perpetuity. The chosen metaphor of «mármoles» works admirably in service of JRJ's purpose, and on a number of different levels. There is, first, its perfect trisyllabic assonance with «árboles»—a phonic equilibrium which conveys the conceptual equilibrium of life/death. Furthermore, it has the advantage of suggesting the coldness, bloodlessness and stasis of death whilst yet denying its finality. This is the central poetic theme. It is achieved by removing the reality, the ugliness of death, by association with the beauty of fine proportion and architectural elegance, so that stasis becomes rather a measured and harmonious stillness—the stillness of sleep, not death. It does so yet further, by association with Petrarchan epithet, (first incorporated into Spanish verse in the sixteenth century), where marble becomes the attribute of the flawless limbs and skin of woman. Such an interpretation is fully in keeping with the poet's intent, for the choice of feminine description is already patent in the plaited locks of hair, the promise of fairskinned complexion once again, and «senos palpitantes», all ascribed to the trees. More importantly however, the metaphor is adroit because in

[23] Miguel de Unamuno, *Del sentimiento trágico de la vida, OC,* 16 vols., Editorial Afrodisio Aguado, Madrid, 1958, XVI, pp. 269-270.

itself it serves to exemplify that «perpetual succession» of which JRJ speaks. It resuscitates and renders eternally present, Antiquity itself. The temples and palaces of classical times are cyclically reborn in the stripped hibernal structure of the trees. History itself becomes a recurrently present phenomenon. And by analogy with the orderly sculptural evocation of «mármoles», the poet stresses the orderliness of a universe motored by an intrinsic purposeful principle: that of eternal renewal. The image of ancient temples, suggested by the metaphor, lends an increasing aura of sanctity to the forest which in turn acquires the nature of a temple where the gods disport themselves and find their home. The entire natural world, embodied in the forest, has become one vast and living Pantheon, the sanctuary of all the gods. This theme of «la selva sagrada» is common also to Rubén Darío.[24] It appears, for example, in «El coloquio de los centauros» *(Prosas profundas)* and is perhaps most clearly of all illustrated in the poem which initiates *Cantos de vida y esperanza,* beginning «Yo soy aquel que ayer no más decía». Stanzas 17 and 20 read:

¡Oh, la selva sagrada! ¡Oh, la profunda
emanación del corazón divino
de la sagrada selva! ¡Oh, la fecunda
fuente cuya virtud vence al destino! [...]

Allí va el dios en celo tras la hembra,
y la caña de Pan se alza del lodo;
la eterna vida sus semillas siembra,
y brota la armonía del gran Todo.

It is this vision, shared by JRJ with Rubén Darío, which enables JRJ to translate into poetry the essence of poetry itself, namely, that of perpetual renewal. The act of reading and re-reading the poem is to re-enact the truth that it expresses. If we return to the poem «Para que yo te oiga» mentioned earlier, we see that in the last stanza JRJ plainly states that in the poem itself lies the perpetuation of its own melody:

¡[...] y la cuento
(para que no se pierda) en la canción
sucesiva del mundo en que va el hombre
llevándote, con él, a su dios solo!

In the telling of the poet—in the poem—perpetuity is achieved. That telling is not the simple reflection of an outer phenomenon, but its embodiment and its realization.

In the Work, JRJ reveals himself to be that «hombre Narciso» of whom he spoke, who is «el panteísta que quiere reintegrarse en la naturaleza». The poem «Nocturno» from *Piedra y cielo* affords a good example.

[24] The theme of the Sacred Forest is similarly one dear to the German nineteenth century Romantics, for example, Hölderlin, Rilke, Novalis. Compare also Pierre Ronsard's «Elégie contre les bûcherons de la forest de Gastine».

It relates a given experience, an epiphany, in which the soul of the poet merges with the heavens:

Mi lágrima y la estrella
se tocaron, y al punto
se hicieron una sola lágrima,
se hicieron una estrella sola.

Me quedé ciego, se quedó
ciego, de amor, el cielo.
Fue todo—y nada más—el mundo
pena de estrella, luz de lágrima. (*LP,* p. 796)

The absoluteness of the fusion is symbolically conveyed in the encounter and mutual metamorphosis of tear with star. Each becomes the other, and in this mutation of identity not two phenomena but one alone results. Star assumes the grief of tear; tear, the light of star: and that union is the product of a mystic love between the poet and the universe. From the starting-point of a star, the poem broadens its horizons to involve the entire cosmos in the experience. By extension with the «estrella», the second stanza amplifies into «cielo» and from there embraces «mundo» itself. Poet and world entire are unified. That blinding love which binds them together signifies a total surrender of individuality and an abandonment of the senses in mutual sacrifice. It is a love which bears a certain profane affinity with the dark night of the soul of San Juan de la Cruz, in which renunciation of the self is the prerequisite to perfect union.[25]

A further example of JRJ as panentheist may be found in the poem «Es mi alma» from *La estación total* (*LP,* p. 1226). Here the poet lists a series of chosen phenomena with which he identifies his soul. The poem is more diffuse than «Nocturno», whose sheer concentration renders it the more intrinsically successful of the two. But the abundance of nature as it is here evoked, aptly serves the underlying theme of the One in the Many. The particular in Nature («ricas aguas»; «frescas alas»; «dulces ramas»; «altas voces») is denied its particularity, to be subsumed into the all-embracing soul of the poet. Where «Nocturno» showed a perfect reciprocity of integration, here the matter is rather one of appropriation and absorption by the soul. Nevertheless, the interpenetration of poet with Nature is total, no less than in «Nocturno», and the two poems clearly exemplify the panentheistic belief of JRJ.

However, this picture does not always entirely cohere in the Work of JRJ. The poet and Nature are not invariably one. A duality does remain. The closing lines of «Arboles hombres» illustrate this duality, in their

[25] With regard to Narcissism and mysticism there are, as with Romantic poets such as Wordsworth, certain problems in the analogy with the mystics' beatific vision. A. Gerard, writing on English Romantic poetry, says that the problem with Wordsworth is that the poet does not submerge his individuality passively and humbly to the divine influx; rather, it is his own individuality that appears to him deified. This Gérard sees as closer to the spirit of Rousseau than to the mystics. See A. GÉRARD, *L'idée Romantique de la poésie en Angleterre. Etudes sur la théorie de la poésie chez Coleridge, Wordsworth, Keats et Shelley,* Les Belles Lettres, Paris, 1955.

sorrowful recognition of the gulf that exists between the essential humanity of the poet and the vegetable category of the trees:

> ¿Cómo decirles que no,
> que yo era sólo el pasante,
> que no me hablaran a mí?
> No quería traicionarles.

Of course the paradox remains, that the problem expressed here should exist at all. For if humanity and vegetation had not a certain common identity, then the question of denying conversation, of self-denunciation or betrayal would be meaningless. But the important point to note is the poet's self-acknowledged «otherness». He cannot renounce his membership of mankind.

In a later poem, indeed, we find that he would not even *wish* to do so. The earlier regret at his own humanity is turned to a positive and proper pride in it. The poem «Del fondo de la vida» from *Una colina meridiana* (*TAP,* pp. 943-944) reveals a JRJ who can by no means be called panentheistic nor pantheistic, such is the clarity of division between himself as man and the hawthorn bush before him. There is mutual contemplation, certainly: «Déjanos a los dos que nos miremos»; and the poem is a most beautiful expression of dignified equality. But it is equality, not identity. In that act of contemplation is the clear recognition—by both parties—of essential otherhood. Under an impartial («igual») sun, man and hawthorn respectfully and quietly appraise each other.[26] It is the equilibrium of the poem's composition which lends it its authority. Just as the hawthorn has «sacado del fondo de la tierra» its organic components of «tronco, hoja, espina» and its «color, su olor, su forma»—so the poet in parallel manner has drawn from those same depths his own being of «carne y hueso» and his own form, colour and odour. Parity exists therefore. But again, not identity. The delineation between what are two separate entities is sharp; each belongs to its own distinct species. The hawthorn, that «oasis de sequera vejetal», is «de una especie diversa, y de otra especie / que tú, mujer, y que yo, hombre».[27] An interesting and somewhat perplexing interrogative punctuates the second line of this poem. It is worthy of some attention: «En el pedral, un sol sobre un espino, mío. / Y mirándolo ¿yo?». The poct sccms to bc questioning his own identity. His doubtfulness however is only temporary for it is rapidly resolved in the ensuing generic self-definition of «yo, hombre» in the seventh line—a definition which is sustained to the very end, in the last stanza: «Y, hombre frente a espino, aquí estoy, con el sol». Nevertheless, the fact that such self-questioning should arise at all brings us to the related major consideration of the way

[26] For an interesting comment on the «krausista» origins—«afición a la naturaleza, cierto espíritu de excursionista dominical»—of JRJ's so-called pantheism or panentheism, see ANGEL GONZÁLEZ, *JRJ: Estudio,* pp. 130-131. González speaks of pantheism in JRJ as being «más aparente que real»—an observation with which I incline to agree.

[27] For further discussion on this poem, see HOWARD T. YOUNG, *The Victorious Expression,* University of Wisconsin Press, Madison, Wisconsin, 1966, p. 122.

in which JRJ regarded his identity, not with Nature this time, but with the Work itself. They are related in the sense that the concept of the natural world as Book and the Book of the world go hand in hand. Our concern now is to discover to what extent JRJ identified himself with his Work.

The poem «Yo no soy yo» from *Eternidades* is a further and more profound exploration of that question of the poet's own identity posed above:

Yo no soy yo.
Soy este
que va a mi lado sin yo verlo;
que, a veces, voy a ver,
y que, a veces, olvido.
El que calla, sereno, cuando hablo,
el que perdona, dulce, cuando odio,
el que pasea por donde no estoy,
el que quedará en pie cuando yo muera. (*LP*, p. 676)

The awareness of two quite separate selves, the self of world-experience and the projected literary self, is here quite evident.[28] The sense of such a dichotomy is of course not unique to JRJ. It is similarly expressed in the poetry of Antonio Machado. A line from the opening poem «Retrato» of *Campos de Castilla,* for example, reads: «Converso con el hombre que siempre va conmigo». Indeed, Machado evolved a whole metaphysic and aesthetic of «otredad». His Abel Martín and Juan de Mairena are themselves literary self-projections—homonyms rather than pseudonyms—created to facilitate the dialectical interplay of their author's thought. With the expression of their opinions in the *Cancionero apócrifo,* they gradually assume an apparently autonomous life. These «alter egos» are the exponents of Machado's theories and counter-theories. Juan de Mairena expatiates on «otredad»:

> De *lo uno a lo otro* es el gran tema de la metafísica. Todo el trabajo de la razón humana tiende a la eliminación del segundo término. *Lo otro no existe:* tal es la fe racional [...] Pero *lo otro* no se deja eliminar; subsiste, persiste [...] Abel Martín, con fe poética [...] creía *en lo otro,* en «La esencial Heterogeneidad del ser», como si dijéramos en la incurable *otredad* que padece lo *uno.*[29]

A basic difference is established by Machado between «el otro» and «lo otro». «El otro» is the means of man's communication with his fellow men; «lo otro» is that inner essence which man seeks within himself in order to justify his existence in the world and to give it meaning. As Segundo Serrano Poncela has pointed out: «esta dialéctica de lo uno a lo otro es análoga [...] a la agonía unamuniana».[30] Certainly, Unamuno too

[28] For an analysis of this and other poems related to the theme of «homo duplex», see L. R. Cole, *The Religious Instinct in the Poetry of JRJ*, p. 60 and pp. 64-66 et seq.

[29] A. Machado, *Obras: poesía y prosa,* p. 357.

[30] Segundo Serrano Poncela, *Antonio Machado, su mundo y su obra,* Losada, Buenos Aires, 1954, p. 112.

was endlessly fascinated and preoccupied by the nature of fictional projection of the self and by «otredad». In his «Prólogo» to *La vida de Don Quijote y Sancho* he affirms the autonomy of literary creation: «los entes que reputamos de ficción tienen una vida propia, independiente y siguen viviendo. Y todos los que al conocerlos los re-creamos, les damos vida».[31] Again, further on we read: «Y como Don Quijote y Sancho son—no es sólo que lo fueron—tan independientes de la ficción poética de Cervantes como lo es de la mía aquel Augusto Pérez de mi novela *Niebla,* al que creí haber dado vida para darle después muerte, contra lo que él, y con razón, protestaba».[32] In every literary genre, not only essay and novel, but in drama and poetry too, Unamuno manifests this continuing theme. In the «Autocrítica», for example, to his dramatic *Misterio en tres jornadas* entitled significantly *El otro,* he writes that the male protagonist of *El otro* «me ha brotado de la obsesión, mejor que preocupación, del misterio—no problema—, de la personalidad».[33] With regard to his poetry, as Manuel Alvar points out: «los poemas, sí, objetivan, pero no para ser contemplados desde lejos, sino para proyectar un subjetivismo, para hacer tantos Unamunos cuantos prosélitos se adhieran a ellos».[34] Unamuno's poem n.° LVI (1) from *De Fuerteventura a París,* beginning «Al frisar los sesenta, mi otro sino», affords a good example of the expression of «otredad». It is accompanied by a gloss in which Unamuno confesses: «Siempre me ha preocupado el problema de lo que llamaría mis "yos ex-futuros", los que pude haber sido y dejé de ser, las posibilidades que he ido dejando en el camino de mi vida».[35]

Again, this is a theme explored in the «masks» of Yeats. The Argentinian writer, Jorge Luis Borges, offers also a yet further instance. Indeed, his prose poem entitled «Borges y yo» could almost serve as a gloss to JRJ's own lines from «Descanso» in *Piedra y cielo:* «Todo tú estás en ti, / aunque te vayas de ti. Basta.» (*LP,* p. 751). An extract from «Borges y yo» confesses:

> Yo vivo, yo me dejo vivir, para que Borges pueda tramar su literatura y esa literatura me justifica [...] Yo he de quedar en Borges, no en mí (si es que alguien soy), pero me reconozco menos en sus libros que en muchos otros [...] No sé cuál de los dos escribe esta página.[36]

JRJ's poem «Yo no soy yo» shows the same paradoxical complexity. For within the initial negation of the self is contained, confusingly enough, an affirmation of that self. Precisely in order to deny it, it must—at least embryonically—exist. Thus the statement «yo no soy yo» is at once a recognition of the poet's own identity and, pursuant upon that recognition,

31 M. de Unamuno, *OC,* IV, p. 29.

32 *Ibid.,* p. 69.

33 M. de Unamuno, *OC,* XII, p. 801.

34 Manuel Alvar, «Prólogo» to Miguel de Unamuno, *Poesías,* Edición Manuel Alvar, Editorial Labor, Textos hispánicos modernos, Barcelona, 1975, p. 43.

35 M. de Unamuno, *OC,* XIV, p. 536.

36 Jorge Luis Borges, «Borges y yo», *El hacedor,* Emecé, Buenos Aires, 1960, pp. 50-51.

a refutation of it. The poem then goes on to offer a progressive definition of that other identity which the first prefers to claim as the true one, backing down in its favour. The tone is almost that of auto-persuasion. The incantatory insistence seems a deliberate design to conjure away the «old Adam» and instal the new. JRJ is in fact disowning here the JRJ of lived experience in honour of this other JRJ of poetic truth. And this should not be the cause of surprise. For it was, without the shadow of a doubt, to the latter that he believed immortality to belong. It is the «poetic JRJ» who is «el que quedará en pie cuando yo muera». In this kind of conflict between the empirical self and the lyrical self we may see that same «quarrel» of which Yeats, in his *Per amica silentia lunae* period of 1917, speaks: «We make out of the quarrel with ourselves, poetry». Or, as he elsewhere says: «No mind can engender till divided into two».[37]

The implications therefore of this distinction between the empirical and the lyrical self are far-reaching. For it is in precisely this distinction that JRJ finds his ultimate redemption. His literary self, the self that is the Work, will prove his salvation. Death will be able to claim only the former, the insignificant JRJ which is but a remnant left over from all that he has poured of his other self into the Work:

> [...] toda mi alma
> —vaciada ya por mí en la Obra plena—
> segura para siempre. (*LP*, p. 884)

The poetic voice of this poem, « ¡Ese día, ese día! » from *Poesía,* is dual. In the first and second stanzas it is that of the empirical «yo» speaking, the «yo» that can declare that it has poured its soul into the Work; the «yo» that can say: « ¡porque haya yo / trabajado en mí tanto, tanto, tanto! ». But in the third and last stanza a subtle shift is made: the «yo» has now become the «yo» of the lyrical self, the voice that survives and can smile in the face of death, knowing that it has bequeathed to the grave nothing but a parcel of bones:

> —y yo sonría ya, sin fin, a todo—,
> porque sea tan poco, huesos míos,
> lo que le haya dejado yo de mí.

Whereas, therefore, at first the empirical self is the subject of its object, the lyrical «yo», it is at last the lyrical self which takes over to reverse the situation. It has become, in its turn, the subject of its object, the empirical «yo». The transition is admirably wrought within the framework of the poem.

Obviously, then, it is essential for a proper understanding of poems such as these to be aware of the ambivalence of JRJ's use of the word «yo», and to decipher its correct identity. Thus, in a slightly earlier poem, beginning «¿Cómo, muerte, tenerte / miedo?», from the same collection

[37] W. B. YEATS, *Autobiographies,* p. 345.

Poesía, the voice of the last three lines must be appreciated as the voice of the lyrical «yo»:

> [...] ¿No seré yo,
> muerte, tu muerte, a quien tú, muerte,
> debes temer, mimar, amar? (*LP,* p. 880)

Only the projected self-within-Work could make such proud defiance, claiming the defeat of Death, threatening and enslaving it.

By contrast, on the other hand, it is the empirical self that we hear in «Otoño corporal» from *Belleza,* affirming that:

> Nada me importa esta muerte
> que es la caída del cuerpo.
> No me moriré al morirme
> de esta manera de aquí. (*LP,* p. 1121)

It is the empirical «yo» speaking, but the affirmation it makes rests wholly on the premise of the lyrical self. In this way, the Work itself has become the enaçtment of a continuous drama between three personae: Death, and the twinned selves of JRJ.[38]

We can now more accurately understand what is meant when we speak of the oneness of JRJ with his Work, and of its anthropomorphic character, as it lives and grows along with that developing self which it incarnates. The metaphor of the Work as a living organism was for JRJ no mere ornament but a reality. Its internal rhythms marked time with the rhythmic breathing of its creator.[39] It is interesting too to note that it is in precisely these terms that JRJ chose to convey the relationship between Bécquer and the poetry of Bécquer, in his tribute to the nineteenth century poet whom he so much admired. JRJ's portrait of Bécquer in *Españoles de tres mundos* uses an extended metaphor in which the poet's heartbeat sets the rhythm and accent of his verse. It is as if the poetic corpus possessed a respiratory apparatus of its own. The fact that such a bodily image as corpus has for long been a commonplace in the general canon of literary terminology is in itself of interest. Its first usage as such in the English language appeared, according to the *Oxford English Dictionary,* in 1727. The Work is—and

[38] A propos of death as an intimately known existential limit, it is worth remembering that JRJ considered ANTONIO MACHADO's «Ultimas lamentaciones de Abel Martín» to be amongst his finest poetry. This is recorded by R. GULLÓN in his *Conversaciones con JRJ,* p. 49: «Hablamos de los papeles póstumos de Machado que están siendo publicados en *Cuadernos hispanoamericanos,* y Juan Ramón dice que en las "Ultimas lamentaciones de Abel Martín" están los más hermosos poemas de aquél». It is possible too that JRJ may have known SANZ DEL RÍO's posthumous *Filosofía de la muerte,* edited by Manuel Sales y Ferré, Sevilla, 1877, which speaks of the existential limits of death and of death as the intimate property of the self and as the expression of life.

[39] This is true even of some of JRJ's earliest compositions. G. PALAU DE NEMES, in her *Vida y obra de JRJ,* II, p. 393, has pointed out as an example the early poem «Lamento de primavera», n.° IX in *Las hojas verdes* written in 1906—a poem whose pentasyllabic rhythms act as a kind of cardiograph, tracing the quickened and irregular beat of a heart «hecho para el amor».

the quotation bears repetition—like «el río de esta sangre que respiramos del mar del aire y la echamos, con el ritmo del corazón y del pulmón nuestro al aire de la tierra y del mar». The muscular dilation and contraction, the inhalation and exhalation of its internal workings, faithfully follow those of its author, and once again reflect that cyclical pattern of recurrence and of self-perpetuating motion which lies at the heart of JRJ's poetic vision.

Notably, it is not only the reflection of his soul but also of his body that JRJ seeks to project in the Work: «Lo que yo busco es reflejar mi alma y mi cuerpo». There is an obvious parallel here with Miguel de Unamuno. The profound admiration which JRJ felt for Unamuno is well known. Indeed he said of him, in his lecture course on «modernismo», that it was from the fusion of «las corrientes representadas por Rubén Darío y Unamuno que nace la poesía española moderna».[40] It is justifiable therefore to note the similar passion manifested by Unamuno for an immortality that should be not only of the soul but of the body also. «Tiemblo ante la idea de tener que desgarrarme de mi carne; [...] y si a Dios me agarro con mis potencias y mis sentidos todos, es para que El me lleve en sus brazos allende la muerte», he confesses in his chapter entitled «El hambre de inmortalidad» in *Del sentimiento trágico de la vida.* Indeed, much of Unamuno's philosophical querying into the desire for personal immortality bears direct comparison with JRJ's conception of the Work as the instrument of this salvation of the self. The shadowy immortality of one's name alone is, for Unamuno and JRJ alike, insufficient without the resurrection of the body. In support of the Catholic Creed («the resurrection of the dead and the life of the world to come»), Unamuno quotes a verse carved on a tombstone in his native Bilbao:

Aunque estamos en polvo convertidos,
en Ti, Señor, nuestra esperanza fía,
que tornaremos a vivir vestidos
con la carne y la piel que nos cubría.

This verse may fittingly be adapted to JRJ's own—unorthodox—creed, if we substitute for «en Ti, Señor» the words «en Ti, mi Obra». For it is, as already cited, in the Work that JRJ wishes to reflect both soul and body—not in a Catholic God. In the «Fragmento tercero» of «Espacio» it would seem that the poet is reconciled to the ultimate abandonment of the body. But it is a partial reconciliation only, betraying a heavy sense of regret and the anticipation of nostalgia:

> Conciencia, yo, el tercero, el caído, te digo a ti (¿me oyes, conciencia?): Cuando tú quedes libre de este cuerpo, cuando te esparzas en lo otro (¿qué es lo otro?) ¿te acordarás de mí con amor hondo; ese amor hondo que yo creo que tú y mi cuerpo se han tenido tan llenamente, con un convencimiento doble que nos hizo vivir un convivir tan fiel como el de un doble astro cuando nace de dos para ser uno?, ¿y no podremos ser por siempre lo que es un astro hecho de

[40] JRJ, *El modernismo,* p. 80.

dos? No olvides que por encima de lo otro y de los otros, hemos cumplido como buenos nuestro mutuo amor. Difícilmente un cuerpo habría amado así a su alma, como mi cuerpo a ti, conciencia de mi alma; porque tú fuiste para él suma ideal y él se hizo por ti, contigo, lo que es.

The corporeal vessel is, to the very last, a divinity of no lesser substance than that of the gods. Why then, the poet protests, shall the soul depart to become incorporated «en otro dios que este que somos mientras tú estás en mí, como de dios?».

Many of Unamuno's pithier statements also cast light on the relationship of JRJ with his Work. One example is his definition of the wish for immortality as the product not of pride, but of the terror of extinction. This is manifestly true of the death-obsessed JRJ. Furthermore, in words peculiarly apposite to JRJ's own attitude to his Work, he states:

El que desprecia el aplauso de la muchedumbre de hoy es que busca sobrevivir en renovadas minorías durante generaciones. «La posteridad es una superposición de minorías», decía Gounod [...] Sacrifica el artista la extensión de su fama a su duración; ansía más durar por siempre en un rinconcito, a no brillar un segundo en el universo todo; quiere más ser átomo eterno y conciente de sí mismo, que momentánea conciencia del universo todo; sacrifica la infinidad a la eternidad».[41]

A great distinction exists, on the other hand, between JRJ and the majority of poets and writers who would embody themselves in their work. For whereas in the latter it is the life of the author that fulfils the book, with JRJ it is the other way about. It is the Work that fulfils and actually creates the life of the poet. It is Unamuno once again who bears closest affinity with JRJ here—most especially in the context of his ideas upon the relation of Cervantes with his great work, *Don Quijote de la Mancha.* For him, it is Don Quijote who is the creator of his author, Cervantes.[42] Of course, this affirmation of Unamuno—that Don Quijote created Cervantes—has to be treated with care. Cervantes created a great literary figure, at once both hero and myth. Into that figure, the unfortunate tax collector that was Cervantes poured his whole genius in order that he might survive and transcend his human condition and circumstances. Thus a chain is set up: the mortal Cervantes, subject to the laws of worldly temporality, creates his Don Quijote, and it is Don Quijote who, in his turn, creates

[41] M. DE UNAMUNO: *OC,* XVI, p. 183.
[42] M. DE UNAMUNO, «Quijotismo y cervantismo», *OC,* V, p. 601:

Con gran acierto se ha dicho y repetido no pocas veces que Don Quijote es el mismo Cervantes. Es Cervantes en cuanto éste tenía de hombre de su tiempo y de su pueblo, es el alma española cuajada en Cervantes.

And again: Para mí la verdadera biografía de Cervantes es su *Quijote.* (*Ibid.,* p. 620.)

Los que conocen nuestra filosofía de la historia [...] saben que creemos que Don Quijote y Sancho tienen más realidad histórica que Miguel de Cervantes Saavedra—y más que la del que esto escribe—y que lejos de ser éste, Cervantes, el que creó a aquéllos, son ellos los que crearon a Cervantes. (*Ibid.,* p. 638.)

the immortal and a-temporal Cervantes. This startling inversion of the norm —the creation of JRJ by and in his Work—is expressed in the tiny poem «Epitafio ideal» from *Poesía (en verso):*

> ¡Libro acabado,
> caída carne mía,
> labrado subterráneo de mi vida! (*LP,* p. 974)

With its suggestion of Adam, of mortality and the Fall, the terms of this poem are certainly surprising.

Speaking in his lecture in Río Piedras in 1954, JRJ testified to the simultaneous development and growth of himself with his Work, in a never-ending succession of new beginnings: «No tengo que añadir que nunca me quedo contento al dar al público un libro. Al contrario. En el momento en que recibo el primer ejemplar impreso deshago su encuadernación y empiezo a cambiarlo todo, es decir, a empezar otra vez». He then aphoristically and quite deliberately fuses in one the development of his personal life with his literary life: «mi biografía es empezar siempre, mi bibliografía siempre empezar». This symbiotic relationship is in a state of perpetual re-growth. But it is the Work which, of the two, emerges as the more vital organism. «Yo no me considero más que un andarín de mi órbita, metamorfoseador en todas mis actividades, y por lo tanto más que en ninguna otra, en Poesía». Such a statement reaffirms, in paraphrase, the Goethian dictum which JRJ adopted and put into practice throughout his creative life:

> Wie das Gestirn,
> ohne Hast,
> aber ohne Rast.

Or, in his own words, «Sin aceleración y sin detenimiento, como los astros gire el hombre alrededor de su propia obra». The Work is indeed the vital body—the Sun—to which its author is a subordinate planet. The Work is the life-giving source, the source of energy.

The significance which JRJ gave to the simultaneity of growth, development and maturation of himself with the Work, within a strictly temporal dimension, is evident from a conversation with Ricardo Gullón on January 28, 1954 in which he stated: «Yo creo que el mejor sistema para ordenar la obra es cronológica. Cada poema va así en la línea del tiempo, en el momento que apareció». In the chronological sequence thus ascribed to the Work is implicit already the idea of autobiography, of diary. However, unlike any ordinary diary, the Work is almost entirely bereft of anecdotal element, and should rather be seen as the record of a spiritual procession. It is true that a certain linear development exists. For instance, one of JRJ's lamentations was that he seriously required—but lacked—a current outlet, some regular review or magazine in which to publish each day's new creations, in order that by so doing he might disencumber himself of his ceaseless day-to-day poetic diary. This would set him free to get on with the ordering and re-working of the total Work. So important was this to him, that he himself founded several such magazines, *Indice* and *Helios* amongst them. It was impossible for him to halt his daily creativity. To Juan Guerrero he confessed:

> Mi gusto sería ir dando, dando siempre a medida que termino las cosas, pues mi gran defecto es que el papel se me pega, y si veo una, dos, tres pruebas siempre encuentro algo que corregir en ellas; de aquí la gran ventaja que para mí tiene el periódico, donde una vez enviado el original no vuelvo a verlo hasta que ya está publicado.

Again, he insists on this need for a daily outlet: «Mi ritmo es dar una cosa diaria, y como una vez terminada no me gusta volver a verla hasta cuando la voy a recoger en libro, necesito un periódico donde darla para que allí quede».[43] Elsewhere too, he is on record as having declared, in December 1952, his intention to publish his Work chronologically: «Voy a dar, por orden cronológico, la obra total».[44]

Nevertheless, despite all these manifestations of an apparently logical and sequential time progression in the Work, they cannot be taken at strict face-value. The Work, on the contrary, cannot be «metred» in so simple a manner. Ultimately, it abides by quite other and more essential time laws. One cogent indication of this fact is JRJ's own explanation of the sub-title which he gave to his publication, *Obra en marcha,* which read: «España. Sin día». That «Sin día» signified the special rhythm of JRJ himself which, in his own words, «no es de reló, ni calendario, sino de tiempo verdadero». The puzzling apparent self-contradiction which this implies is one which has seriously to be taken into account. Those last two words, «tiempo verdadero», afford us the key to the truth. They refer to the chronology of the inner life; and the inner life adheres to no ordinary mundane laws of time. In this connection, it is useful to recall one of JRJ's cryptically telling apothegms: «Mi vida interior, la belleza eterna, mi Obra». The Work is the inner life, and it will follow therefore only that «tiempo verdadero» which is proper to the inner life.

Poems of past experience are constantly revised in the light of subsequent experience and brought cyclically into the present, so that the Work becomes a kind of palimpsest. Never are they left to belong to the definitive past, fixed in the stasis of completion. This constant revision, coupled with the inclusion of new «limbs» to the corpus, effects the cyclical character of the Work operating within its own peculiar time dimension, that of «tiempo verdadero». Furthermore, the incorporation of poems which had not been published elsewhere and individually, meant that both the new additions and the Work as a whole became subject to modification, each influencing the other, and each acquiring a new tone and a new mood, by this mutual interaction and association. Such introductions could set up new vibrations and new reactions in the poetic corpus. Flexibility and fluidity of this sort are of the essence of the Work and of its special inner

[43] Guerrero Ruiz, p. 73.
[44] R. Gullón, *Conversaciones con JRJ,* p. 120.

temporality. The idea of successive regeneration, closely bound with the concept of this inner chronology, is often conveyed by JRJ in metaphors of river and sea. The perpetual renovation of wave upon wave aptly suggests the intrinsic motion of the Work:

> El espíritu es inmanencia en marcha; y cuanto el espíritu concibe para la vida, tiene que ser marcha, devenir; un seguir siendo, como el oleaje o el ondeaje de un mar siempre nuevo sin salir de sus aguas ni de sus playas, y que es nuevo sólo porque cambia de olas constantemente, porque es movimiento y movimiento en marcha.

Just as each serial wave aspires to newness, so likewise poetry is a constant aspiration. The appropriateness of the analogy is still more striking if we recall the overwhelming influence which the sea exerted on the personal life of JRJ and thence upon his entire aesthetic philosophy. The early poetry, it is true, already shows a fine appreciation of the beauty of the sea, the Atlantic, contemplated from JRJ's home town of Moguer—that «nido de gloria [...] el rincón de mi nostalgia». But the real impact of the sea was not to be felt until 30 January 1916, when JRJ set sail for America to marry Zenobia Camprubí. It was during this transatlantic voyage (later to be repeated on 26 August 1936) that JRJ first experienced the ocean directly: nothing but the high seas, the heavens and himself, in one long, solitary, monotonous and rhythmic discourse. It is therefore instructive to observe the very different kind of treatment which the sea receives in the early poetry from that of the later poetry, for it clearly shows the fundamental change in JRJ's conception of that element. In «El mar lejano» from *Baladas de primavera,* written in 1907, the sea is an attractive item in a natural setting, an ornament to be admired. Not only is it spatially distant from the poet, as the title itself tells, but there is a definite emotional distance at operation also between the sea and the poet. Each stanza ends with a parallel two lines:

> ¡Mar de la aurora, mar de plata;
> qué limpio estás entre los pinos! [...]
>
> ¡Mar de la siesta, mar de oro;
> qué alegre estás sobre los pinos! [...]
>
> ¡Mar de la tarde, mar de rosa;
> qué dulce estás entre los pinos! [45]

At this early stage in the Work, the sea is still viewed from a remote terrestrial stand-point, its frame the forest of pine. Emotionally, the poet is no more involved with it than to the extent of simple visual appreciation. However, if we turn to *Diario de un poeta reciencasado,* written in 1916, and inspired by that long sea voyage to the United States, we find amongst

[45] JRJ, *Primeros libros de poesía,* compiled by Francisco Garfias, Aguilar, Madrid, 1973, p. 741. All future references to this edition are given after quotations in the text, in the abbreviated form *PLP*.

the very first poems of the collection the following radical change of treatment. The poem entitled «Soledad» is a good example:

En ti estás todo, mar, y sin embargo,
¡qué sin ti estás, qué solo,
qué lejos, siempre, de ti mismo!

Abierto en mil heridas, cada instante,
cual mi frente,
tus olas van, como mis pensamientos,
y vienen, van y vienen,
besándose, apartándose,
con un eterno conocerse,
mar, y desconocerse.

Eres tú, y no lo sabes,
tu corazón te late, y no lo siente...
¡Qué plenitud de soledad, mar sólo! (*LP*, p. 243)[46]

Physical proximity with the ocean has here become poetically manifest in the identification of self with element, in the second stanza most especially. No longer an object for merely visual delight, the sea has become integral with the poet, a vital phenomenon with which he can converse.

Above all else, it is the influence of this new understanding of the sea upon the poetic diction itself of the Work which most concerns us.[47] The rigid alternating rhyme scheme of the early poem, «El mar lejano», gives way to the freedom of form displayed in the later «Soledad». The conventions of traditional rhyme are broken and a new flexibility—responding to the fluidity of the waters described—makes its appearance in blank verse, activated by its own internal rhythms and inner assonances. The very format and typography of the poem, with its long, self-projecting lines reaching out beyond themselves, only to fall back into the crisp ripples of their curter counterparts, visually suggests the successive advance and retreat of waves. And with a quite new finesse, the lilting free tempo conveys the suck and pluck of the ocean. Henceforth, from the time of his revelatory experience of the ocean, JRJ was to conceive the cyclic and regenerative nature of the entire Work in terms of the perpetual self-renovation of the sea.

This analogy of the Work with the sea perfectly embraces the idea both of linear advance and of cyclical succession, managing to fuse what would otherwise seem to be two mutually exclusive modes of motion.[48] JRJ

[46] For further comment on this poem, see M. P. PREDMORE, *La poesía hermética de JRJ*, p. 127.

[47] The topic of the importance of the sea for JRJ is of course one that has been treated by many distinguished critics, e.g. A. SÁNCHEZ-BARBUDO, *La segunda época de JRJ;* M. P. PREDMORE, *La poesía hermética de JRJ;* D. L. FOGELQUIST, *Juan Ramón Jiménez,* etc. My own reason for doing likewise here is because of its relation to the Work.

[48] It is interesting to compare the English poet, William Blake's conception of the Atlantic Ocean. GEORGE MILLS HARPER, in his book *The Neoplatonism of William Blake,* The University of North Carolina Press, 1961, p. 220, states that «Blake's concept of the Atlantic Ocean as the Sea of Time and Space [...] apparently came

himself bears witness to the immense influence of the sea both upon him personally and upon the Work:

> Mi renovación empieza cuando el viaje a América y se manifiesta con el *Diario.* El mar me hace revivir, porque es el contacto con lo natural, con los elementos, y gracias a él viene la poesía abstracta; así nace el *Diario,* y muchos años después, gracias también al mar, con ocasión del viaje a la Argentina, surge *Dios deseado y deseante.*[49]

The fact that we are able to discern the presence of the sea as a feature in the earliest compositions of JRJ is in itself a corroboration of the growth and unity of the Work as a whole. For those first seminal appearances prophetically foreshadow the developed conception of the sea which was to dominate the Second Epoch and to become symbolic of the very essence of Poetry and of the Work.

Just as the sea knows no termination of what has gone before, so JRJ can similarly claim: «Mi poesía es siempre continuación de mi poesía: —mi verso, de mi verso; mi prosa, de mi prosa—». Even that enigmatic affirmation in the opening lines of the prose poem, «Espacio»: «No soy presente sólo, sino fuga raudal de cabo a fin», becomes intelligible if interpreted in the light of a wave-like succession of aspirations that never quite arrive, and never end.

JRJ's special affinity with the sea is manifest even in his prose portrait of Rubén Darío. Written in 1940, it shows the consistency of his aesthetic vision of the interrelationship between sea and Poetry, in attributing to Darío's poetic technique maritime qualities:

> Mucho mar hay en Rubén Darío, mar pagano. No mar metafísico, ni mar, en él, psicolójico. Mar elemental, mar de permanentes horizontes históricos, mar de ilustres islas. Su misma técnica era marina. Modelaba el verso con plástica de ola: hombro, pecho, cadera de ola; muslo, vientre de ola; le daba empuje, plenitud pleamarinos, altos, llenos de hervoroso espumeo lento de carne contra agua. Sus iris, sus arpas, sus estrellas eran marinos. Todos sus mares, Atlánticos, Pacíficos, Mediterráneos, eran uno: mar de Citeres [...]
>
> Rubén Darío andaba siempre mareado de la ola, de la Venus, de la sal, del tónico.[50]

It is eminently appropriate that JRJ should recapture in images of sea, the essence of a poet so supremely important to him. For the importance of Darío in the poetic development of JRJ may be paralleled perhaps only by that of JRJ's revelatory experience of the ocean. With consummate economy, JRJ resurrects the dead poet thus: «Siempre fue para mí mucho más ente

from the Neo-platonists», and he quotes the following lines from a poetic fragment left by Blake:

> For above Time's troubled Fountains
> On the Great Atlantic Mountains,
> In my Golden House on High,
> There they (Blake's designs) Shine Eternally.

[49] R. Gullón, *Conversaciones con JRJ,* p. 120.
[50] JRJ, *Españoles de tres mundos,* Losada, Buenos Aires, 1942, pp. 41-42.

de mar que de tierra». It is more than a description: it is a tribute. And the choice of its imagery is as revealing of JRJ as of his subject.

The revolution of the Work is its unity, and in its end is to be found its beginning. In the ageing JRJ is to be found the child of Moguer. At the age of seventy, JRJ was writing his *Dios deseado y deseante* in which he was able to trace that same myth of the eternal return of Spring in terms of the perfect cycle of the Work, reflected in the resurrection and return of his own personal childhood. «Con la Cruz del Sur» is a poem which admirably expresses this unity. The constellation which, in the days of Moguer, was for the child the symbolic promise of «la solución de una hermosura» awaiting him, has at the last—so the poem tells—become immediate and accessible. Its promise has been realized in the Work. But that fulfilment—through the passage of time—has brought with it a return to original innocence and a return to infancy, not loss or departure therefrom. In this way JRJ can write, towards the end of his life:

> La Cruz del Sur me está velando
> en mi inocencia última,
> en mi volver al niñodios que yo fui un día
> en mi Moguer de España. (*LP*, pp. 1312-1313)

The Southern Cross still faithfully keeps vigil in the present, thus defeating the remote pastness of «Estuvo, estuvo, estuvo / en todo el cielo azul de mi inmanencia», and bringing the poem full cycle. Immanence has been fulfilled—both the immanent poet in JRJ and the immanent promise of the star—but that progressive realization has proved not unilinear, but gyrate.

This compression of the successive stages of life in a single unified circuit is reminiscent of that which we have already seen in the poem « ¡No le toques ya más, / que así es la rosa! ». In direct parallel with this is the poem «La fruta de mi flor» from *Dios deseado y deseante* in which the cycle of the rose finds its equivalent in the cycle of the self. The «halo of god-consciousness», or Poetry, has become internal, and the poet's body is the mature physical manifestation of it. The ripe «fruit» of the body contains within it the flower and the seed, with the same simultaneity as that of the perfected rose or poem:

> La fruta de mi flor soy, hoy, por ti,
> dios deseado y deseante,
> siempre verde, florido, fruteado,
> y dorado y nevado, y verdecido
> otra vez (estación total toda en un punto)
> sin más tiempo ni espacio
> que el de mi pecho. (*LP*, pp. 1299-1300)

Seasons and stages are all thus united in the single whole.

Perhaps the poem which most successfully of all illustrates the cyclic conception of incipience and fulfilment welded in one, is «La menuda floración» of the same collection. The revolution of the poet's life is one and the same with the revolution of the poetic Work, for they are identified under the one symbol of «niñodiós». The «dios» is the «dios» of his poetic consciousness; the «niño», the child that endures with the man. Together with these, the poem synthesizes the concept of the flower, in which the early bud of childhood and the flowering of manhood parallel the blossoming of the Poetic dream into its own inflorescent prime:

El sueño no fue sueño, era distancia,
y de ella venía la fragancia,
la fragancia que yo, que dios en niñodiós, los dos
le dimos en botón de primavera.
Ella se dilató y hoy llena un mundo
que yo ensanché para este niñodiós.

JRJ the nascent poet, together with the seed of his poetic godhead and the seed of his Work, are caught up in the image of the floret, whose own final emergence similarly turns upon its earliest beginnings:

Por eso vive (el niño) en flor menuda,
en flor del niñodiós, florecilla desnuda,
y en flor del niñodiós desnudo yo lo siento. (*LP*, pp. 1347-1348)

The poem is in fact performing and putting into practice, as we read it, the very process it describes. It is, in itself, the answer to the kind of appeal found in an early «revivido» ballad of 1898, imploring the perpetuation of the idyll that was the poet's childhood in Moguer. The first stanza of this ballad describes the early paradise; the second, the disillusionment experienced upon returning at a later age to the little town; and the third and last is the expression of that longing which was to find its response and resolution in the ultimate poetry of JRJ:

¡Qué tiempo el tiempo! ¿Se fue
con el niñodiós huyendo?
¡Y quién pudiera ser siempre
lo que fue con el primero!
¡Quién no pudiera no caer,
no, no, no caer de viejo;
ser de nuevo el alba pura,
vivir con el tiempo entero,
morir siendo el niñodiós
en mi Moguer, este pueblo! [50 (a)]

Precisely in «La menuda floración», JRJ has arrived at that desired «vivir con el tiempo entero» and that «morir siendo el niñodiós». For the fact is that through the Book and by virtue of the Work, JRJ has been able to transport himself back to the purity and untapped wealth of infancy, his

50 (a) See CARLOS DEL SAZ-OROZCO, *Desarrollo del concepto de Dios en el pensamiento religioso de JRJ,* Editorial Razón y Fe, Madrid, 1966, pp. 12-13.

soul cleansed and made incorruptible by Time. This is the triumphant affirmation made in «Poeta» from *Bonanza:*

> Cuando cojo este libro,
> súbitamente se me pone limpio
> el corazón, lo mismo
> que un pomo cristalino [...]
>
> ¡Qué rico me lo siento! Como un niño
> que no ha gastado nada de su vivo
> tesoro, y aún lo espera todo de sus lirios. (*TAP,* p. 331)

The circle has long been a symbol for perfection, and it is one which offers a universal aesthetic appeal. Ramón del Valle-Inclán, a fellow «modernista» also with linguistic preoccupations, affirms this in his *La lámpara maravillosa,* where he categorically declares: «La expresión estética llena de luz como una estrella, centro de amor y de conocimiento, sólo puede nacer de la visión cíclica». He further stresses the unity which such a vision affords:

> El centro es la unidad, y la unidad es la sagrada simiente del Todo [...] El centro es la razón de la esfera, y la esfera, la forma fecunda que desenvuelve las infinitas posibilidades del centro. La expresión inmutable de la unidad se transforma en la expresión inmutable del Todo. Unidad Potencial es el centro, y la esfera, Unidad Actual. El Verbo es su enlace, la cópula eucarística realizada fuera del Tiempo.[51]

The circle is moreover symbolic of Eternal Time. JRJ employs the concept of the Pythagorean circles in this sense and indeed, in the text itself of his prose poem «Espacio», addresses himself directly to Pythagoras as the «matemático celeste».

Every wheel implies a centre, a mathematical point which itself does not alter position, though such a central point is necessary if there is to be any rotation at all. The world of Time is represented by the turning rim of the wheel; whilst Eternity is the unmoving centre necessarily implied by the movement of Time. This conception of eternal recurrence, symbolically expressed in the figure of the circle is evident in JRJ. It is also apparent in the works of Nietzsche, whom JRJ greatly admired. Nietzsche's Zarathustra, for instance, celebrates recurrence as the wedding-ring of rings: «Oh how should I not lust for eternity and for the wedding-ring of rings—the Ring of Recurrence», he exclaims, in *The Seven Seals.* The gyres of Yeats, and most especially that cyclical conception of history embodied in the diagram at the beginning of Book Five of Yeats's *A Vision,* likewise develop the theme. Nor should the supreme precedent, in the thirteenth century, be forgotten: the great spirals of Dante's «bolgia», conveying the timelessness of infinity. It is with respect to these that Valle-Inclán, once again in *La lámpara maravillosa,* speaks of the frightful sentence meted out to Lucifer to «consumirse en el vértigo del vuelo sin detenerse nunca». He

[51] Ramón del Valle-Inclán, *La lámpara maravillosa,* Editorial Rúa Nueva, Madrid, 1942, pp. 218-219.

continues: «El giro de los círculos infernales apresurado hasta lo infinito haría desaparecer lo pasado y lo venidero trocando en suprema quietud el movimiento. La aspiración a la quietud es la aspiración a ser divino, porque la cifra de lo inmutable tiene el rostro de Dios».[52]

For JRJ the Logos is the centre, the point of Eternity. The poet T. S. Eliot, whose works JRJ knew well, expresses it thus:

> And the light shone in darkness and
> Against the Word the unstilled world still whirled
> About the centre of the silent Word.[53]

Above all, it is the unity of the total design of JRJ's Work which is impressive, rather than any one individual poem. As with Mallarmé and as with Yeats, it is the architecture of the unified opus which chiefly matters. And it is JRJ's particular use of symbols, limited in number but infinite in meaning, which largely contributes to the organization of the unity of the Work. The overall tapestry is woven fundamentally of the same recurrent threads. In his book, *Símbolos y dios en el último JRJ,*[54] Ceferino Santos-Escudero lists an approximate score only of symbols in the Work. This numerical economy not only harmonizes with the general concept of «depuración» and linguistic self-restraint; it also serves the higher interest of unity. For those rich-laden symbols of the later poetry find their origins in the early, and a network of interconnections and accumulated associations is progressively derived. The investment is small; but it is one which gathers increasing returns from the banked capital wealth of the total Work which itself it has promoted. Thus, the early and simple «rosas soñolientas» grow into the incarnation of physical womanly beauty; reappear as love itself; and finally, hoarding up all these prior associations, become the symbol of the perfected Poem, whose essence is the distillation of that Beauty and that Love. The finally achieved Poem therefore brings the circle full round and back again to that «rosa fantástica» which was its origin and source. Again, those early butterflies «de luto, nevadas, blanquiverdes» which depart to the heavens—or the springtime butterfly of *Baladas de primavera* which «está aquí con la ilusión»—will be gathered up into the later «mariposa de luz» of *Piedra y cielo* which has now acquired a far profounder significance as the metaphorical image of evasive Reality.

These are random examples only. But even the concept of the self as child, the «niño» of Moguer, acquires a gradually deeper and larger meaning as it broadens out from personal nostalgic retrospection to assume the symbolic character of mankind itself, thereby uniting the Work with Universal Man:

> El niño es toda la jente,
> el niño soy yo de niño,

52 *Ibid.*, p. 39.

53 T. S. Eliot, «Ash Wednesday», Fifth Section.

54 Ceferino Santos-Escudero, *Símbolos y dios en el último JRJ,* Gredos, Madrid, 1975.

el niño soy yo de viejo,
niño encontrado y perdido. (*TAP*, pp. 928-929)

The paradoxical nature of the very title of this poem, «Niño último», (like the paradox of «inocencia última» in the aforementioned poem, «Con la Cruz del Sur»), betokens the perfect circuit that the span of life has traced. Instances such as these serve to point out the way in which the Work coheres by virtue of a select and recurrent number of symbols. Their genealogy may often be tracked back to simpler images and tropes from which they acquire their ultimate symbolic depth. The difference in function between the early image and its subsequent related symbol is interesting. In its initial role, the image operates as a bridge between the world and the poet's inner emotions. In its development and transition into the later symbol of the Second Epoch, it becomes the stepping-stone that unites an inner and and outer «god-consciousness», in a total apprehension of the cosmos.[55]

The use of symbolism is of course one of the major bonds which relates JRJ with the poets of nineteenth century France. Its pre-eminent virtue, as has been seen, is that of synthesis and unification, as well as promoting the movement toward universals. Another consequence of the use of symbol however—and it is one which was deliberately sought and desired by these poets in common—is a certain impregnability of the poetry for all but a minority of cognoscenti. And here we are further reminded of the intellectual «minoritarismo» of Ortega y Gasset, the élitist sentiments of whom are likewise shared by Rubén Darío. In his «Prefacio» to *Cantos de vida y esperanza,* Darío declares: «Mi respeto por la aristocracia del pensamiento, por la nobleza del Arte siempre es el mismo. Mi antiguo aborrecimiento a la mediocridad, a la mulatez intelectual, a la chatura estética, apenas si se aminora hoy con una razonada indiferencia». For JRJ, as for the French poet Mallarmé, symbolic expression renders the Work accessible only to those prepared actively to collaborate with the poet in their own kind of creative effort toward understanding. That these two poets have much in common is indisputable; but in the following comparison it should nevertheless be remembered that JRJ is by no means as syntactically, or even symbolically, hermetic as Mallarmé. As the poem «Convexidades» illustrates, JRJ is much more «open»:

Vuelve el cielo su espalda,
vuelve su espalda el mar, y entre ambas desnudeces,
resbala el día por mi espalda.

Lo que en el día queda,
es lo que dicen todos todo.
Nuestros tres pechos ¡Dios! están abiertos
contra el todo de todos,
a lo que ignoran todos,
¡hacia todo! (*LP*, p. 441)

[55] For a full analysis of symbolism, see HENRI PEYRE, *Qu'est-ce que le symbolisme?*, Presses Universitaires de France, Paris, 1974.

At the turn of the century, art was becoming increasingly popularized and diffused with the development of the media of press and printing and oral communication, and poetry was becoming prey to an undiscriminating public and a body of journalistic critics altogether too facile and lightweight. A reaction on the part of the ill-served poets themselves was inevitable. The hatred of Mallarmé for the common herd, «le vulgaire», finds its counterpart in JRJ, whose dedication to «la inmensa minoría» is but a thinly disguised and euphemistic equivalent of the French expression. The sentiments expressed by Mallarmé in his lecture entitled «Le "Ten o'clock" de M. Whistler» are unequivocal on the matter of artistic degradation. His proposal, he says, is to speak of Art. With bitter sarcasm he takes up his theme:

> Oui, l'Art—qui depuis peu est devenu, au moins autant que la discussion ou les écrits aient pu en faire cela, une sorte de lieu commun pour l'heure du thé. L'Art court la rue!—un galant de passage lui prend le menton—le maître de maison l'attire à franchir son seuil—on le presse de se joindre à la compagnie, en gage de culture et de raffinement.

Art has suffered slander and defamation by the impertinence and ineptitude of critics and masses alike: «Si la familiarité peut engendrer le mépris, l'Art certainement—ou ce qu'on prend couramment pour lui—en est arrivé à son degré le plus bas d'intimité avec tous». The crass vulgarization of Art is all that its physical accessibility has managed to achieve. Whereas true Art, on the contrary, is not of a public order:

> C'est une divinité d'essence délicate, toute en retrait, elle hait se mettre en avant et ne se propose en aucune manière pour améliorer autrui.

The similarity is striking, here, with that Paterian sentiment:

> For art comes to you professing frankly to give nothing but the highest quality to your moments as they pass, and simply for those moments' sake.

This conception of the absolute non-utilitarianism of Art—a conception manifestly shared by JRJ—was to lend itself to the development of symbolism as a protective barrier against unthinking readership. «Divinité, au-dedans de soi, égoïstement occupée de sa personne seule, n'ayant aucun désir d'enseigner, cherchant et trouvant le beau dans toutes conditions»: such, according to Mallarmé, is the true nature of Art and Poetry. The sanctity of poetry is, then, a religious sanctity, which therefore not only permits but positively demands the envelope of mystery. Hence, it will be incumbent upon the poet to refuse all concessions to the mediocrity of the masses and to abjure all open explanation of his intentions. The symbol will thus provide his refuge and prove the guardian of the holiness of the Poem. Above all, it is the polyvalence of symbolism which achieves these ends. As we have observed, the symbols in the Work of JRJ bear a multiplicity of meanings. They are not mere tokens, each signifying one single specific thing or fact. Their shifting associations require that the reader be constantly working with and alongside their creator in a participatory role which, because of the imaginative and, indeed, creative effort involved, is likely to exclude all but that select «minoría» to whom JRJ adresses himself. Furthermore, the very richness that such polyvalence suggests, means that the symbol can never entirely be exhausted of new possibilities. The Mallarméan «Mystère dans les lettres» is conserved; the indignity of loathsome intimacy circumvented.

This open-ended quality of the symbol, its infinite potential, is of the first magnitude with regard to JRJ's conception of the Work in its entirety. For «una obra», he maintains, «atraerá tanto tiempo cuanto dure su secreto revelado». So long, and no longer. The whole of JRJ's famous lecture on «Poesía cerrada y poesía abierta» stresses the value of open potentiality. And the theme applies not only to the individual life of the poem but to the total life of the Work. Expressing this in a kind of miniature parable, he writes in «Espacio»:

> ¿Un libro, libro? Bueno es dejar un libro grande a medio leer, sobre algún banco, lo grande que termina; y hay que darle una lección al que lo quiere terminar, al que pretende que lo terminemos.

In parenthesis, it is interesting to compare with this the following passage from Mallarmé's «Le livre, instrument spirituel»:

> Sur un banc de jardin, où telle publication neuve, je me réjouis si l'air, en passant, entr'ouvre et, au hasard, anime, d'aspects, l'extérieur du livre: plusieurs—à quoi, tant l'aperçu jaillit, personne depuis qu'on lut, peut-être n'a pensé. Occasion de le faire, quand, libéré, le journal domine, le mien, même, que j'écartai, s'envole près de roses, jaloux de couvrir leur ardent et orgueilleux conciliabule: développé parmi le massif, je le laisserai, aussi les paroles fleurs à leur mutisme et, techniquement, propose, de noter comment ce lambeau diffère du livre, lui suprême. Un journal reste le point de départ; la littérature s'y décharge à souhait.

Closure and termination deal death; the freedom of expansion toward ever new horizons is the source of infinite life for both Poem and Work. Here again, it is the sea which provides the exemplary analogy. Whatever else may have been the differences between JRJ and that other French poet, Paul Valéry, JRJ would surely subscribe to Valéry's concept of the sea «toujours recommencée», in the same way that «un beau vers ne doit jamais s'achever». Not only does JRJ attribute to the sea his own personal «eternidades», but he describes it as «vida sin sueño, siempre abierta; vida sin mar es vida cerrada, poesía cerrada». The circuit of the Work is an open circuit like the circuit of the sea. It admits an infinity of contingencies.

CHAPTER VI

THE IMMANENT NATURE OF JRJ'S POETRY

The Work is neither external nor «other» from JRJ. It is intrinsic or, more accurately, immanent: indwelling in his life and in that Naming which constitutes the very process of creating poetry. The understanding of the last point is of primordial importance and casts the final revealing light on all that has been said up to now.

There are, it may be argued, moments when JRJ himself would appear to refute this. One thinks for instance of the strange «independence» of the Work when, referring to «Espacio» in the prologue to the version given in *Cuadernos americanos,* he says: «Lo que esta escritura sea ha venido libre a mi conciencia poética y a mi expresión relativa, a su debido tiempo, como una respuesta formada de la misma esencia de mi pregunta o, más bien, del ansia mía de buena parte de mi vida, por esta creación singular». Nor, according to the poet, has he any authority over the autonomous «voice» of the Work: «Dentro de mí hay uno que está hablando, hablando [...] No lo puedo callar» («Fragmento tercero»). It would seem from observations such as these that the Work is indeed a quite separate phenomenon from its author. Nevertheless, a closer inspection shows that this «free» poetic advent, possessed of an apparent volition of its own, is in fact simply the result—or «answer»—to an already formulated request: an answer which comes from *within* and which, moreover, stems from the selfsame essence of that initial and so urgent conscious appeal. Request and answer (albeit that the answer comes only in its own good time) are in fact two facets of a single coin. Neither one can therefore truly be said to be autonomous. In the same manner, when JRJ declares his incapacity to control or quieten the voice of his Work it is nonetheless an *inner* voice: integral and integrated. The Work (its poetic tongue) and JRJ remain in indisputable union. «Espacio», that consummate poem in prose, is all the proof required. For all that has been said of its apparent «automatism» («automatic writing»), and of the seeming way in which the Work takes over to result in a Joycean flow of free association, JRJ is still ever in command and abreast of the poetic voice: for they are the same.

The interiority of the Work is expressed in an important letter written from Riverdale, Maryland, by JRJ to Angela Figuera and dated 17 October 1949. «Querida amiga», it begins:

> dios estaba en mí, con inmanencia segura, desde que tuve uso de razón; pero yo no lo sentía con mis sentidos espirituales y corporales que son, naturalmente, los mismos. De pronto, el año pasado, gran año para mí, al poner el pie en el estribo del coche, aquí en Riverdale, camino de New York, camino de la Argentina, lo *sentí,* es decir lo ví, lo olí, lo gusté, lo toqué. Y lo dije, lo canté en el verso que él me dictó. Eso es todo.[1]

In this letter, special caution is needed with reference to the penultimate sentence: «Y lo dije, lo canté en el verso que él me dictó». For it is all too easy to construe this in terms of the nineteenth century Romantic commonplace which purports to make of the poet the tool and passive instrument only of some magically inspired and wholly independent poetic voice from without. This experience of a «divine dictation» should not be allowed to bear the same interpretation as, for example, that of the at first sight comparable experience described by Santa Teresa de Jesús. In chapter XVI of *Su vida* she affirms in not dissimilar terms from those of JRJ that what she writes, she writes at the dictation and inspiration of a perfectly «vocal» and audible God. Her hand, she says, is but the instrument of His voice: «Me dió el Señor hoy [...] esta oración [...] y me puso estas comparaciones y enseñó la manera de decirlo». In his letter, JRJ is describing what is potentially a mystical revelation in which he experiences his «dios» with the same immediacy and intimate totality as does Santa Teresa: a simultaneously spiritual, sensual, physical and almost «geographical» knowledge of the deity. Thus far, it tallies quite remarkably with Santa Teresa's own experience of the God beside her, guiding her pen. Both divinities are apprehended respectively by JRJ and by Santa Teresa with the same totality of the senses—carnal and spiritual alike—and both inspire their receptive listeners in audible dictation. But there is a fundamental difference. The dictating voice of Santa Teresa's God is that of the orthodox Christian God. And He does not reside *within* her. Certainly he is «beside» her, and always so, as she repeatedly tells us. She experiences Him as Christ in His Humanity, a nearly tangible Presence in human shape; but forever distinct, forever separate and other. The «dios» of whom JRJ speaks, on the contrary, is clearly the god of Poetry, the god of the Work. This «dios» of the Work—unlike Teresa's Catholic God—is an immanent and interior deity, part and parcel of the essential JRJ. «Querida amiga», he declares, «dios estaba *en mí*» (my emphasis). The voice of the god of Poetry is, then, no voice from without, belonging to some autonomous god-hood. The revelation experienced by JRJ of what he calls «dios» is neither more nor less than the sudden and total realization of the Work within him: the full apprehension of himself as the Work *in potentia,* and consubstantial with it. The fight to «realize» that god-within was to constitute the very fibre of his life.

It is worth noting that JRJ included Santa Teresa in his enumeration

[1] JRJ, *Cartas literarias,* compiled by Francisco Garfias, Editorial Bruguera, Barcelona, 1977, pp. 175-176.

of those poets whom he regarded as forming the lineage of Spain's authentic poetry, from its beginnings in the *Poema del Cid* through to the works of Antonio Machado. But of the two great mystics, Santa Teresa and San Juan de la Cruz, it should be remembered that it is undoubtedly with the latter that JRJ felt the greater affinity. One possible reason for this may lie just here: in the immanentism which, absent from the works of Santa Teresa, he positively shares in common with the great poet of «Cántico espiritual». « ¡O cristalina fuente! », cries the Esposa who is the poet's own soul:

Si en esos tus semblantes plateados
Formases de repente
Los ojos deseados
Que tengo *en mis entrañas* dibuxados [...] (my emphasis)[2]

Both poets conceive Beauty as immanent in matter, in things material. It lies within, waiting only to be discovered and released. This link with San Juan de la Cruz through the concept of immanentism is further established in their mutual concern with the ineffable. «Poesía inefable existe», JRJ roundly affirms in a conversation with Ricardo Gullón, and continues: «¿Qué es Dios sino un temblor que tenemos dentro, una inmanencia inefable? Los místicos lo hacen, o al menos intentan hacerlo, y lo mismo procura a su manera cada cual, interpretándolo a su modo». The importance of immanentism in JRJ can be adduced from the very frequency with which he makes reference to it in his various critical writings. Thus, for instance, we find in his «Estética y ética estética» the apothegm: «Inmanencia totalmente justa y exacto dinamismo».[3] Indeed, the very organs of Poetry are inherent in the poet: «Número, acento, rima, nunca están en el verso, sino siempre en el poeta». Further, in «La razón heroica» we read that «el que no conciba su inmanencia» is «el que no se da cuenta ni se hace cargo de su destino». Immanentism and the fulfilment of self are inseparables. It is this which explains the «exacto dinamismo» earlier cited as the adjunct of immanentism. For a progressive and mobile development is necessarily the consequence of «inmanencia». In this way, «el espíritu» is quite properly and accurately defined by JRJ as «inmanencia *en marcha*» (my emphasis). Finally, for a conclusive confession of the purely immanent nature of his poetic deity, his Work, we may look to JRJ's «Notas» written for the first edition of *Animal de fondo* in 1949. His statement is unequivocal:

> No que yo haga poesía relijiosa usual; al revés, lo poético lo considero como profundamente relijioso, esa relijión inmanente sin credo absoluto que yo siempre he profesado.

[2] According to St Augustine, the divine spirit is indeed immanent in man, if he look within himself; an opinion probably derived from his neoplatonist leanings. See E. PORTALIÉ's article entitled «Saint Augustin» in the *Dictionnaire de théologie catholique,* Vacant-Mangenot-Amman, I, cols. 2,268-2,472; also 2,506-2,514.

[3] JRJ, «Ideolojía lírica», «Estética y ética estética», *Pájinas escojidas,* p. 144.

Certainly JRJ is one of the most inward-looking writers of his time. A passage from Graciela Palau de Nemes's biography of JRJ corroborates this:

> Despreciando las veleidades exteriores, se había dado gustoso a la vida interior [...] En su ejemplar de *La imitación de Cristo,* de 1882 [...] subrayó los versículos más afines a su conducta. Estos tenían que ver con la concentración en sí mismo [...] Subrayó, entre ellos: «Es cosa laudable que el hombre religioso salga pocas veces, que huya de ser visto y que no quiera ver a los hombres.»[4]

An interesting addendum here is the fact, according to Julián Marías, that this precept of inner withdrawal is close also to the fundamental meaning of phenomenology as extrapolated by Husserl. It is first necessary to lose the world in order to recover it later in the act of consciousness; and this «renueva [...] la frase de San Agustín: Noli foras ire, in te redi, in interiore homine habitat veritas».[5]

The immanence of the poetic Word is described by JRJ—appropriately—in a poem. It is one entitled «Poeta y palabra»:

> La vibrante palabra muda,
> la inmanente,
> única flor que no se dobla,
> única luz que no se estingue,
> única ola sin fracaso. (*LP,* pp. 1171-1172).

Combined with immanence is the concept of emanation, as another poem from the same collection, *La estación total,* exemplifies. It is called «El otoñado»:

> Estoy completo de naturaleza,
> en plena tarde de áurea madurez,
> alto viento en lo verde traspasado.
> Rico fruto recóndito, contengo
> lo grande elemental en mí (la tierra,
> el fuego, el agua, el aire), el infinito.
>
> Chorreo luz: doro el lugar oscuro,
> trasmito olor: la sombra huele a dios,
> emano son: lo amplio es honda música,
> filtro sabor: la mole bebe mi alma,
> deleito el tacto de la soledad.
>
> Soy tesoro supremo, desasido,
> con densa redondez de limpio iris,
> del seno de la acción. Y lo soy todo.

[4] G. Palau de Nemes, *Vida y obra de JRJ,* II, p. 408.

[5] Julián Marías, *Historia de la filosofía,* Revista de Occidente, Madrid, 1964, 17.ª ed., p. 410.

> Lo todo que es el colmo de la nada,
> el todo que se basta y que es servido
> de lo que todavía es ambición. (*LP*, p. 1140)

We may compare the jubilant tone here with the desolate mood of another poem, this time by an English poet. The theme is the same, but the poet is expressing his inadequacy, a moment of dearth. However, before quoting from Samuel Taylor Coleridge's «Dejection, an Ode», it is well to remember a note by Jorge Guillén in his essay entitled «Bécquer o lo inefable soñado» in *Lenguaje y poesía.* Here, Guillén is stressing the same concept of immanentism held by the English Romantic: «Representando a los grandes líricos [...] asienta como verdad fundamental Coleridge: "Todos los verdaderos poetas coinciden en un punto: todos escriben desde dentro, gracias a ese principio interior, y no por algo que se origine fuera"». It is in a passing moment of despair, therefore, that Coleridge, seeking in vain to inspire himself in external natural beauty, cries:

> It were a vain endeavour,
> Though I should gaze for ever
> On that green light that lingers in the west:
> I may not hope from outward forms to win
> The passion and the life, whose fountains are within.
>
> Ah! from the soul itself must issue forth
> A light, a glory, a fair luminous cloud
> Enveloping the Earth—
> And from the soul itself there must be sent
> A sweet and potent voice, of its own birth,
> Of all sweet sounds the life and element.

That «sweet and potent voice» which Coleridge here so urgently desires but which temporarily is denied him, is that selfsame voice of the immanent god of Poetry also honoured by JRJ. JRJ's poem, «El otoñado», expresses the fulfilment of immanence in a moment of perfect plenitude. Coleridge's ode on «Dejection» shows the obverse: the moment of desolation, when the god-within seems absent and silent, denying his own fulfilment. Both poems, however, each in its different way, are celebrations of the concept of immanentism.

In «El otoñado», JRJ is also celebrating that dynamic projection of immanence which results in what may be called «emanation». However, this unilinear outflow from the inner source is not the only trajectory to be traced from immanence. The processional concept that derives from immanentism is one of circularity also, by which the given is received back into its seat of origin. The small poem «Fiesta» will illustrate this better than any attempted paraphrase:

> Las cosas están echadas;
> mas, de pronto, se levantan,
> y, en procesión alumbrada,
> se entran, cantando, en mi alma. (*LP*, p. 879)

Again, this idea of a procession perpetually emanating outwards and then revolving back upon itself to its own source, is to be found reiterated in a phrase from the Coleridge Ode:

> We receive but what we give
> And in our life alone does Nature live.

The theme is one which is given explicit treatment in a number of JRJ's poems. I shall consider briefly four of these, two taken from the first section of *La estación total,* and two from *Diario de un poeta reciencasado.*

The second stanza of the poem «Lo que sigue» reads:

> Entramos y salimos sonriendo,
> llenos los ojos de totalidad,
> de la tarde a la eternidad, alegres
> de lo uno y lo otro. Y de seguir,
> de entrar y de seguir.
> Y de salir. (*LP,* p. 1138)

The «chopo de oro» of the following third stanza draws together the threads of these motions, recognizing «qué bello al ir a ser es haber sido», and thus itself becoming the «síntesis del destino fiel». The poplar tree here exemplifies, in the conversely positive form, that dictum of JRJ that «el que no conciba su inmanencia es el que no se da cuenta ni se hace cargo de su destino». For the poplar is indeed manifestly «aware»—aware, that is, of the beauty of its own inner knowledge of past being, as it goes forth to meet that immanent future of which equally it has full knowledge. It is this conscious conception of «inmanencia» which allows the poplar to become the synthesis of its true destiny.

Again, in «Su sitio fiel», the theme of processional entry and exit points to the perfection of a destiny whose end is in its beginning:

> El fin está en el centro. Y se ha sentado
> aquí, su sitio fiel, la eternidad.
>
> Para esto hemos venido [...]
> Y todos los destinos aquí salen,
> aquí entran, aquí suben, aquí están.
> Tiene el alma un descanso de caminos
> que han llegado a su único final. (*LP,* p. 1170)

My last two examples are two sea-poems from *Diario de un poeta reciencasado,* both of which hinge upon the processional concept. «Soledad» (*LP,* p. 243) stresses the perpetual come-and-go of the waves, metaphorically interchangeable with the ever emanating and returning thoughts of the poet; whilst the poem beginning «No sé si el mar es, hoy» expresses the fusion—and confusion—between the sea and the poet's heart. Their interchangeability is again described in terms of procession:

> Entran, salen
> uno de otro, plenos e infinitos,

como dos todos únicos.
A veces, me ahoga el mar el corazón,
hasta los cielos mismos.
Mi corazón ahoga el mar, a veces,
hasta los mismos cielos. (*LP*, p. 469)

Finally, it should be remembered that the use of vocabulary such as this—emanation and procession—is a profane adaptation of the religious origins from which they derive.[6] The processional concept of Poetry is an extension of the concept of immanentism. It has already been seen that the liturgical procession of «que por mí vayan todos» in the famous poem «¡Intelijencia, dame» reveals an unmistakeable quasi-religious tone. It is not therefore irrelevant to consider in the light of this, the writings of St Thomas Aquinas on the Divine Processus: God, made manifest in His Son, Christ, and thence in the Word, is returned unto Himself, through the Word.[7] Emanating originally from God, the Word duly returns to that First Source. Such, likewise, for JRJ is the Procession of the immanent deity of the poetic Word.

«Espacio»: showcase of the immanent work

The prose poem «Espacio», written in three «Fragmentos» and dated 1941-1942-1954, is the showcase of the Immanent Work. It is the Work in microcosm. Further, it is in «Espacio» that JRJ shows himself to be the liberator of both Spanish verse and prose. In it, he expurgates from the Spanish language certain restrictions which on the one hand late Romanticism and on the other, the prosaic approach of Positivism, had sought to impose.[8] In a sense, his achievement is parallel to that of James Joyce in the English language. Of JRJ's «Espacio» much the same can be said as does Stephen Spender of Joyce's *Ulysses*. In their respective works, each writer invented «one of those systems—like cubism or abstractism—which seem to undermine other work of contemporaries». Each invented «not a literary method but a method», a method whereby interior monologue was to be as convincing as objective realism. The development of this method led along theoretical lines which eventually superseded realism to culminate in the

[6] It may be that JRJ was also drawing on Plotinus' Theory of Emanation. The English poet, William Blake, with whom JRJ manifests certain affinities, undoubtedly did so as George Mills Harper points out in his *The Neoplatonism of William Blake,* University of North Carolina Press, 1961, p. 241.

[7] See my earlier note 21 to chapter II for JRJ's reading of Aquinas. Menéndez y Pelayo, I, pp. 262-265 specifically treats of Aquinas' notion of Procession in connection with aesthetics: «La primera *procesión formal* que se verifica en el entendimiento es la aprehensión de la verdad [...] A la verdad absoluta responde la procesión de la luz [intelectual]», etc. (author's emphasis).

[8] Carlos Bousoño's analysis of linguistic breakthrough in poetry is pertinent to «Espacio», particularly those chapters which deal with «desplazamiento calificativo»; «superposición» («temporal», «espacial», «situacional», «significacional», etc.); and above all «la ruptura del sistema». *Teoría de la expresión poética,* Gredos, Madrid, 1970, chs 5, 8 and 11.

disintegration of reality in fiction, yet with an undeniable logic which quite precluded any turning back.[9]

The breakthrough to the prose poetry of «Espacio» and to JRJ's final announcement of the wish that his entire Work be rendered in «one immense paragraph», had been initiated in that first all-important Atlantic voyage in 1916. The rhythmic waters of that long crossing (30 January to 12 February) inspired the «verso libre» which was to be the hallmark of JRJ's Second Epoch. The culmination of this development, and the decision to move into prose, was to find its full realization in the appearance of «Espacio» together with the conversion into prose of certain of the poems from *Diario de un poeta reciencasado.* That is to say, in the year 1944. An important, although unpublished, note which is cited by Ricardo Gullón in his book *El último JRJ,* merits attention here. It is dated 3 January 1954:

> Hoy, en mis 72 años, y en este Puerto Rico donde me siento más español que en España, harto de tanto verso como se está escribiendo en el mundo y en España concretamente, me hubiese gustado no haber escrito nada en verso, o por lo menos, en verso con rima consonante o asonante, haber escrito sólo en prosa lírica o crítica, más crítica o más lírica, quiero decir. Pero ya que esto no lo puedo arreglar ahora y que tampoco podría borrar lo así escrito ya que ha circulado tanto en tantas partes, me [this part is missing] ... Sin embargo, puedo imponerme un castigo aparte del de revivirlo todo para intentar mejorarlo; voy a imprimirlo todo desde hoy en forma de prosa, como en un archivo inevitable. Por lo menos así tendrá lo mío alguna ventaja: hacer menos vistosa la rima, reducir la superficie impresa con los poemas y enseñar a leer y a decir el verso a muchos que no lo saben. Y sobre todo a quienes lo recitan en público.

Despite the fact that this was written at so late a date in his life, nevertheless a full eleven years earlier JRJ was already claiming an entire lifetime of preoccupation with this new form of prosody. From his prologue to the first stanza of «Espacio», published in *Cuadernos americanos,* vol. XI, n.º 5, September-October 1943, we read:

> Toda mi vida he acariciado la idea de un poema seguido (¿cuántos milímetros, metros, kilómetros?) sin asunto concreto, sostenido sólo por la sorpresa, el ritmo, el hallazgo, la luz, la ilusión sucesiva, es decir, por sus elementos intrínsecos, por su esencia.

The logical conclusion to this was the view that prose and verse were not two separate genres in themselves, but that the sole differentiating factor between them was «la rima». «Si no la hay, todo es prosa, y ésta puede recortarse y escribirse en verso». He gives a lively illustration to this argument by using an extract from the opening lines of *Don Quijote.* The famous Cervantine prose is rendered in octosyllabics, thus:

En un lugar de La Mancha
de cuyo nombre no quiero

[9] STEPHEN SPENDER, *The Making of a Poem,* W. W. Norton, New York, 1962, pp. 89-90.

acordarme, no ha mucho
tiempo que vivía un
hidalgo de los de lanza
en astillero, adarga
antigua, rocín flaco y
galgo corredor. Una olla... etc.

The example adequately confirms JRJ's assertion that the «romance octosílabo» is indeed «el pie con que camina toda la escritura española en verso y prosa». Discussing the business of writing poetry, and in particular the ballad form, in «Dos líneas permanentes de la poesía española», he declares:

> Es claro que el verso del romance octosílabo puede ser, lo mismo que es ahora y ha sido mucho (con consonante o asonante alternados), un verso de dieciséis con asonante o consonante par, pues el ritmo, naturalmente, permanece el mismo, y un ciego no sabría distinguir entre uno y otro. Para un ciego el verso y la prosa serían iguales. Y en realidad no existe el verso más que por el consonante o el asonante, por la rima. El ciego es siempre una gran autoridad para la escritura poética. Si no se viese escrita la poesía, ¡qué distintas serían las opiniones sobre ella!

It is now that he expresses his regret at having adopted the foreign techniques of the Parnassian and Symbolist schools in his youth, and lauds instead the intrinsically Spanish « ¡Romance, "riomío de mi huir"; canción con todas mis alas, verso libre sólo mío, y prosa, prosa mía enamorada! ».

The justification for this new departure into prose is above all, for JRJ, the rule of the ear over the rule of the eye:

> Tome un poema y recítelo pensando que todos los oyentes son ciegos. Precisamente, la mayoría de los lectores se hacen cargo del poema, en primer término, por como lo ven. El verso libre es prosa y puede escribirse como tal. Si no fuera por la rima no habría verso, y no encuentro inconveniente en que el poema se escriba seguido.

In substantiation of this, JRJ again refers to the ballad and its history. Initially written in prolonged lines of sixteen syllables, it was simply in order to accommodate it to the narrow pages on which the «juglares» transcribed the text that it was chopped into the shorter octosyllables. A measure of practical expediency; not of aesthetics. What JRJ means in pointing this out is that the division of poetry into interrupted lines is of no especial aid to the reader. On the contrary, the most efficient yardstick whereby to test true poetry is to render it into prose. Neither music nor poetry—those two so closely related arts—is visual in character, he declares. In short, «al escribir en prosa un poema, al escribirlo seguido, la poesía gana». This is precisely what he will do with «Espacio».

However, it should not be thought that this conception of poetry represented any sudden volte face, nor that it was some merely arbitrary caprice of a man reaching the end of his life. From a conversation held between JRJ and Guerrero Ruiz as early as June 1915, there is evidence that this apparently new conception had in fact been incubating throughout a lifetime. «A veces», he confessed to his friend in that early year in his career, «pienso que tal vez esté en las postrimerías de mi obra poética, porque al fin y al cabo encuentro algo artificioso en la forma poética, y me pregunto: ¿es honrado esto? Acaso no, a pesar de su belleza. Por eso tal vez escriba ya prosa solamente, una prosa que, claro está, sea poética, elevada, pura [...] Debemos escribir como se habla, de una manera clara, elevada, natural». Significantly enough, the exquisite prose of *Platero y yo* had already by this time made its first appearance, in 1914, in the Biblioteca Juventud, published by *La lectura,* Madrid, with the completed edition coming out in 1916. In January of 1931, moreover, Guerrero Ruiz records that «ahora le interesa más la prosa, y su gusto sería trabajar unos cuantos años en prosa para dejar una labor equivalente a la que ha realizado en verso». Already JRJ was experiencing the feeling that he had exhausted all the traditional poetic forms, and that he must move on: «Cuando él mira hacia su obra no se siente "satisfecho"; no es ésta la palabra», says Guerrero Ruiz, «es más bien contento lo que siente, pues en realidad ha creado todas las formas posibles. El ciclo poético queda completado desde el romance a la canción, hasta el verso desnudo».

Again, it is worth noting that *La colina de los chopos,* one of JRJ's most lyrical prose collections, was composed between the early years of 1914 and 1920; whilst the prose poems which were to become part of his book, *Cuadernos,* were composed and variously published in magazines between the years 1925 and 1935. Finally, JRJ's early inclination toward prose poetry can find no better witness than the poet's own description of the very first poem he wrote: «Mi primera poesía fue en prosa y se llamaba "Andén"».[10] Graciela Palau de Nemes also records that JRJ's very next composition, his second only, was similarly a prose piece: «Riente cementerio», published in the journal *Córdoba.* As she states: «En Juan Ramón primero fue la prosa, después el verso».[11] Evidence enough exists therefore to establish the fact that «Espacio», epitomizing the final Juanramonian aesthetics, is the outcome of early and seminal thinking which slowly and consistently had been maturing over the years.

According to JRJ, it was the physical and visual aspect of Miami which provided the final trigger of inspiration to the uninterrupted prose form of «Espacio»:

> (Miami) es un arrecife de coral que se presenta como una línea horizontal, recta. Pues bien: esa línea y ese paisaje me hicieron concebir según es el poema «Espacio» [...] El poema quiere ser también algo de horizontes ilimitados, sin obstáculos; dar la impresión de que podría seguir sin fin, continuamente [...] Yo lo compararía también con un friso. Miami es como el poema: llano, amplio, sin una colina ni un obstáculo que se oponga a la vista; todo es espacio abierto, libre.

This geographical impact on the literary creation is given further emphasis by the majority of JRJ's critics, and notably by Graciela Palau de Nemes in her biography.

[10] JRJ, *El modernismo,* p. 54.
[11] G. Palau de Nemes, *Vida y obra de JRJ,* I, pp. 75-77.

I have described «Espacio» as the showcase of the Immanent Work, and the microcosm of the entire corpus of JRJ's poetry. A close analysis of the prose poem is necessary in order to justify such a claim. First, however, we should be aware that precisely this fact—that «Espacio» draws together the Work in its entirety—has been the object of some adverse criticism. Bernardo Gicovate, for instance, finds fault with the prose poem on the grounds that it cannot properly be apprehended without a close knowledge of all that precedes it, so strict is the inter-relationship. The reader approaching «Espacio» without an acquaintance of the total preceding Work, he argues, «no comprendería más que las palabras en su esqueleto de significado, ya que sólo existe el poema ("Espacio") en función de lo que ya se ha leído. Por consiguiente, tendremos que admitir que "Espacio" no tiene existencia en sí».[12] Certainly we may agree that «Espacio» demands of its reader a certain literary cultural background; but to deny its independent poetic value must surely be mistaken.

In synopsis, the poem is structured on a chain of questions. The poet, finding himself in the world of real phenomena, seeks the reason for the existence of these, and—more importantly—their essence. That is, he queries the how and the why of the essence of the cosmos, as also of the human condition itself. «¿Por qué», he demands, «comemos y bebemos otra cosa que luz o fuego?» Or again, he speculates: «¿Esperan más (las plantas) que verdear, que florear y que frutar; [...] más que quedarse sin luz, más que dormirse y despertar?» Further, he seeks to know his own relationship with the universe. How does his essential being relate with the essential world? Or how, indeed, does his physical body relate to space? In attempting the resolution of these incertitudes, he claims not parity with the gods, but that the gods have parity with him, in a jubilant self-affirmation of divinity. Through the god of his own consciousness, he will conquer the inexplicable and will transcend both Space and Time: «Nada es la realidad sin el Destino de una conciencia que realiza». The implication is that the gods themselves could not have gone any further than JRJ in *their* achievements or in *their* consciousness. A declaration of the purely immanent nature of the Work is heard in the words: « ¡Espacio y tiempo y luz en todo yo, en todos y yo y todos! »

In the very opening sentence of the poem, JRJ measures himself against the gods. Significantly, he relegates them to a closed past, whilst placing himself by contrast in a present which is clearly intended to be understood as the eternal present:

> Los dioses no tuvieron más sustancia que la que tengo yo [...] ¿Quién sabe más que yo, quién, qué hombre o qué dios puede, ha podido, podrá decirme a mí qué es mi vida y mi muerte, qué no es? Si hay quien lo sabe, yo lo sé más que ése, y si quien lo ignora, más que ése lo ignoro.

The pride of the poet is, in a way, the pride of Job in confrontation with the God of *The Old Testament*. The parallel, of course, bears the difference

12 B. Gicovate, *La poesía de JRJ*, p. 168.

that whilst Job acknowledges himself to be a creature of God, JRJ categorically denies any such thing. Nevertheless, the comparison is an interesting one. The language of JRJ is not dissimilar from the language of Job. Although again, it should be remembered that Job limits himself to questioning God, whereas JRJ is challenging the very superiority of God. Proudly Job cries:

> Todo esto lo ven mis ojos, lo ha oído mi oído y lo entendió.
>
> Lo que vosotros sabéis, lo sé yo también; no soy menos que vosotros.
>
> Pero yo quisiera hablar con el Omnipotente y quisiera venir a cuentas con Dios.[13]

If we pursue for a moment—and with due caution—the interest of this biblical parallel, bearing in mind that JRJ certainly read the Bible with close attention,[14] could we not interpret «Espacio» as JRJ's own personal answer to questions similar to the ones set before Job by God? In chapters XXXVIII to LVI of *The Book of Job,* God asserts his omnipotence and the helplessness of mere man. An extract reads:

> Voy a preguntarte, respóndeme tú.
>
> ¿Dónde estabas al fundar yo la tierra? Dímelo, si tanto sabes.
>
> ¿Quién determinó, si lo sabes, sus dimensiones? ¿Quién tendió sobre ella la regla?
>
> ¿Sobre qué descansan sus cimientos o quién asentó su piedra angular entre las aclamaciones de los astros matutinos y los aplausos de todos los hijos de Dios?

The answer of Job to these and other interrogations proving the debility of man and his dependence upon The Almighty, is one of total submission:

> ¡Cuán pequeño soy! ¿Qué voy a responder? Pondré mano a mi boca. Una vez hablé, no hablaré más. Dos veces, no añadiré palabra.

Let us now compare this with the imprecations of JRJ to the whole assembly of the gods. Far from the humility of Job, his reply could not be more different in tone. He is not only the equal, but the superior of the gods:

> Yo tengo, como ellos, la sustancia de todo lo vivido y de todo lo porvenir. No soy presente sólo, sino fuga raudal de cabo a fin.

In other words: Yes! he would indeed affirm that he was present at the laying of the foundations of the earth; Yes! he knows the measures of it,

[13] *Job,* 13. 1-3. The Spanish version is given here and in the following biblical citations in order to point out more clearly the affinity between the biblical language and that of JRJ. E. Nácar Fuster and A. Colunga, Biblioteca de Autores Cristianos, Madrid, MCMLV.

[14] There are no less than twelve biblical works and exegeses in the personal library of JRJ in Moguer. Three of these works are by Ernest Renan, who considered the Gospels in the light of his own scepticism.

its fastening and its corner stone. Yes! he was there when the morning stars sang together, and all the sons of God shouted for joy. He is not inferior. And his poem in prose will reveal his transcendental power over Time and over Space, precisely through the unique god that is his own consciousness. As Rubén Darío says, in *El canto errante:* «La actividad humana no se ejercita por medio de la ciencia y de los conocimientos actuales, sino en el vencimiento del tiempo y del espacio. Yo he dicho: Es el Arte el que vence el espacio y el tiempo».[15]

For JRJ, the only evidence of God is *his* (JRJ's) own personal relationship with the universe. No other proof exists for him—(and in this he is not far from existentialist philosophers, most especially Ortega). «Espacio», therefore, in which JRJ subsumes the very Nature of God, must ultimately be seen as a supreme blasphemy—a blasphemy expressed in very fine poetry.

A quotation from Unamuno's *Del sentimiento trágico de la vida* will help to clarify to some extent some of the problems of consciousness and godhood that the poem «Espacio» poses. In the chapter «De Dios a Dios», Unamuno says:

> Y es que sentimos a Dios, más bien que como una conciencia sobrehumana, como la conciencia misma del linaje humano todo, pasado, presente y futuro, como la conciencia colectiva de todo el linaje, y aún más, como la conciencia total e infinita que abarca y sostiene las conciencias todas [...] La divinidad que hay en todo, desde la más baja, es decir, desde la menos conciente forma viva hasta la más alta, pasando por nuestra conciencia humana, la sentimos personalizada, conciente de sí misma, en Dios.[16]

All this finds expression in the parabolic encounter in «Espacio» of JRJ with the crab—one of those «lowest of living forms» mentioned by Unamuno. It is the poet's heedless crushing of this creature into a «cáscara vana» which brings home the realization of the heroism and divine sanctity of what is now nothing but a «hueco». Here is the sudden awareness of the essential identity of consciousness between crab and man, between invertebrate and vertebrate organism, both enveloped in the universal consciousness of God: «Y en el espacio de aquel hueco inmenso y mudo, dios y yo éramos dos». But it must be realized that this is not a mystic

15 RUBÉN DARÍO, *El canto errante, Poesías completas,* edited by Alfonso Méndez Plancarte and Antonio Oliver Belmás, Aguilar, Madrid, 1967, p. 698.

16 M. DE UNAMUNO, *OC,* XVI, pp. 302-303. On divinity as the projection of the consciousness of the human race, see Sanz del Río's translation of Krause's *Ideal de la humanidad para la vida.* In her study of *Helios* and other «modernista» periodicals, P. O'Riordain draws attention to the influence of «krausista» thought on the founders of *Helios:* «Si el espíritu de Rubén preside la revista en primer término, al fondo se adivina la figura de Giner de los Ríos». She further quotes R. Pérez de Ayala as saying: «Ningún libro mejor que el *Ideal de la humanidad para la vida* de Krause para inquerir cuál sea mi deber». There is a review by P. de AYALA in *Helios* of a book by ALVARO DE ALBORNOZ called *No liras, lanzas,* in which P. de Ayala quotes extensively from *Ideal de la humanidad para la vida.* There is no doubt too that JRJ's interest in oriental religions and readings of Rabindranath Tagore must have been influential in this matter.

fusion between God and man. That «dos» is strongly positioned, and they remain emphatically separate entities. The fact that it is precisely the *space* of that hollow husk which jolts the poet into the knowledge of his own divinity, is supremely important. It relates directly with the title and totality of the poem.

In this and other ways, the poet discovers his relationship with the world of phenomena: that of universal harmonious identity. It is the absoluteness of this self-integration with phenomena that gives him the grounds for his self-appointed godhood. Equivalence with the poplar tree in Madrid, advising him to follow its own example: «Termínate en ti mismo, como yo»; intimacy with the pine tree of Fuentepiña: « ¡Qué amigo un árbol, aquel pino [...] junto a la casa de mi Fuentepiña! »; tender integration with a sea of love, seeking the touch of his hands «como un cordero blanco»; self-identification—«tronco de invierno soy»—with an uprooted stump on a beach; or oneness with a bird: «tú y yo, pájaro, somos uno»:—all these are manifestations of a divine unity with the world of natural phenomena. They represent, in effect, that «ritmo vejetativo» which JRJ calls «mi tercer ritmo, más cercano [...] al de la poesía». JRJ is at the centre of this cosmic harmony: «Unidad de unidades es lo uno», he says, and «Espacio» is the hymn of praise to that perfect universal concordance whose corollary is Love and Beauty. It is the song of a bird, toward the end of the «Fragmento primero», which triggers off a definitive vision of world concord and an evocation of peace in the cosmos, akin both in theme and lyricism to that other—biblical—vision of reconciliation. « ¡El canto! », exclaims JRJ; and immediately, conjured before his eyes, he sees «jugando al pájaro y la ardilla, al gato y la gallina, al elefante y al oso, al hombre con el hombre». Curiously comparable with this apotheosis is the following extract from *Isaiah* 11. 6-7:

> Habitará el lobo con el cordero, y el leopardo se acostará con el cabrito, y comerán juntos el becerro y el león [...]
>
> La vaca pacerá con la osa, y las crías de ambas se echarán juntas, y el león, como el buey, comerá paja.

Profane, and divine, both are the expression of apocalyptic Peace and Unity.[17]

It is notable that JRJ's vision is immediately subsequent upon music,

17 There is a parallel here in the admixture of the profane with the divine in the poems of William Blake. George Mills Harper quotes Northrop Frye on the subject: «Blake's "feeling that the Bible does not exhaust the Word of God" accounts for what Northrop Frye calls "contrapuntal symbolism, that is, the use of un-Christian mythology, usually Classical, to supplement and round out a Christian poem"». G. M. Harper, *The Neoplatonism of William Blake,* p. 201. With regard to JRJ as an apocalyptic poet, Frank Kermode's *The Sense of an Ending,* Oxford University Press, New York, 1967, gives a useful general discussion of Apocalypse in literature, the early chapters being the most relevant here. «Apocalypse», he says, «depends on a concord of imaginatively recorded past and imaginatively predicted future» (p. 8). Further on he discusses the «virtual time» of books as, in Suzanne K. Langer's phrase, a «man-centred model of world-time, and the book as world-model» (p. 52).

the music of a bird. Harmony and music are inseparables in «Espacio». Moreover, they are of the very fabric of the poem, lending it literary unity as a recurrent motif. Already, in his «Epílogo» to «Poesía cerrada y poesía abierta», JRJ had observed the role of music in the revelation of the universe: «Y este es el drama poco pensado del poeta: que tiene que descifrar el secreto hermoso del mundo, cantando, y cantando de un modo sacro, gracioso y dado al mismo tiempo, como quiso Platón, siendo como es un hombre.» The cortex or surface of the world embraces a hidden nucleus which is its true meaning and origin, and it is for the poet with his divine Orphic endowments to reveal this. The pre-eminent importance of song is corroborated similarly by Rubén Darío: «La necesidad del canto: el canto es lo único que libra de lo que llama Maeterlinck lo trágico de todos los días. A medida que el tiempo pasa y a pesar del triunfo de los adelantos materiales, la omnipotencia órfica se acentúa y se hace cada vez más invencible.»[18] The sacred singing of the poet to which JRJ alludes is not an empty metaphor, nor is the idea of cosmic harmony other than authentically true for him. His own fusion with the natural phenomena of the world, intermittently expressed in the poetic voice, is the manifestation of this fundamental «concors». Not for nothing does JRJ say of his beloved poet, San Juan de la Cruz, that he «habló la música que es armonía de eternidad y vida, sustancia y esencia». «Espacio» itself is a transcribed poem of the lyrical harmony of the universe—the concept of which was developed by the Neoplatonists of the ancient world from root-ideas in the Pythagoreans and, of course, in Plato himself. Hence, the «matemático celeste» to whom JRJ addresses himself in the «Fragmento primero» is a referential signpost to Pythagorean harmonies—harmonies which underscore the poem and which are lyrically manifest in phrasings of such incantatory quality as the following: «Alas, cantos, luz, palmas, olas, frutas me rodean, me envuelven en su ritmo, en su gracia, en su fuerza delicada; y yo me olvido de mí entre ello, y bailo y canto y río y lloro por los otros, embriagado.» The music of the spheres, in its Boethian triplicate of «musica mundana», «humana» and «instrumentalis», permeates «Espacio»: «Yo oigo siempre esa música que suena en el fondo de todo, más allá; ella es la que me llama desde el mar, por la calle, en el sueño.» The nightingale is «sólo un calumniado prólogo» to that grand orchestration. The oneness of all beings derives from this quintessence of world-melody, and time and again the poet takes up the refrain: «Tú y yo, pájaro, somos uno; cántame, canta tú, que yo te oigo, que mi oído es tan justo por tu canto. Ajústame tu canto más a este oído mío que espera que lo llenes de armonía. ¡Vas a cantar! toda otra primavera, vas a cantar. ¡Otra vez tú, otra vez la primavera! » In song and in music, Time is vanquished: eternal recurrence triumphs.

It has been said earlier that amongst the questions posed by the poet in «Espacio» is that of the reason for the existence of things, their essence. It is a notable feature of «Espacio» that the particular is frequently suppressed in favour of the universal. The generic is used to such an extent as to

[18] RUBÉN DARÍO, «Unamuno, poeta», *La Nación,* Buenos Aires, 1909.

imply a deliberate attempt to capture the essence that lies behind the specific. The famous example of « ¡No le toques ya más, / que así es *la* rosa! » (my emphasis) has already elsewhere been cited. But it is in «Espacio» that the Platonic theory of Ideas (essences) is perhaps best exemplified. The following extract amply shows the use of the generic to attain the intrinsic essence: « ¡Pobre del hombre si la mujer oliera, supiera siempre a rosa! ¡Qué dulce la mujer normal, qué tierna, qué suave (Villon), qué forma de las formas, qué esencia, qué sustancia de las sustancias, las esencias; qué lumbre de las lumbres; la mujer, madre, hermana, amante! ».

It is to the title itself of the poem that we should now address our attention: «Espacio». It is interesting to note that the concept of space is a preoccupation also of Antonio Machado. Through the mouthpiece of his alter ego, Juan de Mairena, he says:

> Meditando sobre la cuarta dimensión del espacio, llegué yo a dudar de las otras tres, a descubrir que el espacio en que yo pensaba, un gran vacío de toda materia, la nada primigenia anterior a todo cuerpo y a toda forma geométrica imaginable, no podía tener ninguna dimensión. El día que comprenda—pensaba yo—que ese espacio pueda tener tres dimensiones, ¿por qué no comprender que tenga cuatro?[19]

The word «space» has for us, nowadays, daring connotations. Scientific investigations, astronautical explorations, advances in the knowledge of Physics and Mathematics, all have to do with the great phenomenon of Space. Moreover, the concept not only of Space but of Time also, has undergone a revolution within the twentieth century. The discoveries of the Quantum Theory have proved the inseparability of Space and Time. Physicists now speak of Space-Time. The work of Planck (1858-1947), of Rutherford (1871-1937), of Einstein (1879-1955), of Fermi (1901-1954) and of very many others, have upturned all former understanding of the dimensions of Space and Time. The extraordinary achievement of JRJ in «Espacio» is to have intruded with the poetic Word into the new scientific conception of the universe. He is ahead of his era. Indeed, we may venture to say that with the poetic language of «Espacio», he most closely parallels the language of the scientists—the language, that is, of Physics and Mathematics. The modernity of «Espacio», properly understood, is such as to shock. That modernity shocks poetically, just as modern scientific visions of the universe shock the layman. It is vital to our understanding of the daring literary adventure that is «Espacio», to remember that from 1913 to 1915 JRJ lived in the Residencia de Estudiantes in Madrid, and that in this atmosphere of intellectual and spiritual liberalism, he came into contact with many of the most forceful thinkers, artists and scientists of the time, from all over Europe. Alberto Jiménez-Fraud, in an article about the Residencia which appeared in a special issue of the *Texas Quarterly* entitled *Image of Spain,* stresses the spirit of intellectual adventure fostered by the institution: «The continual relationship with these eminent

[19] A. MACHADO, *Juan de Mairena, Obras: poesía y prosa,* pp. 497-498.

scholars, far from distracting the Residencia from its two fundamental activities, the educational and the didactic, contributed towards lending these activities not only an intellectual stimulus but also that spirit of adventure without which a true liberal education cannot exist.»[20] JRJ was undoubtedly influenced by this atmosphere of stimulation and scholarly daring throughout at least three of the most important years of his life. Remarkably significant too, to our study of «Espacio» and its extraordinary new contribution to literature, is the fact (recorded by Jiménez-Fraud in the same article) that Einstein himself attended the Residencia as did also the famous science-fiction writer and novelist, H. G. Wells. Contact, direct or indirect, with men such as these must almost certainly have counted for something in the shaping of the poet.

In his lecture course on «modernismo», JRJ was already drawing the parallel between poetic and scientific advance: «[El] poeta [es un] inventor hacia el futuro. Lo mismo ocurre con [el] científico. Se ataca más mientras más precursor. Einstein pide a astrónomos demuestren teoría de la relatividad. Un inventor es un tío raro, extraño.»[21] Later on, in the same course of lectures, he stressed the innovatory nature of the twentieth century in every realm: poetry, science and philosophy alike. Poetry, no less than science, was making supreme new progress: «Lo que ocurre es que en ese momento hubo un gran renacimiento poético [...] Porque el siglo xx, comienzos del siglo xx, es un gran siglo en todo el mundo, lo mismo en la ciencia, la física, por ejemplo, Einstein.»[22] The analogy that I have been implying between the significance of «Espacio» and the Einsteinian theory of Relativity is an admittedly risky one—even arguably extravagant. JRJ's knowledge of contemporary Physics was unlikely to be profound or detailed. Nevertheless there is little reason to suppose that he should not have been acquainted with the broad outlines of the special theory of Relativity, formulated in 1905, to the effect that all movement is related to the system of references in which the observer, who is measuring it, is situated. On this premise, Space and Time are no longer absolute entities; they are subject to the principle of relativity. It is a principle which, moreover, likewise governs the simultaneity of events. The classical notion of simultaneity supposes absolute Time. The relativist notion, on the contrary, posits that what may appear to be simultaneous to one observer may not appear so to another. The works of Einstein were certainly available in Spain. His *Uber die spezielle und die allgemeine Relativitätstheorie, gemeinverständlich* (1917) was translated into Spanish as *Teoría de la relatividad especial y general* in 1921 with further editions appearing in 1923 and 1925. In 1939 *La física, aventura del pensamiento* came out, translated from *Die Physik als Abenteuer der Erkenntnis,* published in 1938; and in 1948 appeared *El significado de la relatividad,* translated

20 ALBERTO JIMÉNEZ-FRAUD, «The "Residencia de Estudiantes"», *Image of Spain, Texas Quarterly,* The University of Texas, Austin, edited by Ramón Martínez-López, IV, núm. 1, 1961, p. 51.

21 JRJ, *El modernismo,* p. 97.

22 *Ibid.,* p. 201.

from the second edition of the English version, *The Meaning of Relativity.* Suffice it to add two more works by different authors which found their way into Spanish translation, to show the availability of literature on these subjects to meet the demands of interest. Bertrand Russell's *The ABC of Relativity* was translated in the same year as its publication, 1925, under the title *El ABC de la relatividad;* and *Relativitätstheorie und Philosophie,* published in 1924 by H. Driesch, was available in Spain in 1927 as *La teoría de la relatividad y la filosofía.*

If analogies upon the relativity of Space and Time are to be drawn, it is however probably safer to cease speculating on Einsteinian influence on «Espacio» and turn to the surer ground of Bergsonian philosophy.

That JRJ was familiar with the writings of Henri Bergson is evidenced by a number of allusions to him in *El modernismo* (p. 53; p. 114; p. 175 and p. 223) amongst which, moreover, JRJ signals Bergson as a «modernista». Bergson's major works were all available in Spanish translation: *Essai sur les données immédiates de la conscience* (1889); *Matière et mémoire* (1896); *L'évolution créatrice* (1907); *L'énergie spirituelle* (1919); *Durée et simultanéité. A propos de la théorie d'Einstein* (1922); and *La pensée et le mouvant* (1934). A good number of books and articles were also published in Spain on the subject of Bergson and his philosophy, of which a representative selection would include the following: M. García Morente, *La filosofía de Bergson* (1917); Alejandro Korn, «Bergson» and «Bergson en la filosofía contemporánea» in his *Obras,* II, pp. 111-143; and E. Molina, *Proyecciones de la intuición. Nuevos estudios sobre la filosofía bergsoniana* (1935). In 1936 a variety of authors contributed to *Homenaje a Bergson* (University of Córdoba, Argentina); and in 1941 another *Homenaje a Bergson* appeared with the composite authorship of J. Gaos, O. Robles, J. Vasconcelos and J. Xirau. 1941 saw also the publication of J. Zaragüeta's *La intuición en la filosofía de Henri Bergson;* whilst in 1943 Joaquín Xirau brought out his *Vida, pensamiento y obra de Bergson,* and Diamantino Martins, his *Bergson: la intuición como método de la metafísica.* Bergsonian philosophy was evidently readily accessible.

The importance of Bergson's work is that it marks the transition from positivism to metaphysics or, in other terms, from the thinking of the nineteenth century to that of the twentieth. His ideas on Space and Time differ radically from those of Kant. According to Bergson, they should no longer be thought of as comparable and parallel terms. Space, he argues, is an aggregate of points, from any one of which we can pass to any other; Time, however, is irreversible in that every moment is an irreplaceable, true creation to which it is impossible to return. Nevertheless, this Time is not clock-time or—in Bergson's own words—«spatialized» time. It is «living» time, as apprehended in its immediate reality by the consciousness: that is, «durée réelle». Space and Time are to each other as matter to memory, as the body to the soul. They correspond to the two basically differing intellectual modes of thought and intuition, and it is this latter alone which is capable of apprehending «real duration», conceptual thought being impotent to seize the meaning of life and real Time. As an interpolation at this point, we may note here the reason for Ortega's scrupulous choice of the term «vital reason»: he had learned the value of the Bergsonian concept of «élan vital».

Bearing in mind this brief outline of Bergson's work, let us look at a passage from «Espacio»: «No es el presente sino un punto de apoyo o de comparación, más breve cada vez; y lo que deja y lo que coje, más, más grande.» Already within this sentence are the two joint concepts of Time and Space. The first half speaks of the relativity of Time, real Time. And in the second half, the word «grande» unites the concept of psychological depth (greatness, importance) with spatial size (largeness). The statement then initiates a series of reflections on the spatial and temporal significance of things absent. The recollection of a certain dog in Moguer gives the poet cause to meditate thus: «No, ese perro que ladra al sol caído no ladra en el Monturrio de Moguer, ni cerca de Carmona de Sevilla, ni en la calle Torrijos de Madrid; ladra en Miami, Coral Gables, La Florida, y yo lo estoy oyendo allí, allí, no aquí, no aquí, allí, allí.» Here in this passage is geographical simultaneity, together with the transcendence of orthodox time. It is in Space-Time that the poet is able to hear the dog, multiple yet single, ubiquitous yet stationary. In fact it is the displacement of the poet himself rather than of the animal, that most astonishes: «Yo lo estoy oyendo allí». It is as if the atoms of his body are disassembled and translated to the place of the dog, there to be reintegrated. He has also transcended Time: «Yo te oí, perro, siempre, desde mi infancia, igual que ahora». The poet can recognize, moreover, the point of Eternity, of perfect unchanging stasis, at the centre of Space-Time, for he adds: «tú no cambias en ningún sitio, eres igual a ti mismo, como yo». It is in fact the interior life of the consciousness which achieves this apparent miracle, the combination of intuition and memory *within.* An extract from Bergson's «L'âme et le corps» in *L'énergie spirituelle* illustrates exactly this:

> Or je crois bien que notre vie intérieure tout entière est quelque chose comme une phrase unique entamée dès le premier éveil de la conscience, phrase semée de virgules, mais nulle part coupée par des points.

(In parenthesis here, note the curiously parallel concept in JRJ of translating the uninterrupted flow of the inner life in an equivalently single and continuous phrase of poetic prose.)

> Et je crois par conséquent aussi que notre passé tout entier est là, subconscient, —je veux dire présent à nous de telle manière que notre conscience, pour en avoir la révélation, n'ait pas besoin de sortir d'elle-même ni de rien s'adjoindre d'étranger: elle n'a, pour apercevoir distinctement tout ce qu'elle renferme ou plutôt tout ce qu'elle est, qu'à écarter un obstacle, à soulever un voile.[23]

That «veil» is indeed lifted in «Espacio», and the inner life of the conscience with its hidden accumulations from the past revealed in a transcendence

[23] Henri Bergson, «L'âme et le corps», *L'énergie spirituelle, Oeuvres,* Presses Universitaires de France, Paris, 1959, p. 858.

of Time and Space. The whole of the «Fragmento segundo» is a corroboration of Bergson's thinking. Beneath Washington Bridge flow the yellow fields of the poet's childhood days; and New York is the same as Moguer, the same as Seville or Madrid. The wind blows alike on the corners of Broadway and on the corner of the street in Moguer, «La Esquina de las Pulmonías». In the garden of St John the Divine in New York, the poet discovers the green poplars of Madrid.[24] There, too, he speaks in Spanish with a dog and a cat, while young choristers sing in the eternal, universal language of music. The «Fragmento» ends in a fusion of sun and moon; a sun simultaneously present and absent, as it rises anew: «un sol de gloria nueva, nueva en otro este». In space perception, as in thought, there are evidently a number of differing levels which are nevertheless synergistically at work.[25] In «Espacio» we find exemplified Bergson's palimpsestic concept of the consciousness.

For Bergson, it is intuitive thought alone and not conceptual thought, which arrives at reality. According to José Ferrater Mora's synopsis of Bergsonian philosophy, «el método intuitivo, que representa, como la reducción fenomenológica de Husserl, "una inversión de la dirección habitual del pensamiento", se dirige, consiguientemente, a lo real»—in a way that pragmatic thought never can. It is quite clear that the author of «Espacio» is practising the intuitive approach to reach psychological truth—the only possible method to do so, in Bergson's view. As Ferrater Mora continues: «En la vida psíquica se encuentra, más que en ninguna otra parte, el carácter esencialmente cambiante y huidizo que posee lo real en su entraña; el asociacionismo, que Bergson somete a una incisiva crítica, es un ejemplo de la espacialización de lo psíquico, el cual se resuelve, en última instancia, en temporalidad y, por tanto, en duración—duración *real*.»

In «Espacio», whose composition ranges over the period 1941 to 1954, JRJ has tried to accomplish what he counselled in his lecture, «La razón heroica», in 1948:

> Pero tenemos que unir el mundo separado. Unirnos todos en una obra universal (que yo no sé si sería aún una representación teatral planetaria, pero

[24] There are obvious Proustian affinities here; but also an interesting parallel in THOMAS WOLFE's *The Story of a Novel* (1936) in which Wolfe makes a similar Space/Time leap to discover himself and his native America in Paris, through a flow of free associations.

[25] See RICHARD MÜLLER-FREIENFELS, *The Evolution of Modern Psychology*, translated by W. Béran Wolfe, Yale University Press, New York, 1935. The role of eidetic phenomena in the psychology of perception and conceptualization is discussed, in particular in connection with members of the Göttingen School of phenomenologists. JRJ is unlikely to have been directly familiar with these, but much of their work bears interestingly upon «Espacio». The «illogical» logic of eidetic imagery, especially in poetry, is analyzed by HANS MEYERHOFF in *Time in Literature*, University of California Press, Berkeley and Los Angeles, 1960, pp. 23-24. «The logic of images or association», he says, «is an attempt to show that, so far as the temporal sequences and *order* of events within the inner world of experience and memory are concerned, we must employ symbols of *disorder* that violate the strictly "logical" order and progression of events to which we have become accustomed by science and common sense».

> que, en el caso de que lo fuera, tendría que aceptarse y representarse como la única verdad posible hoy al hombre) en la que todos participemos por igual, tomando cada parte por igual, repartiéndonos lo mejor y lo peor equitativamente, lo agradable y lo desagradable, con un sentimiento inherente de belleza.

The statement bears an evidently «krausista» stamp, and has parallels in Giner de los Ríos and in Sanz del Río's *Ideal de la humanidad para la vida.* Its sentiments are basic to Idealist/Romantic thinking, as shown for instance in Schelling in Germany or Wordsworth, Shelley and Keats in Great Britain. It is, however, within the reality of *disunity* that the poet of «Espacio» must seek this transcendental Unity. This is what accounts for the paradox of the poem: whilst the very theme and burden of «Espacio» is Unity, both its presentation and its diction appear fragmentary and discontinuous. Two passages of writing, the first by Bergson and the second by Georges Poulet in his book *La distance intérieure* may help us to reconcile this apparent paradox.

In the section entitled «L'âme et le corps» in *L'énergie spirituelle,* Bergson has the following to say on the subject of literary composition:

> Les mots auront beau alors être choisis comme il faut, ils ne diront pas ce que nous voulons leur faire dire si le rythme, la ponctuation et toute la choréographie du discours ne les aident pas à obtenir du lecteur, guidé alors par une série de mouvements naissants, qu'il décrive une courbe de pensée et de sentiment analogue à celle que nous décrivons nous-mêmes [...] C'est quelque chose comme l'art du musicien; mais ne croyez pas que la musique dont il s'agit ici s'adresse simplement à l'oreille [...] il s'agit de tout autre chose que d'une harmonie matérielle des sons. En réalité, l'art de l'écrivain consiste surtout à nous faire oublier qu'il emploie des mots. L'harmonie qu'il cherche est une certaine correspondance entre les allées et venues de son esprit et celles de son discours, correspondance si parfaite que, portées par la phrase, les ondulations de sa pensée se communiquent à la nôtre et qu'alors chacun des mots, pris individuellement, ne compte plus: il n'y a plus rien que le sens mouvant qui traverse les mots [...] Le rythme de la parole n'a donc d'autre objet que de reproduire le rythme de la pensée; et que peut être le rythme de la pensée sinon celui des mouvement naissants, à peine conscients, qui l'accompagnent?[26]

Unity, then, is to be found in the overall flow of thought which makes itself felt through the words, overriding the apparent disconnectedness of the individual word or phrase. It is interesting that the Mallarméan critic, Henri Mondor, has much the same thing to say with regard to the technique of the French poet: «Tous les mots se reflètent les uns sur les autres jusqu'à paraître ne plus avoir leur couleur propre, mais n'être que les transitions d'une gamme».[27]

An extract from Georges Poulet's penetrating analysis of the work of this other poet, Mallarmé, similarly open to the charge of disconnected

[26] H. Bergson, «L'âme et le corps», *Oeuvres,* pp. 849-850.
[27] Henri Mondor, *Vie de Mallarmé,* Gallimard, Paris, 1941, p. 238.

and non-sequential writing—is helpful to our understanding of JRJ's «Espacio». The disorder in Mallarméan poetry is, he says, an effect of art:

> Art qui consiste avec des réminiscences et des suggestions, avec l'emmêlement orageux du passé et du futur, à créer autour de ce qui n'est jamais présent, de ce qui n'est qu'éternel et illusoire, une fiction de durée. Aussi, dans un sens, le poème mallarméen consiste-t-il en cette durée. Son manque apparent de cohérence, le fait que l'esprit y est sans cesse obligé de se porter en avant ou en arrière, le fait aussi qu'il y est assailli tour à tour par des impulsions contradictoires, tout cela donne au poème une sorte de substance temporelle qui est faite du temps même qu'il faut à l'esprit pour en percer le sens et en vivre la fiction. Mais inversement et finalement tous ces «dégagements multiples» peuvent être «résumés d'un regard», ramenés à une «vision simultanée de la Page».[28]

It is probably above all the «Fragmento tercero» which mystifies most for its apparent incoherence. Scarcely does its disconnected discourse, shifting in rapid dreamlike non-sequiturs, seem appropriate to the revelation of essential Unity. And yet it would be not only facile but positively wrong to explain this away with the tag of Surrealism. The Surrealists maintained that the intellect was irrelevant to poetic art and that the subconscious alone was the source of creation. In «Espacio», on the contrary, there is a distinct train of thought—metaphysical thought—evident in the sequence of enquiry and interrogation. JRJ's principle of art as «lo espontáneo sometido a lo consciente» is as true of «Espacio», if we care to look for it, as of the rest of his Work. Moreover we have evidence that JRJ (as also Antonio Machado) was himself critical of the Surrealists. An example of this is his «Recuerdo al primer Villaespesa» in *El Sol* (Madrid, 10 May 1936) with its mordant comments on all «—isms» including «sobrerrealismo». Or again, in the passage from «Poesía española contemporánea» in *El Sol* (24 May 1936) he scathingly alludes to the disjointed compilation of anthologies in terms of a Surrealistic hotchpotch: «Uno de esos cuerpos sin cabeza, o con otras cosas, zapatos, guitarras, coles, cucharas, peces, en vez de cabezas, tan propios del sobrerrealismo, imitado jeneral, con gran talento a veces, de naturales ruinas».

It may of course be contested here that no less a biographer and critic of JRJ than Graciela Palau de Nemes has detected, for example in «Balada del corazón hipertrofiado» from *Primeras prosas,* what she claims to be «tendencias surrealistas al imitar con el ritmo cronométrico el latido del corazón, y con la puntuación, las pausas»;[29] and that again she attributes surrealistic features to some of the prose passages describing New York in *Diario de un poeta reciencasado:* «Debido a la carencia de elementos naturales amables a los sentidos, en esta prosa juanramoniana irrumpen expresiones descriptivas nuevas, algunas caricaturescas con rasgos surrea-

[28] GEORGES POULET, *La distance intérieure,* Plon, Paris, 1952, p. 349. The three quotations within the extract are from S. MALLARMÉ, *Oeuvres complètes,* p. 309; p. 286; p. 455 respectively.

[29] G. PALAU DE NEMES, *Vida y obra de JRJ,* II, p. 393.

listas».[30] My own contention however is that the hermeticism of «Espacio», its break with the norms of tradition, its anarchy and independence are not to be attributed to Surrealism.[31] «Espacio» ought not to be placed within the canon of Surrealist writings. If we are to «explain» it, it is better done in the light of Bergsonian philosophy. In «Espacio» JRJ is attempting to reveal the workings of his own psyche, to capture the essence of his being in its fluid passage across Time and through Space. In other words, his «real duration». It is precisely this «continuité d'écoulement» which is made up of the seemingly disparate succession of states. But note that it *is* a continuity. For each of these states «annonce ce qui suit et contient ce qui précède». In the words of Bergson:

> A vrai dire, ils ne constituent des états multiples que lorsque je les ai déjà dépassés et que je me retourne en arrière pour en observer la trace. Tandis que je les éprouvais, ils étaient si solidement organisés, si profondément animés d'une vie commune, que je n'aurais su dire où l'un quelconque d'entre eux finit, où l'autre commence.[32]

Just as the innovation of radiography (discovered in 1895 by Röntgen) revealed the inner physiology of the body, so concomitant scientific advances were being made in human psychology. Abreast of these, «Espacio», with its innovatory language is an artistic attempt to bring to light inner psychological truths. JRJ's prose poem may be seen as the exposition in art of the following psychological finding of Bergson:

> Il n'y a pas d'état d'âme, si simple soit-il, qui ne change à tout instant, puisqu'il n'y a pas de conscience sans mémoire, pas de continuation d'un état sans l'addition, au sentiment présent, du souvenir des moments passés. En cela consiste la durée. La durée intérieure est la vie continue d'une mémoire qui prolonge le passé dans le présent, soit que le présent renferme distinctement l'image sans cesse grandissante du passé, soit plutôt qu'il témoigne, par son continuel changement de qualité, de la charge toujours plus lourde qu'on traîne derrière soi à mesure qu'on vieillit davantage. Sans cette survivance du passé dans le présent, il n'y aurait pas de durée, mais seulement de l'instantanéité.[33]

«Espacio» is, in Mallarméan terms, the «moi projeté absolu»[34] of JRJ. The egocentricity of such an exploration is, as Michel de Montaigne pointed out however, the sole possible method of exploring Universal Man. For only through self-knowledge can one arrive at an understanding of mankind. That the poem's breadth does extend beyond the self is evident. An extract from the «Fragmento tercero», for example, shows a pre-eminent concern with the dichotomy that exists between the actual condition of the world and the ideal:

[30] *Ibid.*, pp. 625-626.
[31] In this, I concur with the opinion of D. F. FOGELQUIST, *JRJ*, pp. 99-100.
[32] H. BERGSON, «Introduction à la métaphysique», *La pensée et le mouvant, Oeuvres*, p. 1397.
[33] *Ibid.*, p. 1411.
[34] S. MALLARMÉ, *Oeuvres complètes*, p. 434.

> La vida es este unirse y separarse, rápidos, de ojos, manos, bocas, brazos, piernas, cada uno en la busca de aquello que lo atrae o lo repele. Si todos nos uniéramos en todo [...] estos claros del campo nuestro, nuestro cuerpo, estas caras y estas manos, el mundo un día nos sería hermoso a todos, una gran palma sólo, una gran fuente sólo, todo unido y apretado en un abrazo como el tiempo y el espacio, un astro humano, el astro del abrazo por órbita de paz y de armonía.

JRJ's intuitive understanding of the new concept of Space-Time has earlier been suggested; and it is precisely this «embrace of Time with Space» which here he posits as the exemplar of the universal embrace of the brotherhood of Man. Moreover, the vocabulary of this passage seems to corroborate the analogy between the language of «Espacio» and the world of science: astronomical terms («astro»; «órbita») are wedded to humanistic concepts («abrazo»; «paz»; «armonía»).

I have suggested that JRJ's endeavour to explore his own essential self, his «durée réelle», is thereby the endeavour also to penetrate the essence of Man and of Life. For, as Hans Meyerhoff points out in his study *Time in Literature,* the «self» is experienced and known only against the background of the succession of temporal moments and changes which constitute one's biography and therefore the question, what is man?, is inextricably linked with the question of what is time. At the opening of the «Fragmento tercero» an implicit self-identification is proposed, at least momentarily, between JRJ and the first created man, Adam: «El mar, el sol, la luna, y ella y yo, Eva y Adán». From this deliberate equation, we are to infer that the poet of «Espacio» is the representative of all men, of human Life itself. He is, in a way, the Adam of Ortega's «Adán en el Paraíso», the essay which Ortega published in 1910. That is to say, every man and no man: Life. «¿Quién es Adán?», Ortega asks, and then replies: «Cualquiera y nadie particularmente: la vida». The Adam of «Espacio» and the Adam of Ortega share in common the same metaphysical burden: «Para Adán la vida existe como un problema». Just as JRJ in «Espacio», so Ortega's «Adán en el Paraíso es la pura y simple vida, es el débil soporte del problema infinito de la vida [...] VIDA, concretado, condensado en cada una de sus pulsaciones. El corazón de Adán, centro del universo, es decir, el universo íntegro en el corazón de Adán, como un licor hirviente en una copa. Esto es el hombre: el problema de la vida.» The very pullulation of Ortega's language to convey the teeming variety of life recalls that of «Espacio»: «La gravitación universal», writes Ortega, «el universal dolor, la materia inorgánica, las series orgánicas, la historia entera del hombre, sus ansias, sus exultaciones, Nínive y Atenas, Platón y Kant, Cleopatra y Don Juan, lo corporal y lo espiritual, lo momentáneo y lo eterno y lo que dura [...] todo gravitando sobre el fruto rojo, súbitamente maduro del corazón de Adán». Such accumulative lists of disparate things, names and places; the combination of the real with the fictitious; the fusion of geographical and temporal differences: all these are of the essence of the vision of «Espacio» too.

Ortega, like JRJ later, posits the question of the location of Paradise:

«¿Dónde está el Paraíso?» Is it a northern or southern landscape? «No importa: es el escenario ubicuo para la tragedia inmensa del vivir.» As for JRJ, «Paradise» is nothing but a false and interim title (as are also «Edén», «Oasis» and «Cielo») for a place as yet undiscovered. Meanwhile, the natural and geographical setting of «Espacio» remains as ambiguous and all-comprehensive as that «escenario ubicuo» of Ortega. For Ortega, clearly, Adam in Paradise signifies man in the world; but in a world which is a stage («escenario»), since man's life is something he must perform, as a drama. Bearing this in mind, we should observe the following sentence from JRJ's «Fragmento tercero»: «Todos somos actores aquí, y sólo actores, y el teatro es la ciudad, y el campo y el horizonte, ¡el mundo! »

The synthetic vision of the cosmos which JRJ evokes bears yet further affinity with the view of Ortega that «cada elemento [...] necesita de todos los demás: es la relación mutua entre los otros». Thus, «la esencia de cada cosa se resuelve en puras relaciones». In other words, the whole of life is an «exchange of substances» in which it is necessary to «coexistir, tramarse en una red sutilísima de relaciones, apoyarse lo uno en lo otro, alimentarse mutuamente, conllevarse, potenciarse». With this quotation, we are returned to the earlier quotation from JRJ given above, in which he too envisages a similar universal «network»: «La vida es este unirse y separarse [...]»

Like the Adam of Ortega «con la verdura del Paraíso en torno, circundado de animales», so JRJ in «Espacio» is also surrounded by a world of pristine luxuriance. But circumstantial reality matters only insofar as it is a component part of the man. The reabsorption of his own past, present and even future circumstances, which JRJ imaginatively realizes in «Espacio», is his own concrete destiny.[35] Emphatically he declares: «Mi Destino soy yo y nada y nadie más que yo».

Ortega's essay is ostensibly concerned with an aesthetics of painting; but it is a thin disguise to what is in effect, as Julián Marías has pointed out, the first philosophical formulation of the doctrine of Life.[36] Perhaps even more interesting than the similarity of the metaphysical problems raised in Ortega's «Adán en el Paraíso» and in JRJ's «Espacio» is the expression of those problems. «Pero la vida de nuestro espíritu es sucesiva, y el arte que la expresa teje sus materiales en la apariencia flúida del tiempo», states Ortega. These words, written some forty years before the composition and publication of the «Fragmento tercero» of «Espacio», seem to anticipate it, so directly are they relevant to the method by which JRJ was to explore that «real duration» of the self, the successive and fluid character of the Bergsonian «élan vital».

It is important to make clear that the parallels indicated above are not intended as anything other than coincidences—albeit very interesting ones. Obviously JRJ knew Ortega's essay. But no claim is here made to the effect that «Espacio», or more specifically the «Fragmento tercero», owed any conscious debt to the Ortegan essay or was openly influenced by it. It

[35] This concept is developed in ORTEGA's *Meditaciones del Quijote.*

[36] JULIÁN MARÍAS, *La escuela de Madrid: Estudios de filosofía española,* Emecé, Buenos Aires, 1959, p. 185.

remains nevertheless worthy of notice that Ortega the philosopher uses in his essay an eminently poetic language, the central artistic metaphor of which is Adam in Paradise, in order to probe the problem of man in the world. To a not dissimilar purpose, JRJ the poet carries that diction in «Espacio» to its furthermost limits of linguistic art.

The question remains, to what extent is the new method inaugurated in «Espacio» a success? The «Fragmento primero» and the «Fragmento segundo» certainly appear more achieved than the last. In the «Fragmento tercero», JRJ seems to come close to the case of Joyce's Bloom and Stephen Dedalus, ceasing to be the subjective thinker of «I» to become instead «an object through which external forces pass: history, landscape, myths» —with a resultant dissolution of individuality.[37] The «segundo yo» of JRJ turns into an unbridled power, so that the now minimized «I» of the man cries out helplessly:

> Dentro de mí hay uno que está hablando, hablando, hablando ahora. No lo puedo callar, no se puede callar [...] Quiero el silencio en mi silencio, y no lo sé callar a éste, ni se sabe callar. ¡Calla, segundo yo, que hablas como yo y que no hablas como yo; calla, maldito!

The «Fragmento tercero» is distinctly lacking in the control of the earlier two, and gives «Espacio» a provisional and unfinished character. This unfinished condition is equally true of JRJ's Work in its entirety. He did not, ultimately, accomplish his desired aim: the aim, that is, of re-writing the total Work in one immense, uninterrupted paragraph of poetic prose. It may indeed be that such a proposition of achieving the Perfect Immanent Work is the proposition of The Impossible—likewise worthy of capital letters. There also exists the possibility, however, that the provisional character of «Espacio» is a deliberate one, concealing a profound truth. The fact that JRJ gives the name «Fragmento» to each of the three sections suggests a real awareness of the necessarily fragmentary nature of his great attempt at the salvation of the world in and through the Word. Perhaps his undertaking is the deliberately partial «saving»—bit by bit— of the intricate puzzle that is the universe. The assembly of all the pieces would finally constitute the salvation of its totality. These three fragments are just the beginning of the End. And this, JRJ knew. It is in this light that we should perhaps understand the meaning of the name «Fragmento», triply applied to «Espacio». For JRJ is carrying out, poetically, the same kind of work of restoration as the archaeologist who, gathering up and re-assembling the broken fragments of an ancient vase, seeks to reconstruct and resurrect a whole era of History. It is in the naming of the world and of its component parts—and therein only—that salvation lies. That is why, in the «Fragmento primero», JRJ stresses the anonymity of the ideal world: «Enmedio hay, tiene que haber un punto, una salida; el sitio del seguir más verdadero, con nombre no inventado, diferente de eso que es diferente e inventado que llamamos, en nuestro desconsuelo, Edén, Oasis, Paraíso,

[37] See STEPHEN SPENDER, *The Making of a Poem,* W. W. Norton, New York, 1962, p. 90.

Cielo, pero que no lo es». Not until that perfect place is given its rightful Name can it be truly apprehended or truly reached. «Paradise» is a mere approximation of a sign to indicate a stage along the way to that as yet imperfectly apprehended Place. On the positive side, the perfect love of Eloïsa for Abelard, for example, finds its perfection precisely because it is capable of nomination. It is nameable, and it is named: «Todo claro y nombrado con su nombre en llena castidad».

In the Name is our salvation, and the salvation of the world. Thus, we have come full circle to the significance of the Word and Work in JRJ. If that salvation has not proved finally consummated, nevertheless the grandeur of the undertaking of the Work and the extraordinary achievements even within its own limitations remain.

APPENDIX

The preoccupation with temporality and a-temporality is one which JRJ and his contemporaries share in common. Antonio Machado, Gabriel Miró, Valle-Inclán, Azorín—for example—all are concerned with the aesthetic revelation of time and the passage of time in a-temporal terms. I shall consider each of these four briefly in that order.

Antonio Machado's poem «Renacimiento» (*Galerías,* LXXXVIII) is a good illustration:

> Tal vez la mano, en sueños,
> del sembrador de estrellas,
> hizo sonar la música olvidada
> como una nota de la lira inmensa,
> y la ola humilde a nuestros labios vino
> de unas pocas palabras verdaderas.

Machado's scepticism of objective time is expressed by Juan de Mairena, his alter ego, in the following way: «Nuestros relojes nada tienen que ver con nuestro tiempo, realidad última de carácter psíquico, que tampoco se cuenta ni se mide»; and again, considering the uncertainty of «lo pretérito», he says:

> ¿Quién sabe lo que ha pasado? No dudo que haya en nuestra conciencia una pretensión a fijar lo pasado, como si las cosas pudieran hacerse inmutables al pasar de nuestra percepción a nuestro recuerdo. Pero si lo miramos más de cerca, veremos que el devenir es *uno,* y que es su *totalidad* (porvenir-presente-pasado) lo sometido a constante cambio. También es cierto que, como el punto de mira y los puntos de referencia varían de continuo—cuantitativa y cualitativamente—, ningún acontecimiento de nuestro pasado ha de aparecernos dos veces como exactamente el mismo. De suerte que ni el porvenir está escrito en ninguna parte, ni el pasado tampoco.

It is this a-temporal expression of time which Machado praises in Bécquer, the precursor of twentieth century Spanish poetry, of whom the apocryphal Juan de Mairena says: «Es palabra en el tiempo, el tiempo psíquico irreversible, en el cual nada se infiere ni se deduce. En su discurso rige un principio de contradicción propiamente dicho: "sí, pero no; volverán, pero no volverán"» (*Obras: poesía y prosa,* p. 498).

A poem from JRJ's *Eternidades* coincides with the synthetic concept of time expressed by Machado:

> ¡Oh tiempo, dame tu secreto,
> que te hace más nuevo cuanto
> más envejeces!
>
> Día tras día, tu pasado
> es menor, y tu porvenir más grande,
> —y tu presente
> ¡lo mismo siempre que el instante
> de la flor del almendro!—
>
> ¡Tiempo sin huellas:
> dame el secreto con que invade,
> cada día, tu espíritu a tu cuerpo! (*LP*, p. 564)

In a tribute to the early work of JRJ called *Ninfeas,* Machado recognizes its a-temporal quality, defining it as:

> Un libro de olvido divino
> que dice fragancia del alma, fragancia
> que puede curar la amargura que da la distancia,
> que sólo es el alma la flor del camino.

The treatment of a-temporal time in Machado's own work—and most notably in his *Soledades y galerías*—has already received full discussion by major critics. My object here is simply to show the prevalence of the theme amongst JRJ's contemporaries as a whole. Before going on to consider Miró, Valle-Inclán and Azorín, however, it seems necessary to note a certain growing divergence between JRJ and Machado with regard to a-temporal expression. For the fact is that the poet of *Soledades* gradually gave way to a poet of circumstance and «littérature engagée» quite alien to JRJ. Ricardo Gullón cites, in his *Relaciones entre Antonio Machado y JRJ,* Università di Pisa, 1964, p. 16, the following note written by JRJ in July 1921:

> Antonio Machado, este [falta una palabra] de poesía, se anduvo siempre buscando, y antes se encontraba siempre. Ahora se ha perdido a sí mismo. ¿Dónde se ha perdido a sí mismo, en Baeza, en Soria, en Segovia, en Madrid? Pero ya se encontrará, y si no se encuentra más, ya se ha encontrado bastante.

From this it is clear that JRJ detected in Machado a departure from the a-temporal essence of «poesía pura». Confirmation of this is to be found in an excellent work of criticism by Antonio Blanch:

> El magisterio y padrinazgo de Jiménez sobre los poetas jóvenes es un hecho indiscutible, y esto desde que comienza a ser evidente en su obra una firme voluntad de poesía pura. Precisamente esta nueva tendencia de depuración y de introspección iba a alejarle de su antiguo amigo Antonio Machado, cada vez más escéptico y más dado a una poesía *temporal y naturalista.* (my emphasis) (*La poesía pura,* p. 95)

Blanch then quotes from a letter written in 1924 (three years after the note quoted above) in which JRJ rejects a copy of Machado's *Nuevas canciones*. His reasons may have been personal ones, but more probably it was because he could not accord with the later tendencies of Machado toward occasional verse, naturalism and temporality; in other words, all that was opposed to «poesía pura». Fundamentally in this criticism JRJ was accurate, because in the late years of his life, Machado did indeed adopt a clear cut line as a political «engagé». Even though he held similar views during the Civil War, the eminent critic Antonio Sánchez-Barbudo is nevertheless obliged to recognize that the majority of the poems written «a la altura de las circunstancias» are not of Machado's best. His remarks on one of the war poems are illuminating with regard to the departure from the a-temporality of «poesía pura»: «Fue pues escrito el día en que parecía inminente la caída de Madrid; el mismo día que, obedeciendo órdenes, salió él para Valencia, acompañado de su familia. Es difícil juzgar este poema si no tenemos en cuenta las *circunstancias* en que nació» (my emphasis) (*Las poesías de Antonio Machado,* Editorial Lumen, Barcelona, 1969, p. 451). Such are the dangers of aesthetic loss incurred when the temporal interiority of pure poetry is abandoned. *Soledades y galerías,* above all, remains nevertheless exemplary of the generation's concern with the a-temporal expression of the passage of Time.

Turning to Miró, we find another master of such expression, this time in a poetry that takes the shape of prose. In an article entitled «Gabriel Miró y "el mundo según es"», *Papeles de Son Armadans,* Madrid, Palma de Mallorca, LXII, May 1961, Edmund L. King has observed of Miró that he knew how to «complacerse en morar morosamente en lo recóndito del alma». It may be that this is a key to the magical revelation of «el fluir del tiempo» as a constant—the constant of a present eternity—which is the hallmark of the entire corpus of Miró's work. It is again a matter of that search for the essential timeless self, to which JRJ referred in his note about Machado, quoted above. An extract from the opening scene, «La llegada», of Miró's *Años y leguas* will provide an illustration:

> Después de muchos años, lo primero que encontraba en su campo, era a sí mismo, atravesándolo, estampándose en todo como su sombra prolongada por el sol poniente. Había de sumergirse y de perderse en la visión como en el sueño que no nos gana sino cuando perdemos la conciencia de nuestra vida y de nuestra postura.

The timeless present of the land to which Sigüenza is nostalgically returning is expressed in the salt breeze, the running water, the quivering poplars, in age-old sounds and smells and sights that yet are pristine, as in his first youth:

> Pero no pareciendo que «fuese ayer», o pareciéndolo precisamente porque entonces sentimos todo lo contrario. Y porque nos oprime la verdad del tiempo devanado tuvo más fuerza alucinante la emoción de esta hora que se había quedado inmóvil para Sigüenza desde entonces.

So substantial, so immediately real, is this a-temporal present hour that «hasta hizo un ademán suave de tocarla, de empujarla, queriendo que volviese a caminar a su lado».

In this «recherche du temps perdu», the passage of time is dissolved. It is not, however, that Sigüenza achieves a resurrection of the past, as such; but rather that the past becomes transformed and embodied in the present, as one and the same, eternally. It is precisely by means of a-temporal expression that this fusion is brought about: a mysterious meeting of eyes across time and space:

> Una lente lírica le acercaba a sí mismo [...] y ahora, entre todo, se le presentaba, no el recuerdo óptico y casuístico, sino la misma mirada, la sensación de su vida, que se había envejecido allí, y ahora le salía para verle pasar, a veinte años de distancia [...] Ahora, al verse, se consustanciaban en el tiempo y se pertenecían.

A single further example of Miró's handling of the phenomenon of time must suffice here. The scene of «Doña Elisa y la eternidad», from the same book, is a masterpiece of the a-temporal portrayal of time's flow. Lifting the cardboard lid of an old box in an attic, Sigüenza discovers the funeral wreath of doña Elisa's daughter. It is as if the box were the repository of time itself; and the action of its opening, the trigger which releases the pent-up years: «Le parece a Sigüenza que haya abierto un pomo de olor de años, de años de una virginidad ya sin cuerpo. Y vuelve a poner la losa de tiempo y de cartón». The harmless everyday item of a cardboard cover, devoid in itself of any temporal significance, has become the slabstone of time and of tomb. Miró's entire depiction of doña Elisa herself is an expression, rendered in the similarly a-temporal terms of her physical appearance, her gestures and speech, of eternity. «Se le para en sus ojos la bruma de la quietud perdurable. ¡Es la desgana de lo de ahora; es la eternidad, es la eternidad! ».

The precision and economy of language, the exactitude of the perfect adjective, are the means whereby Miró achieves the sense of the flow of time; and it is this which links him stylistically and thematically with the poetry of JRJ. The fact that JRJ appreciated the work of Miró is evident. Ricardo Gullón testifies that JRJ possessed work dedicated personally to him by Miró (*Conversaciones con Juan Ramón,* p. 177). Guerrero Ruiz tells how JRJ wished to include Miró as a contributor in the founding of a new review entitled *Poesía española 1930-1931* (*JR de viva voz,* p. 60); and relates JRJ's appraisal of Miró's prose as above all musical (p. 54).

It is this notion of musicality as the essence of a pure poetry in which the passage of time can find expression in a-temporal form, which will serve as a link with that other contemporary man of letters, Ramón del Valle-Inclán. In the chapter «El milagro musical» from *La lámpara maravillosa,* he speaks of the temporal synthesis achieved through the poetic form:

> La rima junta en un verso la emoción de otro verso con el cual concierta: Hace una suma, y si no logra anular el tiempo, lo encierra y lo aquilata en el

instante de una palabra, de una sílaba, de un sonido [...] Como la piedra y sus círculos en el agua, así las rimas en su enlace numeral y musical. (p. 62)

I should like to cite two passages from this same book in order to show the particular resemblance they bear to the quotations already taken from Miró with respect to the a-temporal treatment of the «fluir del tiempo». First, let us bear in mind Sigüenza's re-encounter with his past in *Años y leguas* as we read the following similarly personal anecdote from «El anillo de Giges» of *La lámpara maravillosa:*

> Era yo estudiante, y un día contemplando el juego de algunos niños que danzaban como los silvanos en los frisos antiguos, peregrinó mi corazón hacia la infancia y tornó revestido de una gracia nueva. Al caminar bajo la sombra sagrada de los recuerdos, no experimenté la sensación de volver a vivir en los años lejanos, sino algo más inefable, pues comprendía que nada de mi psiquis era abolido. Hasta entonces nunca había descubierto aquella intuición de eternidad que se me mostraba de pronto al evocar la infancia y darle actualidad en otro círculo del Tiempo.

The affinity between the temporal/a-temporal experience of the two contemporaneous writers is self-evident. It is the inner psyche, unrelated to chronological time, which fuses the flow of time from past youth to the present in a single eternity. Valle-Inclán then gathers up this experience to connect it directly with his definition of the time-transcendence of poetry, which we have already noted:

> Toda la vida pasada era como el verso lejano que revive su evocación musical al encontrar otro verso que le guarda consonancia, y sin perder el primer significado entra a completar un significado más profundo. ¡Aun en el juego bizantino de las rimas, se cumplen las leyes del Universo! Con los ojos vueltos al pasado, yo lograba romper el enigma del Tiempo [...] Vivía intensamente la hora anterior, y a la par conocía la venidera, estaba ya morando dentro de su círculo. A lo largo de los caminos por donde una vez había pasado, se hacía tangible el rastro de mi imagen viva.

As in the case of the cardboard box of Miró's story, whose opening released the almost palpable years of the past, Valle-Inclán uses the image of a sesame seed, with its «Open Sesame! » connotations, as the repository of time. For him, «el momento más pequeño era un sésamo que guardaba sensaciones de muchos años». In much the same way as Miró, he can say: «Hallé y gocé como un pecado místico la mudanza de las formas y el fluir del Tiempo», whilst nevertheless transcending it, converting the temporal into the a-temporal: «Yo conocía fuera de la razón utilitaria, transmigraba amorosamente en la conciencia de las cosas y rompía las Normas. Mis ojos y mis oídos creaban la Eternidad».

The following precept, again taken from *La lámpara maravillosa,* applies to the great majority of Valle's work: «El inspirado», he says, «ha de sentir las comunicaciones del mundo invisible, para comprender el gesto en que todas las cosas se inmovilizan como en un éxtasis, y en el cual late el recuerdo de lo que fueron y el embrión de lo que han de ser». Valle's early composition of the four *Sonatas,* published between 1902 and 1905 and bearing the closest affinity with the «modernista» style, show in practice this aesthetic concept. They are novels of the interior psychological time-piece of a personality rather than the chronology of circumstance. As Allen W. Phillips has pointed out in his «Estudio preliminar» to his edition of the *Sonatas* (Editorial Porrúa, México, 1972, p. xxvii), «En ellas se refieren sucesos pero los esquemas narrativos se diluyen, y Valle se desinteresa del mundo real para crear el suyo propio, acercándose de modo indirecto a las cosas, con técnica de poeta, para extraer de ellas su sentido misterioso». It is not temporal objective reality, but the a-temporal reality of atmosphere and mood, which concerns Valle-Inclán. He suppresses the society of the nineteenth century in favour of creating another, quite artificial one, of his own. His protagonist, the Marqués de Bradomín, is not subject to the social norms of the time, nor does he even belong to his century. He lives and behaves according to the ideals of other eras, as is frequently emphasized in the *Sonata de invierno.* Thus, although the *Sonatas* do depict the «fluir del tiempo» in the gradual ageing of the person of Bradomín and in his nostalgic evocation of the past, nevertheless it is achieved in purely a-temporal terms. The real time of the *Sonatas* does not reside in the chronology of the episodes in Bradomín's life. It is the constant factor of the psyche—the continuing sensitivity and fidelity to Beauty—of Bradomín, which detains objective time and creates its own: a static time, in which the character of Bradomín seems forever smiling, forever sceptical and roguish, but always the essential gentleman honouring the a-temporal principles of chivalry and Beauty.

In a very different work, *Tirano Banderas* (1926), we find the same aesthetic principles concerning the expression of time. There is a deliberate lack of linearity in the narrative, and objective time is dislocated, fragmented, or superimposed upon itself in the case of simultaneous events. Valle himself affirmed that his aim, within the three-day duration of the novel, was to fill time to the full, in the way that El Greco filled to full the dimension of space. In this particular aspect of the genius of Valle-Inclán—the ability throughout the canon of his work to convey the passage of time in artistically and poetically a-temporal form—is realized Valle's own aesthetic injunction, namely, that the poet «como el místico, ha de tener percepciones más allá del límite que marcan los sentidos, para entrever en la ficción del momento, y en el aparente rodar de las horas, la responsabilidad eterna». (*La lámpara maravillosa,* VI). As Ricardo Gullón corroborates: «El tiempo de la creación poética fundirá el ayer y el presente, según ocurre en las leyendas de Valle-Inclán. El tiempo abolido resucita a través de un lenguaje donde el arcaísmo, como purgación de lo prosaico cotidiano, tiene significado renovador». (*Direcciones del modernismo,* Gredos, Madrid, 1971, p. 48).

Lastly, Azorín, another master of poetic prose, searches also for the eternal present. A good example is the following opening to chapter XVI of his novel, *Doña Inés* (1925):

> Un íntimo desasosiego conturba a don Pablo. El sentido del tiempo, hora por hora, minuto por minuto, le ha llevado paulatinamente a adelantarse al

> tiempo. No se puede perdurar en la percepción de la hora, del minuto y del segundo, sin acabar por tener la visión total del tiempo. Del pasado venimos al presente; del presente habremos de caminar hacia el porvenir.

Don Pablo is the artist, the writer, who is seeking to apprehend the substance of life through the detention of Time. What is of interest here once more is the fact that in prose writing no less than in poetry the theme was to become pervasive in the generation of JRJ.

FINAL NOTE

Since completing this book, there has come to my notice the publication by Antonio Sánchez Romeralo of Juan Ramón Jiménez's *Leyenda (1896-1956)* (Colección Goliárdica, Madrid, 1978). The importance of Sánchez Romeralo's scrupulous edition of Juan Ramón's projected final poetic anthology, interrupted by the poet's death in 1958, cannot be too highly stressed. The last years of Juan Ramón's life were devoted to the organization of his Obra according to subject matter in seven volumes under the general title of *Metamórfosis. Leyenda* was to have figured not only as the first of these volumes, but as the sole volume of poetry. The unique character of *Leyenda* is therefore patent, in the context of Juan Ramón's conception of the total Obra. It is my hope that the present study of this conception may complement our understanding of the poetic enterprise initiated in *Leyenda* but unrealized in the fullness of its magnitude.

BIBLIOGRAPHY

I. Juan Ramón Jiménez: Works cited

Jiménez, J. R.: *Cartas literarias,* compiled by F. Garfias, Editorial Bruguera, Barcelona, 1977.
— *Cartas de Zenobia Camprubí y Juan Ramón Jiménez,* ed. by R. Gullón, *La Torre,* núm. 27, 1959.
— *Crítica paralela,* ed. by A. del Villar, Narcea, Madrid, 1975.
— *Cuadernos,* ed. by F. Garfias, Taurus, Madrid, 1971.
— «De siglos», *Rueca,* V, México, 1954.
— *Diario poético,* Poética, I, La Plata, 1943.
— *El modernismo, notas de un curso (1953),* ed. by R. Gullón, Aguilar, México, 1962.
— «El romance, río de la lengua española», *El trabajo gustoso (Conferencias),* sel. by F. Garfias, Aguilar, Madrid-México-Buenos Aires, 1961.
— *En el otro costado,* ed. by Aurora de Albornoz, Ediciones Júcar, Madrid, 1974.
— *Españoles de tres mundos,* Editorial Afrodisio Aguado, Madrid, 1960.
— *La colina de los chopos,* ed. by F. Garfias, Taurus, Madrid, 1966.
— *La corriente infinita,* Aguilar, Madrid, 1961.
— *La obra desnuda,* ed. by A. del Villar, Aldebarán, Sevilla, 1976.
— *Libros de poesía,* ed. by A. Caballero, Aguilar, Madrid, 1972.
— *Olvidos de Granada, La Torre,* 1960.
— *Pájinas escojidas; prosa,* sel. by R. Gullón, Gredos, Madrid, 1958.
— *Pájinas escojidas; verso,* sel. by R. Gullón, Gredos, Madrid, 1958.
— *Platero y yo,* Biblioteca Juventud, *La lectura,* Madrid, 1914.
— *Primeros libros de poesía,* compiled by F. Garfias, Aguilar, Madrid, 1973.
— *Segunda antolojía poética,* Espasa-Calpe, Madrid, 1922.
— *Tercera antolojía poética,* compiled by E. Florit, Editorial Biblioteca Nueva, Madrid, 1970.

II. Critical works on Juan Ramón Jiménez cited and consulted

Bo, C.: *La poesía de Juan Ramón Jiménez,* Editorial Hispánica, Madrid, 1943.
Campoamor González, A.: *Vida y poesía de Juan Ramón Jiménez,* Ediciones Sedmay, Madrid, 1976.
Cano, J. L.: «Juan Ramón Jiménez y la revista *Helios*», *Clavileño,* VII, núm. 42, 1956.
Cardwell, R. A.: *Juan R. Jiménez, The Modernist Apprenticeship 1895-1900,* Colloquium Verlag, Berlin, 1977.
Cernuda, L.: «Juan Ramón Jiménez», *Estudios sobre poesía española contemporánea,* Madrid, 1957.
Cole, L. R.: *The Religious Instinct in the Poetry of Juan Ramón Jiménez,* The Dolphin Book C.° Ltd., Oxford, 1967.
Crespo, A.: *Juan Ramón Jiménez y la pintura,* Universidad de Puerto Rico, San Juan, 1974.
Díaz-Plaja, G.: *Juan Ramón Jiménez en su poesía,* Aguilar, Madrid, 1958.

DÍEZ-CANEDO, E.: *Juan Ramón Jiménez en su obra,* El Colegio de México, México, 1944.
FIGUEIRA, G.: *Juan Ramón Jiménez, poeta de lo inefable,* Biblioteca Alfar, Montevideo, 1944.
FLORIT, E.: «Nota preliminar», Juan Ramón Jiménez, *Tercera antolojía poética,* Editorial Biblioteca Nueva, Madrid, 1970.
— «The Modernist Prefigurement in the Early Work of Rubén Darío», transl. by J. Wilcox, *Rubén Darío: Centennial Studies,* ed. by M. González-Gerth and G. D. Schade, University of Texas, Austin, 1970.
FOGELQUIST, D. L.: *Juan Ramón Jiménez,* Twayne Publishers, Boston, 1976.
— «Los cinco elementos del universo poético de Juan Ramón Jiménez», *Revista Hispánica Moderna,* núms. 2-3, April-July 1958.
FONT, M. T.: *Espacio: autobiografía lírica de Juan Ramón Jiménez,* Insula, Madrid, 1972.
GARFIAS, F.: *Juan Ramón Jiménez,* Taurus, Madrid, 1958.
GICOVATE, B.: *La poesía de Juan Ramón Jiménez,* Ediciones Ariel, Barcelona, 1973.
GÓMEZ DE LA SERNA, R.: *Juan Ramón Jiménez, Retratos contemporáneos, Retratos completos,* Aguilar, Madrid, 1961.
GONZÁLEZ, A.: *Juan Ramón Jiménez: estudio,* Ediciones Júcar, Madrid, 1973.
GOULARD, M.: *Juan Ramón Jiménez y la crítica en Escandinavia,* Insula, Madrid, 1963.
GUERRERO RUIZ, J.: *Juan Ramón de viva voz,* Insula, Madrid, 1961.
GULLÓN, R.: *Conversaciones con Juan Ramón,* Taurus, Madrid, 1958.
— *El último Juan Ramón Jiménez,* Alfaguara, Madrid-Barcelona, 1968.
— *Estudios sobre Juan Ramón Jiménez,* Losada, Buenos Aires, 1960.
— *Juan Ramón Jiménez y el modernismo,* Aguilar, Madrid, México-Buenos Aires, 1962.
— *Monumento de amor, La Torre,* núm. 27, 1959.
— *Relaciones entre Antonio Machado y Juan Ramón Jiménez,* Università di Pisa, 1964.
Homenaje a Juan Ramón Jiménez, La Torre, núms. 19-20, July-December 1957.
LIRA, O.: *Poesía y mística en Juan Ramón Jiménez,* Editorial Universidad Católica, Santiago, 1969.
MACRÍ, O.: «El segundo tiempo de la poesía de Jiménez», *La Torre,* núms. 19-20, July-December 1957.
MONCY, A.: *Juan Ramón Jiménez y el modernismo, La Torre,* núm. 43, July-September 1963.
NEDDERMAN, E.: *Die symbolistischen Stilelemente im Werke von Juan Ramón Jiménez,* Hamburg, 1935.
OLSON, P. R.: *Circle of Paradox. Time and Essence in the Poetry of Juan Ramón Jiménez,* The Johns Hopkins Press, Baltimore, Maryland, 1967.
PABLOS, B. DE: *El tiempo en la poesía de Juan Ramón Jiménez,* Gredos, Madrid, 1965.
PALAU DE NEMES, G.: *Vida y obra de Juan Ramón Jiménez,* 2 vols., Gredos, Madrid, 1974.
PREDMORE, M. P.: *La poesía hermética de Juan Ramón Jiménez,* Gredos, Madrid, 1973.
RIBBANS, G.: «Recaptured Memory in Juan Ramón Jiménez and Antonio Machado», *Studies in Modern Spanish Literature and Art presented to Helen F. Grant,* Tamesis, London, 1972.
SÁNCHEZ-BARBUDO, A.: *La segunda época de Juan Ramón Jiménez 1916-1953,* Gredos, Madrid, 1962.
— *La segunda época de Juan Ramón Jiménez: Cincuenta poemas comentados,* Gredos, Madrid, 1963.
SANTOS-ESCUDERO, C.: *Símbolos y Dios en el último Juan Ramón Jiménez,* Gredos, Madrid, 1975.
SAZ-OROZCO, C. DEL: *Desarrollo del concepto de Dios en el pensamiento religioso de Juan Ramón Jiménez,* Editorial Razón y Fe, Madrid, 1963.
SCHONBERG, J.-L.: *Juan Ramón Jiménez ou le chant d'Orfée,* Neuchâtel, A la Baconnière, 1961.

TORRE, G. DE: «Cuatro etapas de Juan Ramón Jiménez», *La Torre,* núms. 19-20, July-December 1957.
VERHESEN, F.: «Tiempo y espacio en la obra de Juan Ramón Jiménez», *La Torre,* núms. 19-20, July-December 1957.
YOUNG, H. T.: *The Victorious Expression,* University of Wisconsin Press, Madison, Wis., 1966.

III. OTHER WORKS CITED OR CONSULTED

ALBERTI, R.: *La arboleda perdida,* Seix-Barral, Barcelona, 1977.
ALBORNOZ, ALVARO DE: «Aristocracia y democracia (Carlyle, Ruskin, Nietzsche)», *Nuestro Tiempo,* May 1905.
ALONSO, D.: *La poesía de San Juan de la Cruz,* Consejo Superior de Investigaciones Científicas, Madrid, 1942.
ASTRADA, C.: *Idealismo fenomenológico y metafísico existencial,* Imprenta de la Universidad, Buenos Aires, 1936.
AZORÍN: *Doña Inés, Obras completas,* vol. IV, Aguilar, Madrid, 1948.
BÉCQUER, G. A.: *Obras completas,* Aguilar, Madrid, 1961.
BENSON, A. C.: *Walter Pater,* Macmillan, New York and London, 1906.
BERGSON, H.: *Oeuvres,* Presses Universitaires de France, Paris, 1959.
BLANCH, A.: *La poesía pura española,* Gredos, Madrid, 1976.
BLEIBERG, G.: «Algunas revistas literarias de hacia 1898», *Arbor,* XI, núm. 36, 1948.
BORGES, J. L.: *El hacedor,* Emecé, Buenos Aires, 1960.
BOUSOÑO, C.: *Teoría de la expresión poética,* Gredos, Madrid, 1970.
BROOKS, C.: *The Hidden God,* Yale University Press, New Haven and London, 1963.
BRUNS, G. L.: *Modern Poetry and the Idea of Language,* Yale University Press, New Haven and London, 1974.
CARLYLE, T.: *On Heroes, Hero-Worship and the Heroic in History,* vol. V, Ams Press, New York, 1974.
CELMS, T.: *Der phänomenologische Idealismus Husserls,* Riga, 1928.
CERVANTES: *Don Quijote de la Mancha,* text and notes by Martín de Riquer, Editorial Juventud, Barcelona, 1958.
CHILD, R. C.: *The Aesthetic of Walter Pater,* Wellesley College Publication, Octagon Books, New York, 1969.
CHIPP, H. B.: *Theories of Modern Art; a Source Book by Artists and Critics,* University of California Press, Berkeley, 1971.
CHISHOLM, A. R.: *Mallarmé's Grand Oeuvre,* Manchester University Press, 1962.
CIPLIJAUSKAITÈ, B.: *El poeta y la poesía,* Insula, Madrid, 1966.
COLERIDGE, S. T.: *Biographia Literaria,* ed. by G. Watson, Dent, London, 1975.
COROMINAS, P.: «On Emerson and Carlyle», *La revista blanca,* año III, 1900.
COSSÍO, M. B.: «El arte de saber ver», *Boletín de la Institución Libre de Enseñanza,* núm. 65, Madrid, October 1879.
CRUZ, SAN JUAN DE LA: *Obras,* 3 vols., J. Peláez, Toledo, 1912-1914.
DANTE, A.: *The Divine Comedy,* transl. by J. D. Sinclair, Bodley Head, London, 1958-1964.
DARÍO, R.: *Poesías completas,* Aguilar, Madrid, 1967.
— «Unamuno, poeta», *La Nación,* Buenos Aires, 1909.
DAVIE, D.: *Articulate Energy, an Enquiry into the Syntax of English Poetry,* Routledge & Kegan Paul, London, 1955.
DAVIS, L. E.: «Oscar Wilde in Spain», *Comparative Literature,* n.° 25, 1973.
DELFEL, G.: *L'esthétique de Stéphane Mallarmé,* Flammarion, Paris, 1951.
DÍAZ, J. S.: *Manual de bibliografía de la literatura española,* Gustavo Gili, Barcelona, 1966.
DÍAZ-PLAJA, G.: *Modernismo frente a noventa y ocho,* Espasa-Calpe, Madrid, 1951.
DÍAZ-RODRÍGUEZ, M.: *Camino de perfección,* Editorial Cecilio Acosta, Caracas, 1942.
Dictionnaire de théologie catholique, Vacant-Mangenot-Amman, Paris, 1931.
DONOGHUE, D.: *Yeats,* Collins, Glasgow, 1971.

DRIESCH, H.: *Relativitätstheorie und Philosophie,* G. Braun, Karlsruhe, 1924.
EINSTEIN, A.: *Die Physik als Abenteuer der Erkenntnis,* A. W. Sijthoff, Leiden, 1938.
— *The Meaning of Relativity,* Methuen, London, 1922.
— *Uber die spezielle und die allgemeine Relativitätstheorie, gemeinverständlich,* F. Vieweg, Braunschweig, 1917.
ELIOT, T. S.: *Ash-Wednesday,* G. P. Putnam's Sons, New York and London, 1930.
— *Four Quartets,* Harcourt, Brace & C.°, New York, 1943.
ELTON, O.: *Biography of F. Frederick York Powell,* Clarendon Press, Oxford, 1906.
FARINELLI, A.: *Il romanticismo nel mondo latino,* Fratelli Bocca, Turin, 1927.
FERRÁN Y FORNIÉS, A.: *La soledad, Obras completas,* La España Moderna, Madrid, 1893.
FERRATER, J. M.: *Diccionario de filosofía,* Editorial Sudamericana, Buenos Aires, 1958.
— «Wittgenstein o la destrucción», *Realidad,* núm. 13, 1949.
FERRERES, R.: *Los límites del modernismo y del 98,* Taurus, Madrid, 1964.
FLETCHER, I.: *Walter Pater,* Longman, London, 1959.
GARCÍA MORENTE, M.: *La filosofía de Bergson,* Publicaciones de la Residencia de Estudiantes, Madrid, 1917.
— *Lecciones preliminares de filosofía,* Losada, Buenos Aires, 1952.
GÉRARD, A.: *L'idée Romantique de la poésie en Angleterre, études sur la théorie de la poésie chez Coleridge, Wordsworth, Keats et Shelley,* Les Belles Lettres, Paris, 1955.
GINER DE LOS RÍOS, F.: *Estudios de literatura y arte,* V. Suárez, Madrid, 1876.
— *Ensayos,* ed. by J. López-Morillas, Alianza, Madrid, 1969.
GÓMEZ DE LA SERNA, R.: *Morbideces,* Madrid, 1908.
GÓNGORA, L. DE: *Fábula de Polifemo y Galatea, Obras completas de don Luis de Góngora y Argote,* ed. by Juan and Isabel Millé y Giménez, Aguilar, Madrid, 1961.
GUILLÉN, J.: *Lenguaje y poesía,* Alianza, Madrid, 1972.
GULLÓN, R.: *Direcciones del modernismo,* Gredos, Madrid, 1971.
— *La invención de 98 y otros ensayos,* Gredos, Madrid, 1969.
GURVITCH, G.: *Les tendances actuelles de la philosophie allemande,* Bibliothèque d'Histoire de la Philosophie, Paris, 1949.
HAMBURGER, M.: *The Truth of Poetry,* Weidenfeld & Nicolson, London, 1969.
HARPER, G. M.: *The Neoplatonism of William Blake,* The University of North Carolina Press, 1961.
HEBREO, L. (JUDAS ABRAVANEL): *Diálogos de amor,* transl. by El Inca Garcilaso de la Vega, Espasa-Calpe Argentina, Austral, Buenos Aires, 1947.
HEIDEGGER, M.: *On the Way to Language,* transl. by P. D. Hertz, Harper & Row, New York, 1971.
— *Poetry, Language and Thought,* transl. by A. Hofstadter, Harper & Row, New York, 1971.
— *The End of Philosophy,* transl. by J. Stambaugh, Harper & Row, New York, 1973.
HENRÍQUEZ UREÑA, P.: *Estudios griegos,* Escalante, México, 1908.
HOFMANNSTHAL, H. VON: *Selected Prose,* Pantheon Books, New York, 1952.
Homenaje a Bergson, University of Córdoba, Argentina, 1936.
Homenaje a Bergson (J. Gaos, O. Robles, J. Vasconcelos, J. Xirau), 1941.
HOUGH, G.: *The Last Romantics,* Duckworth, London, 1949.
HUGO, V.: *Les contemplations,* Garnier, Paris, 1969.
HUSSERL, E.: «Die Krisis der europäischen Wissenschaften und die transzendentale Phänomenologie», *Philosophia,* ed. by A. Liebert, Beograd, 1936.
— *Ideen zu einer reinen Phänomenologie und phänomenologische Philosophie,* M. Niemeyer, Halle, 1913.
— *Méditations cartésiennes. Introduction à la phénoménologie,* transl. by Mlle. G. Peiffer and M. E. Levinas, A. Colin, Paris, 1931.
— *Vorlesungen zur Phänomenologie des inneren Zeitbewusstseins,* ed. by M. Heidegger, M. Niemeyer, Halle, 1929.

JACKSON, H.: *The Eighteen Nineties,* Cape, London, 1913.
JIMÉNEZ-FRAUD, A.: «The "Residencia de Estudiantes"», *Image of Spain, Texas Quarterly,* The University of Texas, Austin, ed. by R. Martínez-López, IV, n.º I, 1961.
JOSIPOVICI, G.: *The Lessons of Modernism,* Macmillan, London, 1977.
— *The World and the Book,* Stanford University Press, Stanford, California, 1971.
JOYCE, J.: *Ulysses,* Bodley Head, London, 1962.
KEMPIS, THOMAS À: *De la imitación de Cristo y menosprecio del mundo,* transl. by P. Juan Eusebio Nieremberg, Editorial Apostolado de la Prensa, Madrid, 1951.
KERMODE, F.: *The Sense of an Ending,* Oxford University Press, New York, 1967.
KING, E. L.: «Gabriel Miró y "el mundo según es"», *Papeles de Son Armadans,* Madrid, Palma de Mallorca, LXII, May 1961.
KNOX, I.: *The Aesthetic Theories of Kant, Hegel and Schopenhauer,* Columbia University Press, New York, 1936.
KORN, A.: «Bergson» and «Bergson en la filosofía contemporánea», *Obras,* II.
KRAUSE, K. C. F.: *Compendio de estética,* transl. by F. Giner de los Ríos, V. Suárez, Madrid, 1883.
— *Ideal de la humanidad para la vida,* introduced by J. Sanz del Río, Facultad de Filosofía y Letras de la Universidad de Madrid, 1871.
LEDESMA MIRANDA, R.: «Maeztu en mi recuerdo. Homenaje a Don Ramiro de Maeztu», *Cuadernos hispanoamericanos,* núms. 33-34, September-October 1952.
LEÓN, FRAY L. DE: *De los nombres de Cristo,* Clásicos Castellanos, Madrid, 1914.
LONERGAN, B. J.: *Verbum: Word and Idea in Aquinas,* University of Notre Dame Press, South Bend, Indiana, 1967.
LÓPEZ-MORILLAS, J.: *El krausismo español,* Fondo de Cultura Económica, México, 1956.
LOVEJOY, A. O.: *The Great Chain of Being,* Harper & Row, New York, 1960.
LOWELL, A.: in *Some Imagist Poets,* Constable, London, 1915.
MACHADO, A.: *Obras: poesía y prosa,* ed. by Aurora de Albornoz and Guillermo de Torre, Losada, Buenos Aires, 1964.
MALEVICHT, K.: *The Non-Objective World,* transl. by H. Dearstyne, P. Theobald, Chicago, 1959.
MALLARMÉ, S.: *Oeuvres complètes,* Gallimard, Paris, 1945.
MAPES, E. K.: *La influencia francesa en la obra de Rubén Darío,* Managua, Nicaragua, 1966.
MARÍAS, J.: *El método histórico de las generaciones,* Revista de Occidente, Madrid, 1949.
— *History of Philosophy,* transl. by S. Appelbaum and C. C. Strowbridge, Dover Publications, New York, 1967.
— *Introducción a la filosofía,* Revista de Occidente, Madrid, 1963.
— *La escuela de Madrid: estudios de filosofía española,* Emecé, Buenos Aires, 1959.
MARTINS, D.: *Bergson: la intuición como método de la metafísica,* transl. by José Hermida López, Madrid, 1943.
MENÉNDEZ Y PELAYO, M.: *Antología de poetas hispanoamericanos,* Real Academia Española, Madrid, 1893-1895.
— *Historia de las ideas estéticas en España,* 9 vols., Imprenta de los Hijos de Tello, Madrid, 1920.
MEYERHOFF, H.: *Time in Literature,* University of California Press, Berkeley and Los Angeles, 1960.
MICHAUD, G.: *La doctrine symboliste,* Nizet, Paris, 1947.
— *Mallarmé,* Hatier, Paris, 1971.
— *Mallarmé, l'homme et l'oeuvre,* Hatier-Boivin, Paris, 1953.
MIRÓ, G.: *Obras completas,* Biblioteca Nueva, Madrid, 1943.
MOLINA, E.: *Proyecciones de la intuición. Nuevos estudios sobre la filosofía bergsoniana,* 1935.
MONDOR, H.: *Vie de Mallarmé,* Gallimard, Paris, 1941.
MÜLLER-FREIENFELS, R.: *The Evolution of Modern Psychology,* transl. by W. Béran Wolfe, Yale University Press, New York, 1935.
NERVAL, G. DE: *Oeuvres,* Garnier, Paris, 1966.

NIETZSCHE, F. W.: *The Birth of Tragedy,* transl. by W. Kaufmann, Vintage Books, New York, 1967.
— *Nietzsche, aforismos y sentencias,* compiled by R. Baeza, Colección Microcosmos, 1920.
— *Nietzsche, poeta (interpretaciones líricas),* compiled by F. A. de Icaza, 1921.
ONG, W. J.: *The Presence of the Word,* Yale University Press, New Haven, Conn., 1967.
O'RIORDAIN, P.: *«Helios» and «Alma española»: Two Spanish Literary Reviews of 1903-04,* Liverpool, Ph. D., 1965.
ORTEGA Y GASSET, J.: «Las dos grandes metáforas» (in El segundo centenario de Kant), *Obras completas,* vol. II, Revista de Occidente, Madrid, 1957.
— *Obras completas,* 11 vols., Revista de Occidente, Madrid, 1958-1969.
PANIAGUA, D.: *Revistas culturales contemporáneas,* Ediciones «Punta Europa», Madrid, 1964.
PATER, W. H.: *Appreciations,* Macmillan, London and New York, 1889.
— *Essays on Literature and Art,* ed. by J. Uglow, Dent, London, 1973.
— *Marius the Epicurean,* Macmillan, London, 1910.
— *Plato and Platonism, a series of lectures,* Greenwood Press, New York, 1969.
— *The Renaissance,* Collins, Glasgow, 1961.
PAZ, O.: *El arco y la lira,* Fondo de Cultura Económica, México, 1956.
PEYRE, H.: *Qu'est-ce que le symbolisme?,* Presses Universitaires de France, Paris, 1974.
PLATO: *Seventh Epistle, The Works of Plato,* vol. IV, G. Bell & Sons, London and New York, 1911-1915.
PLOTINUS: *The Enneads,* transl. by S. MacKenna, Faber, London, 1969.
POE, E. A.: «The Power of Words», *The Complete Poems and Stories of Edgar Allan Poe,* vol. II, Alfred H. Knopf, New York, 1958.
PORTALIÉ, E.: «Saint Augustin», *Dictionnaire de théologie catholique,* Vacant-Mangenot-Amman, Paris, 1931.
POULET, G.: *La distance intérieure,* Plon, Paris, 1952.
— *Studies in Human Time,* transl. by E. Coleman, Harper & Bros., New York, 1959.
PRAZ, M.: *The Romantic Agony,* transl. by A. Davidson, Oxford University Press, London and New York, 1970.
QUEVEDO Y VILLEGAS, F. G. DE: *Obra poética,* 3 vols., ed. by J. M. Blecua, Editorial Castalia, Madrid, 1969-1971.
— *Poesía amorosa,* sel. by J. M. Blecua, Ediciones Anaya, 1965.
RAY, N.: *An Artist in Life,* University of Kerala, Trivandrum, India, 1967.
REYES, A.: *Mallarmé entre nosotros,* Ediciones Tezontle, México, 1955.
ROSENBLATT, L. M.: *L'idée de l'art pour l'art dans la littérature anglaise pendant la période victorienne,* H. Champion, Paris, 1931.
RUSSELL, B.: *The ABC of Relativity,* K. Paul, Trench, Trubner & C.° Ltd., London, 1925.
SALINAS, P.: *Ensayos de literatura hispánica,* Aguilar, Madrid, 1967.
— *Literatura española siglo XX,* Antigua Librería Robredo, México, 1949.
SÁNCHEZ-BARBUDO, A.: *Las poesías de Antonio Machado,* Editorial Lumen, Barcelona, 1969.
SANZ DEL RÍO, J.: *Filosofía de la muerte, estudio hecho sobre manuscritos de D. Julián Sanz del Río por M. Sales y Ferré,* Carlos Bailly Baillière, Madrid, 1877.
SAYCE, R. A.: *Style in French Prose,* Clarendon Press, Oxford, 1965.
SCHENK, H. G.: *The Mind of the European Romantics,* F. Ungar, New York, 1967.
SCHOPENHAUER, A.: *Parerga and Paralipomena,* 2 vols., transl. by E. F. J. Payne, Clarendon Press, Oxford, 1974.
SERRANO PONCELA, S.: *Antonio Machado, su mundo y su obra,* Losada, Buenos Aires, 1954.
SILVER, P.: *Ortega as Phenomenologist,* Columbia University Press, New York, 1978.
SOBEJANO, G.: *Nietzsche en España,* Gredos, Madrid, 1967.
SPENDER, S.: *The Making of a Poem,* W. W. Norton, New York, 1962.

TAGORE, SIR R.: *Creative Unity,* Macmillan, London, 1922.
— *Gitanjali,* Macmillan, London, 1920.
TAYLOR, M. E. J.: *Greek Philosophy,* Oxford University Press, 1924.
TERESA DE JESÚS: *Su Vida,* Espasa-Calpe, Madrid, 1971.
THORLBY, A.: *The Romantic Movement,* Longman, London, 1966.
TILLYARD, E. M. W.: *The Elizabethan World Picture,* Chatto & Windus, London, 1960.
ULLMAN, S.: *Style in the French Novel,* Barnes & Noble, New York, 1964.
UNAMUNO, M. DE: «La dignidad humana», *Ciencia social,* Barcelona, January 1896.
— «Maese Pedro. Notas sobre Carlyle», *La España moderna,* núm. 161, Madrid, May 1902.
— *Obras completas,* 16 vols., Editorial Afrodisio Aguado, Madrid, 1958-1964.
— *Poesías,* ed. by M. Alvar, Editorial Labor, Textos hispánicos modernos, Barcelona, 1975.
VALLE-INCLÁN, R. DEL: *La lámpara maravillosa,* Editorial Rúa Nueva, Madrid, 1942.
— *Memorias del Marqués de Bradomín, Sonatas,* Editorial Porrúa, México, 1972.
— *Tirano Banderas, Obras completas,* vol. I, Rivadeneyra, Madrid, 1944.
VALVERDE, J. M.: *Estudios sobre la palabra poética,* Ediciones Rialp, Madrid, 1958.
VAN TIEGHEM, P.: *Le romantisme dans la littérature européenne,* Michel, Paris, 1948.
VIGNAUX, P.: «Nominalisme», *Dictionnaire de théologie catholique,* Vacant-Mangenot-Amman, Paris, 1931.
WARD, A.: *Walter Pater: The Idea in Nature,* Macgibbon & Kee, London, 1966.
WELLEK, R.: *A History of Modern Criticism 1750-1950,* 4 vols., Yale University Press, New Haven, 1955-1965.
WILDE, O.: *The Picture of Dorian Gray,* Oxford University Press, London and New York, 1974.
WILSON, E.: *Axel's Castle,* C. Scribner's Sons, New York and London, 1954.
— *The Wound and the Bow,* Oxford University Press, New York, 1970.
WINDELBAND, W.: *Historia de la filosofía,* transl. by F. Larroyo, Editorial Pallas, México-Quito, 1941.
WITTGENSTEIN, L.: *Philosophische Untersuchungen,* Blackwell, Oxford, 1958.
— *Tractatus Logico-Philosophicus,* Routledge & Kegan Paul, London, 1961.
WOLFE, T.: *The Story of a Novel,* C. Scribner's Sons, New York and London, 1936.
WORDSWORTH, W.: *Lyrical Ballads,* ed. by W. J. B. Owen, Oxford University Press, London, 1969.
XIRAU, J.: *Vida, pensamiento y obra de Bergson,* Editorial Leyenda, México, 1943.
YEATS, W. B.: *Autobiographies,* Macmillan, London, 1955.
— *The Collected Poems of W. B. Yeats,* Macmillan, London, 1977.
ZARAGÜETA, J.: *La intuición en la filosofía de Henri Bergson,* Espasa-Calpe, Madrid, 1941.
ZARDOYA, C.: *Poesía española contemporánea,* Ediciones Guadarrama, Madrid, 1961.